Practical Database Auditing for Microsoft SQL Server and Azure SQL

Troubleshooting, Regulatory Compliance, and Governance

Josephine Bush

Apress®

Practical Database Auditing for Microsoft SQL Server and Azure SQL: Troubleshooting, Regulatory Compliance, and Governance

Josephine Bush
Boulder, CO, USA

ISBN-13 (pbk): 978-1-4842-8633-3   ISBN-13 (electronic): 978-1-4842-8634-0
https://doi.org/10.1007/978-1-4842-8634-0

Managing Director, Apress Media LLC: Welmoed Spahr
Acquisitions Editor: Jonathan Gennick
Development Editor: Laura Berendson
Coordinating Editor: Jill Balzano

Cover photo by Clark Van Der Beken on Unsplash

Distributed to the book trade worldwide by Springer Science+Business Media LLC, 1 New York Plaza, Suite 4600, New York, NY 10004. Phone 1-800-SPRINGER, fax (201) 348-4505, e-mail orders-ny@springer-sbm. com, or visit www.springeronline.com. Apress Media, LLC is a California LLC and the sole member (owner) is Springer Science + Business Media Finance Inc (SSBM Finance Inc). SSBM Finance Inc is a **Delaware** corporation.

For information on translations, please e-mail booktranslations@springernature.com; for reprint, paperback, or audio rights, please e-mail bookpermissions@springernature.com.

Apress titles may be purchased in bulk for academic, corporate, or promotional use. eBook versions and licenses are also available for most titles. For more information, reference our Print and eBook Bulk Sales web page at http://www.apress.com/bulk-sales.

Any source code or other supplementary material referenced by the author in this book is available to readers on GitHub (https://github.com/Apress). For more detailed information, please visit http://www. apress.com/source-code.

Printed on acid-free paper

For my husband, Jim, who somehow managed to be nothing but supportive about a book that would put him to sleep.

Table of Contents

About the Author

 **Josephine Bush** has more than ten years of experience as a database administrator. Her experience is extensive and broad based, including experience in financial and energy data systems using SQL Server, MySQL, Oracle, and PostgreSQL. She is a Microsoft Certified Solutions Expert: Data Management and Analytics. She holds a BS in Information Technology, an MBA in IT Management, and an MS in Data Analytics. She is the author of *Learn SQL Database Programming*. You can reach her on Twitter @hellosqlkitty.

About the Technical Reviewer

Kathi Kellenberger is a Customer Success Engineer at Redgate and a Data Platform MVP. She has worked with SQL Server since 1998 and has authored, co-authored, or tech-reviewed over 20 technical books. Kathi is a volunteer at LaunchCode in St. Louis where she teaches T-SQL in the LaunchCode Women+ program. When Kathi isn't working, she enjoys spending time with family and friends, cycling, singing, and climbing the stairs of tall buildings.

Acknowledgments

Thank you to my technical reviewer, Kathi, whose careful review and thoughtful suggestions improved the book.

Thank you to the team at Apress, especially Jonathan Gennick and Jill Balzano, who were instrumental in bringing this book to publication.

Thank you, dear reader, for reading this book. My hope is that you will come to love auditing as much as I do, but if nothing else, your life is made a bit easier with the guidance I've provided.

Introduction

People usually think of auditing as scary or boring. Scary because the auditors will see you doing something wrong and you will get in trouble. Boring because you picture pencil pushers digging through piles of paper searching for some little error.

I worked at a financial company with very strict auditing requirements. I tried my hand at SQL Server Audit and extended events (XEvents) for PCI compliance. It was a nice surprise when the skeptical PCI auditors reviewed my implementation and said it passed with flying colors. This bolstered my growing love of auditing.

What's in This Book?

This book gives you concrete examples of how auditing can make your life easier. You aren't in the dark after setting up auditing. I set up auditing at my current job because I got tired of people blaming problems on database changes. I had no idea if there were any changes at all because I wasn't auditing. Now, I can say exactly what changed and work with users to determine if this change broke something.

This book gives you a high-level overview of why you need auditing and what types of auditing exist. It goes into detail on the types of auditing available in SQL Server, Azure SQL, and AWS RDS SQL Server. You will learn how to use SQL Server Audit and extended events to track changes to schema, security, and configurations. Not all changes can be captured with these features, so the book covers other features like change data capture (CDC), temporal tables, and common criteria compliance.

Next, the book covers auditing methods in both Azure SQL Database and Azure SQL Managed Instance. There are differences in how you audit those compared to SQL Server. Additionally, you will learn how to use SQL Server Audit and extended events in AWS RDS SQL Server.

After reading this book, you will have many use cases and scripts at your disposal to help you implement your auditing strategy.

Intended Audience

For database administrators who need to know what's changing on their database servers, and who are making those changes. For database-savvy DevOps engineers and developers who are charged with troubleshooting processes and applications. For developers and administrators who are responsible for generating reports in support of regulatory compliance reporting and auditing.

Contacting the Author

I tried to ensure the accuracy of all the scripts and descriptions. I know there may be issues that come up anyway. Feel free to email me at hellosqlkitty@gmail.com with comments or questions.

PART I

Getting Started with Auditing

## CHAPTER 1

Why Auditing Is Important

Auditing is an official examination and verification of accounts or records. A lot of times people are referring to financial audits, but auditing applies in many more areas than finance. Here in America when people hear auditing, their first natural thought might be the Internal Revenue Service (IRS). Pretty much everyone feels queasy if the IRS contacts them because they are being audited. It happened to me one time, and the auditor said, "Hold on, we think we owe you money!" When you are audited, it's the assumption that it will end up costing you.

There is also the kind of auditing when internal or external auditors come speak to you to find out if you are following proper procedures. Those can be scary, too, so it's no wonder auditing may have a bad reputation. Auditing in and of itself isn't a bad thing. I would say, it's a good thing. You want to make sure people are following proper procedures. Whether it's the IRS or auditors at your company, some rules, regulations, procedures, and laws need to be followed. Sometimes, there need to be consequences to ensure compliance.

The point of auditing isn't to punish people or get people in trouble, at least not with the database auditing I will be discussing throughout this book. It's to shed light on possible issues or areas where you may need to follow guidelines more strictly.

Why Should You Audit?

Some companies may not value auditing and some are required to audit because of regulations. Even if your company isn't required to audit, that shouldn't stop you from auditing. There is value in auditing: it allows those who have the responsibility to know what's going on the ability to know what's going on.

The reason I set up auditing at the business I worked at was because I would often have people come to me saying something is broken, and they couldn't figure out why. We also had many environments where too many people have access to and can

© Josephine Bush 2022
J. Bush, *Practical Database Auditing for Microsoft SQL Server and Azure SQL*,
https://doi.org/10.1007/978-1-4842-8634-0_1

change too many things. By setting up and configuring auditing, I was able to see who was changing what. What a relief! No more "why did this happen?", and I can't provide any insights. I could say to them, "I don't see any changes in the database, or this user changed the schema on the 5th."

In the end, my company was acquired by a more heavily regulated company, and they needed the systems to be audited with proper reports reviewed weekly. My new company was very pleased that I had already done the legwork making it easy for us to do the auditing. Originally, the management at my company didn't think this was a priority, but I worked on it in between other projects and built exactly what the new parent company needed without knowing they would need this. It wasn't something magical I was doing or that I could somehow predict the future. I was following basic auditing principles. They pay off!

Types of Audits

The types of audits you will have to do will vary depending on the business you work with. Regardless of the type of business you are in, auditing will help you. Listed in the following are the types of audits you may encounter:

Internal – This type of audit is initiated by the business itself. This helps the business maintain standards that may or may not be required by external auditors or government regulations. Reasons you may want to do this type of auditing, even if you aren't required to do more official types of auditing, are to make sure your business is running as smoothly and efficiently as possible. Internal audits can also be used to ensure you will be ready for external audits.

External – This type of audit is conducted by a third party such as a governmental regulatory body or an accountant. These external auditors will be familiar with the types of rules and regulations you need to be following and will ensure that you are following them precisely.

Tax – In America, the Internal Revenue Service (IRS) will sometimes audit tax returns of individuals or businesses to ensure accuracy, making sure you haven't overpaid or underpaid your taxes. These audits tend to be selected randomly, but there may be things you pay taxes on that make you more likely to be audited.

Financial – This type of audit is conducted by external auditors to ensure that financial statements and/or payroll payments are accurate.

Compliance – This type of audit may be conducted by internal or external auditors and ensures that the business is compliant with internal or external auditing standards. This can be broken down into regulatory compliance and corporate compliance. Corporate compliance is internal rules and guidelines, and regulatory compliance is adhering to government laws and regulations.

Operational – This type of audit is generally conducted by internal auditors, but there may be cases where they are conducted by external auditors. This audit is meant to help determine ways to improve business operations.

Information Systems – This type of audit may be conducted by internal or external auditors to ensure that the systems are providing accurate data to users and to make sure that systems are secure so that unauthorized users aren't able to access or alter them.

Types of Regulatory Compliance

Regulatory compliance is when a business must follow state, federal, and international laws relevant to its operations. The specific regulations that are required vary from business to business. Listed in the following are the types of regulatory compliance you may encounter:

California Consumer Privacy Act (CCPA) – Enacted in 2018, this law protects consumers' personal information and how it's used by businesses that collect that information.

General Data Protection Regulation (GDPR) – This strengthens the data protection for citizens of the European Union (EU). Enacted in 2018, it requires businesses to protect the privacy of EU citizens for any transactions that occur in the EU member states.

Health Insurance Portability and Accountability Act (HIPAA) – Enacted in 1996, this is a standard to protect sensitive health-related information. This requires anyone with medical data to ensure it's safe from accidental release or hacking.

Payment Card Industry Data Security Standard (PCI DSS) – This is a set of standards that ensures the security of credit card data. Enacted in 2004, it outlines how payment data is stored, transmitted, and processed.

Sarbanes-Oxley Act (SOX) – Enacted in 2002, this is an accounting and compliance framework. Publicly traded companies must adhere to the creation and maintenance of secure computing systems.

What Is Database Auditing?

Database auditing is when you utilize database tools and auditing strategies to record changes on your database servers. Database auditing is typically used to

- Gather data on specific database activities

- Track changes to database servers

- Report on changes to auditors

- Investigate suspicious activity

The different types of database auditing you can do are

- **Server-level auditing** – This includes things like tracking the creation of a linked server, a SQL Agent job, or a database.

- **Security auditing** – This includes things like creating a login or modifying a user's permissions.

- **Data definition language (DDL) auditing** – This includes things like creating or dropping a table.

- **Data manipulation language (DML) auditing** – This includes things like selecting, inserting, deleting, or updating from a table.

Database Problems Auditing Can Solve

Auditing can help you solve a lot of problems. The following list outlines some scenarios auditing can help you with:

- **Who broke this?** People come to you saying something is broken, why? You are in the dark without auditing. If you have the auditing set up, you can see who changed something which may be the change causing the issue.

- **Who is using this login?** You can also see if someone used something in the case of a table or a login. We had a scenario where the SQL Server sysadmin (sa) password was handed out like candy. A SQL login may have been set up for one purpose, but now it's been shared around, and we don't want different users using the same login ever. To do this, we had to know who was using sa. You can't just ask around and say, "Are you using sa on this server?" You either get people who don't respond, who just don't know, or say they don't have time to look. We audited sa, got a list of users, and those users and their managers were contacted and told, "We must move you off sa. We see you are doing these things with sa, so let's get you a username/password set up so you can continue to do the work you need to do."

- **Who is using this database object?** There was another case where the development team was trying to figure out what login was writing to a table. They could see updated data but had no idea where it came from, so it's another way auditing can help you.

- **What permission does a user need?** As part of this sa auditing, we also examined what people were doing to see if we could pare down on the level of permissions they were granted in a production system with the goal of granting the least permissions required. Most of these users didn't even realize the power they had using sa, and all of them just used it in a way that was in alignment with their own work.

- **Are users misusing the database?** We did catch one guy sharing out his domain user and password to allow someone else to perform his job duties while he was out of the office, which is a huge no-no.

- **What changed?** Many times, internal or external auditors need proof that you had approval before making changes, or they require reports listing out changes. With the auditing in place, providing this documentation is much easier.

In summary, you can see how auditing can be very powerful and, in many cases, required by law. Auditing isn't something you need to be afraid or avoid. It can help you make sure your database systems are being used in accordance with laws and regulations. Even if you aren't required by law to audit your databases, you can use auditing as a sanity check for yourself and your team. Plus, auditing can help you develop policies and procedures and help you determine if everyone is following those procedures.

## CHAPTER 2

Types of Database Auditing

The starting point of any good auditing strategy is knowing the auditing options you have at your disposal. This chapter gives you a high-level description of each auditing tool that is covered in this book.

SQL Server Audit

SQL Server Audit is a built-in SQL Server auditing feature that can be used to set up auditing with SQL Server Management Studio (SSMS). You can also set it up with SQL scripts, which makes it easier to apply the same auditing strategy to many servers.

This feature makes it easy to see what is changing on your SQL Server. You can audit everything that is changing or parts and pieces of those things that are changing.

To make SQL Server auditing work, you need two or three things depending on what you want to audit. You are required to create an *audit specification*. This will determine where you store audit data. You will also need one *server specification* and/ or one *database audit specification* for audit data to write to the audit specification. The server audit specification can audit server activities, and it can also audit all the database activities in the same way. Each audit specification can have one server and/or one database audit. Those server and database audits are not dependent on each other.

The server audit specification is generally good for auditing server-level changes and/or all the databases at the same time. The database audit specification is good for auditing one database or a subset of activities in one database.

Figure 2-1 shows where you can set up SQL Server Audit via SQL Server Management Studio.

© Josephine Bush 2022
J. Bush, *Practical Database Auditing for Microsoft SQL Server and Azure SQL*,
https://doi.org/10.1007/978-1-4842-8634-0_2

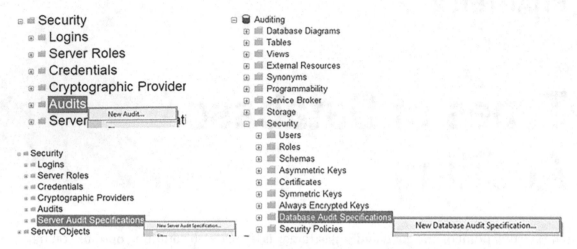

Figure 2-1. *Setting up SQL Server Audit*

Chapter 3, "What Is SQL Server Audit?", provides more details on SQL Server auditing. Chapters 4, "Implementing SQL Server Audit via the GUI," and Chapter 5, "Implementing SQL Server Audit via SQL Scripts," take you through implementing SQL Server auditing.

Extended Events

Extended events is a built-in SQL Server auditing feature that can be used to set up auditing with SQL Server Management Studio. You can also set it up with SQL scripts, which makes it easier to apply the same auditing strategy to many servers.

Extended events makes it easy to see what is changing on your SQL Server. It doesn't have auditing capabilities as nuanced as SQL Server Audit, so if you are looking to audit a subset of activities for a user or database, then it's best to use SQL Server Audit for that instead.

Extended events is very good at capturing everything a specific user does. It's also very good at capturing anything happening in a database.

To make extended events work, you need to set up a session. That's the only piece that's required, instead of the two or three pieces for SQL Server Audit.

Additionally, extended events has a wizard to walk you through setup, or you can create a session without a wizard. It also has templates to help you set up a session without needing to know all the configuration settings to make it work.

Figure 2-2 shows where you can set up extended events via SQL Server Management Studio.

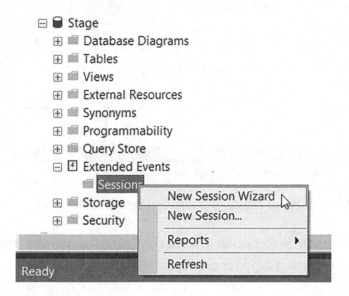

Figure 2-2. *Setting up extended events*

Chapter 6, "What Is Extended Events?", provides more details on configuration options. Chapters 7, "Implementing Extended Events via the GUI," and Chapter 8, "Implementing Extended Events via SQL Scripts," take you through implementing extended events.

Tracking SQL Server Configuration Changes

There are multiple ways you can track SQL Server configuration changes. These are the type of changes you make to server settings like changing the maximum memory setting or showing advanced options. All of these options, including additional options, are covered in Chapter 9, "Tracking SQL Server Configuration Changes."

Extended events is one way you can capture these types of changes. Figure 2-3 shows you a cross-section of how it captures configuration changes if you query it via the SQL Server Management Studio GUI. You can also query it via scripts, which is covered in Chapter 9, "Tracking SQL Server Configuration Changes."

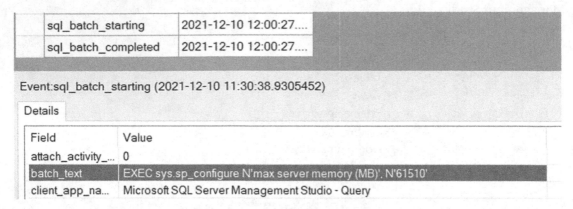

Figure 2-3. *Extended event capturing configuration change*

You can also use SQL Server Audit to track configuration changes. Figure 2-4 shows you a cross-section of how it captures configuration changes.

	event_time	audit_action	statement	succeeded	database_name
1	2022-04-24 19:03:51.3038436	EXECUTE	EXEC sys.sp_configure N'max server memory (MB)', N'5688'	1	master

Figure 2-4. *SQL Server Audit capturing configuration change*

Lastly, you can also query the *SQL Server Log* directly. The SQL Server Log contains system events. Figure 2-5 shows an example result of this.

	LogDate	ProcessInfo	Text
1	2022-04-24 11:28:49.730	spid53	Configuration option 'max server memory (MB)' changed from 5666 to 5667. Run the RECONFIGURE statement to install.
2	2022-04-24 12:28:19.780	spid56	Configuration option 'user connections' changed from 0 to 100. Run the RECONFIGURE statement to install.

Figure 2-5. *SQL Server Log query results*

Change Data Capture

Change data capture will allow you to track changes to data instead of who is querying the data. It uses the SQL Server Agent to record data changes made by inserting, updating, or deleting data in a specific table. It reads the changes from the transaction log of the database. The details of the changes are stored in a change table that mimics the structure of the original table.

There are multiple steps for configuration that are covered in Chapter 10, "Additional SQL Server Auditing and Tracking Methods." Figure 2-6 shows you the original table and its CDC table.

Figure 2-6. *CDC table structure*

When you query the cdc.dbo_ErrorLog_CT table, which is where CDC is storing the changes to the dbo.ErrorLog table, you will see something like the query results in Figure 2-7. Figure 2-7 was taken after one update to one row.

	_$update_mask	ErrorLogID	ErrorTime	UserName	ErrorNumber	ErrorSeverity	ErrorState	ErrorProcedure	ErrorLine	ErrorMessage	__$command_id
1	<0004	1	2021-12-15 00:00:00.000	jbush	1000	5	3	4	10	testing	1
2	<0004	1	2021-12-15 00:00:00.000	testing	1000	5	3	4	10	testing	1

Figure 2-7. *CDC results*

Change Tracking

SQL Server Change Tracking is a lightweight way to track DML changes to SQL Server database tables. These changes are tracked once the DML statement is committed to the database. It differs from change data capture in that it tracks changes synchronously, whereas change data capture reads from the transaction log file, which causes a delay while reading the changes. Also, Change Tracking doesn't require the SQL Agent to be started, unlike change data capture that does.

Figure 2-8 shows how to enable Change Tracking on a database.

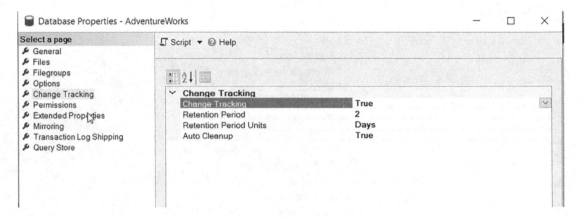

Figure 2-8. *Enabling SQL Server Change Tracking on a database*

Once you have Change Tracking enabled at the database level, you can enable it for a table. Figure 2-9 shows how to enable Change Tracking on a database table.

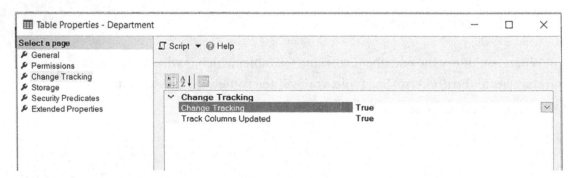

Figure 2-9. *Enabling SQL Server Change Tracking on a database table*

To see the changes that are captured, you will query an internal table to get results. This query is covered in Chapter 10, "Additional SQL Server Auditing and Tracking

Methods." Figure 2-10 shows how DML changes would be captured in this internal table. The first row in the results is an insert statement, and the second and third rows are update statements.

	SYS_CHANGE_VERSION	SYS_CHANGE_OPERATION	DepartmentID	Name	GroupName	ModifiedDate
1	2	I	17	testing	testinggroup	2022-01-05 16:32:20.140
2	3	U	1	Engineering1	Research and Development	2008-04-30 00:00:00.000
3	4	U	2	Tool Design1	Research and Development	2008-04-30 00:00:00.000

Figure 2-10. *Querying Change Tracking information*

Additional information about Change Tracking is covered in Chapter 10, "Additional SQL Server Auditing and Tracking Methods."

C2 Audit and Common Criteria Compliance

C2 and *Common Criteria compliance* are internationally recognized to follow specific security guidelines when auditing. These types of auditing are a comprehensive type of logging of all activities on your database server. If you don't have an auditor requiring you to turn this on, leave it off. It can be very impactful to server performance. They assign a unique generated ID to each group of related auditing activities. You can enable these at the server level. Figure 2-11 shows you where you can enable these.

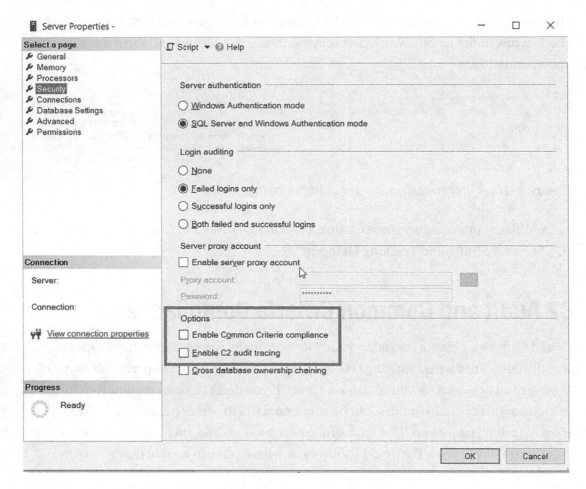

Figure 2-11. *Enabling C2 or Common Criteria compliance*

Additional information about C2 and Common Criteria compliance is covered in Chapter 10, "Additional SQL Server Auditing and Tracking Methods."

Temporal Tables

This built-in database feature allows you to see data stored in the table at any point in time. It's a system-versioned table that keeps a full history of data changes. The validity of each row is managed by the system, which is the database engine. The versioning is implemented as a pair of tables, current and history. Each of these tables has two datetime2 type columns to define the period of validity for each row. They are called the PERIOD columns. The current table contains the current value for each row. The history table contains each previous value for each row and the start time and end time for which it was valid.

Figure 2-12 shows you a temporal table and its history table.

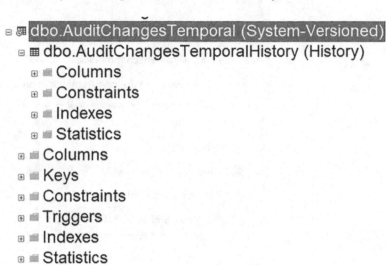

Figure 2-12.   *Temporal table with its history table*

Additional information about temporal tables is covered in Chapter 10, "Additional SQL Server Auditing and Tracking Methods."

Successful and Failed Login Auditing

There are a couple of ways you can implement *successful and failed login auditing*. When you track logins, you will see any successful logins, failed logins, or both in the SQL Server Log. One way is via SSMS in the Server Properties as shown in Figure 2-13. Once configured, the successful and/or failed logins will appear in the SQL Server Log.

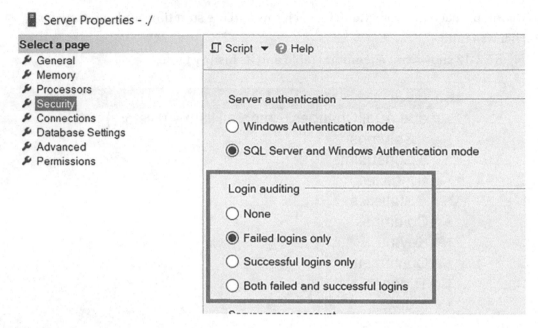

Figure 2-13. *Changing login auditing*

Another way you can capture this information is with extended events. Additional information about login auditing is covered in Chapter 10, "Additional SQL Server Auditing and Tracking Methods."

Auditing Azure SQL Databases

Auditing Azure SQL databases is quite a bit different than auditing SQL Server databases, especially when it comes to SQL Server Audit. SQL Server Audit isn't available in Azure SQL Database. You need to use the Azure portal to set up your audits. You can't use SQL Server Management Studio for this. Figure 2-14 shows you how you can enable auditing that is similar to SQL Server Audit in the portal.

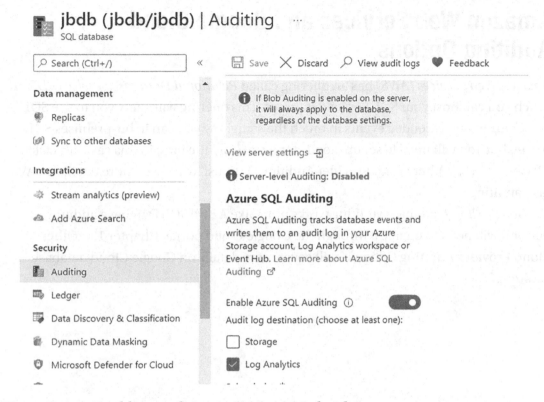

Figure 2-14. *Enabling auditing on Azure SQL database*

Auditing Azure SQL Managed Instance

Auditing Azure SQL Managed Instance is much the same as auditing on-premises SQL Server. The main difference is you don't have access to the virtual machine under the database server, so you will need to set up cloud storage to hold the audit or event files. Refer to the sections on SQL Server Audit and extended events to help you understand how they work. Azure SQL Managed Instance auditing will be covered in more detail in Chapter 14, "Auditing Azure SQL Managed Instance."

Amazon Web Services and Google Cloud Auditing Options

Amazon Web Services (AWS) has an offering called *Relational Database Service (RDS)* in which you can host your SQL Server databases. This offering will allow you to use SQL Server Audit and extended events in much the same way you can in on-premises SQL Server, but you will need to set up cloud storage to hold the files; in this case, it's called S3. Chapter 15, "Other Cloud Provider Auditing Options," will cover more details on AWS RDS auditing.

Google Cloud database auditing works more like Azure SQL Database auditing in that you will need to enable it through the Google Cloud portal. Chapter 15, "Other Cloud Provider Auditing Options," will cover more details on Google Cloud database auditing.

PART II

Implementing Auditing

## CHAPTER 3

What Is SQL Server Audit?

SQL Server Audit is built-in auditing functionality available via SQL Server Management Studio GUI or SQL scripts. You can set it up and configure it to capture pretty much anything that happens on SQL Server. It's quite flexible and easy to set up.

SQL Server Audit Availability

The first version of SQL Server Audit was available in 2008, and it was only in Enterprise edition. As of the 2012 version, Microsoft expanded it to be available in server-level audits with all editions, but database auditing was still only in Enterprise. By 2016 and since, you can do server and database auditing with any edition, which is so much nicer since a lot of people don't use Enterprise edition only. Table 3-1 outlines the availability of SQL Server Audit.

Table 3-1. *SQL Server Audit availability by version*

Version	Server audit availability	Database audit availability
2008	Enterprise	Enterprise
2012, 2014, and 2016 before SP1	All editions	Enterprise
2016 SP1, 2017, and 2019	All editions	All editions

© Josephine Bush 2022
J. Bush, *Practical Database Auditing for Microsoft SQL Server and Azure SQL*,
https://doi.org/10.1007/978-1-4842-8634-0_3

SQL Server Audit Requirements

To make SQL Server auditing work, you need two or three things depending on what you want to audit. You are required to create an audit. This will determine where you store audit data. You will also need one server and/or one database audit specification that defines what you want to capture. Each audit can have one server specification and/or one database specification per database. Those server and database audits are not dependent on each other.

The screenshot in Figure 3-1 shows you the locations of the audits.

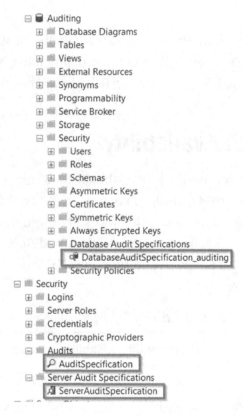

Figure 3-1. *SQL Server audits*

Note that the SQL Server audits highlighted in Figure 3-1 aren't there by default. I created those to give you a point of reference for where you can find them.

The audit specification is where you will configure where to store your audit, how much data to keep, if you want to filter to capture only certain kinds of data, and what you want to happen on audit logging failure. You can set up an audit specification under Security ➤ Audits in SQL Server Management Studio. You can have multiple audit specifications, and each of them can hold one server audit specification and one database audit specification per database. You can have an audit specification hold only one server audit, one database audit per database, or both.

The server audit specification is where you will configure what you want your audit to collect at the server level and, optionally, at the database level. You can set up a server audit specification under Security ➤ Server Audit Specifications in SQL Server Management Studio. You can have multiple server audit specifications, but they will each need a separate audit specification since each audit specification can only hold one server specification audit. This server audit can audit server-level objects, but it can also audit all your database the same way. If you have more specific auditing needs for each of your databases, you will want to use only server-level actions in your server audit specification. There's more information on audit actions later in this chapter.

The database audit specification is where you will configure what you want your audit to collect at a database level. You can set up a server audit specification under each database under Security ➤ Database Audit Specifications in SQL Server Management Studio. You can have multiple database audit specifications on each database, but they will each need a separate audit since each audit specification can only hold one database audit specification per database.

Setting up and configuring the audit specifications will be covered in Chapter 4, "Implementing SQL Server Audit via the GUI."

Note   You don't need sysadmin permissions to set up SQL Server Audit, but you will need some custom permissions to set it up. For the audit and the server audit specifications, you will need either CONTROL SERVER or ALTER ANY SERVER AUDIT permission. For the database audit specification, you will need ALTER ANY DATABASE AUDIT or CONTROL SERVER permission. Of course sysadmin permissions will also work to set up all the audit components.

SQL Server Audit Use Cases

The server audit is generally good for auditing server-level changes and/or all the databases at the same time. The database audit is good for auditing one database or a subset of activities in one database. The following list takes you through some scenarios for auditing with multiple audit specifications and server and database audits:

- **Auditing schema and permissions changes at the server and all databases the same way**

  This will require an audit specification and a server audit specification.

- **Auditing everything a specific user does**

  This will require an audit specification with a filter to capture only that user's activities and a server audit specification.

- **Auditing everyone querying or modifying a table**

  This will require an audit specification and a database audit specification that specifies this one table with the associated actions you want to capture.

- **Auditing schema and permissions changes at the server level and only a specific database**

  This will require an audit specification, a server audit specification, and a database audit specification.

Audit Categories

There are three categories of audit actions: server, database, and audit.

- **Server-level actions** – Captures permission changes and the creation of databases. Includes any audit action that doesn't start with SCHEMA_ or DATABASE_

- **Database-level actions** – Captures DML and DDL changes, which includes auditing actions at the database level. Includes audit actions that start with SCHEMA_ or DATABASE_

- **Audit-level actions** – Captures actions in the auditing process, such as creating or dropping an audit specification. This is the AUDIT_CHANGE_GROUP option.

Audit Action Groups

Within each of these audit categories, there are groups of actions you can capture. Some actions are audited automatically, and you don't need to set up any auditing actions to capture them, such as Server Audit State Change (setting State to ON or OFF). This corresponds to when you start or stop an audit.

Server Audit Action Groups

For server audits, these are the groups I find the most useful for auditing changes at the server level. They can only be chosen in a server audit specification. The following list outlines these groups:

- **AUDIT_CHANGE_GROUP** – Captures when an audit is created, modified, or deleted
- **DBCC_GROUP** – Captures when a user executes a DBCC command
- **SERVER_OBJECT_OWNERSHIP_CHANGE_GROUP** – Captures when the owner of a server object is changed
- **SERVER_OBJECT_PERMISSION_CHANGE_GROUP** – Captures when GRANT, REVOKE, or DENY on a server object permission
- **SERVER_OPERATION_GROUP** – Captures changes like altering settings, resources, external access, or authorization
- **SERVER_PERMISSION_CHANGE_GROUP** – Captures when GRANT, REVOKE, or DENY for permissions are set at the server level
- **SERVER_PRINCIPAL_CHANGE_GROUP** – Captures when server principals are created, altered, or dropped
- **SERVER_ROLE_MEMBER_CHANGE_GROUP** – Captures when a login is added or removed from a fixed server role, like sysadmin

- **SERVER_STATE_CHANGE_GROUP** – Captures when the SQL Server service state is modified, like when it's restarted after patching

- **LOGIN_CHANGE_PASSWORD_GROUP** – Captures when a login password is changed

---

Note   Additional server audit action groups can be used. Descriptions of each are available in the following link:

`https://docs.microsoft.com/en-us/sql/relational-databases/security/auditing/sql-server-audit-action-groups-and-actions?view=sql-server-ver15#server-level-audit-action-groups`

Database Audit Action Groups

For database audits, these are the groups I find the most useful for capturing schema and permission changes at the database level. They can be chosen in a server audit specification, which will allow for auditing of all the databases on the server the same way. If you only want to audit one database with these actions, don't use them in your server audit, and instead only set them up in your database audit. The following list outlines these groups:

- **DATABASE_CHANGE_GROUP** – Captures when a database is created, altered, or dropped

- **DATABASE_OBJECT_ACCESS_GROUP** – Captures when database objects such as certificates and asymmetric keys are accessed

- **DATABASE_OBJECT_CHANGE_GROUP** – Captures when CREATE, ALTER, or DROP statements are executed on database objects, such as schemas

- **DATABASE_OBJECT_OWNERSHIP_CHANGE_GROUP** – Captures when a change of owner for objects occurs within a database

- **DATABASE_OBJECT_PERMISSION_CHANGE_GROUP** – Captures when a GRANT, REVOKE, or DENY has been issued for database objects, such as assemblies and schemas

- **DATABASE_OWNERSHIP_CHANGE_GROUP** – Captures when you use the ALTER AUTHORIZATION statement to change the owner of a database

- **DATABASE_PERMISSION_CHANGE_GROUP** – Captures when a GRANT, REVOKE, or DENY is issued for a statement permission

- **DATABASE_PRINCIPAL_CHANGE_GROUP** – Captures when principals, such as users, are created, altered, or dropped from a database

- **DATABASE_ROLE_MEMBER_CHANGE_GROUP** – Captures when a login is added to or removed from a database role

- **APPLICATION_ROLE_CHANGE_PASSWORD_GROUP** – Captures whenever a password is changed for an application role

- **DBCC_GROUP** – Captures when a user executes a DBCC command

- **SCHEMA_OBJECT_CHANGE_GROUP** – Captures when a CREATE, ALTER, or DROP operation is performed on a schema

- **SCHEMA_OBJECT_OWNERSHIP_CHANGE_GROUP** – Captures when the permissions change to the owner of a schema object

- **SCHEMA_OBJECT_PERMISSION_CHANGE_GROUP** – Captures whenever a grant, deny, or revoke is issued for a schema object

The following actions can be used when you want to capture everything happening in a database or on a database server. I only use these action types if I'm filtering the audit to get only one user or to see if a schema or database is no longer in use. Be very careful with these actions, though. They can quickly get out of control collecting so much audit data that you will never be able to weed through.

- **DATABASE_OBJECT_ACCESS_GROUP** – Captures when any action is taken in the database being audited

- **SCHEMA_OBJECT_ACCESS_GROUP** – Captures when any action is taken in the schema being audited

> **Note**   Additional database audit action groups can be used. Descriptions of each are available in the following link:
>
> https://docs.microsoft.com/en-us/sql/relational-databases/
> security/auditing/sql-server-audit-action-groups-and-
> actions?view=sql-server-ver15#database-level-audit-
> action-groups

When you are working with database audits, you have some actions that aren't available at the server audit level. These will capture actions taken on the database schema and schema objects such as tables, views, stored procedures, and functions. The following list outlines these groups:

- **SELECT** – Captures SELECT statements
- **UPDATE** – Captures UPDATE statements
- **INSERT** – Captures INSERT statements
- **DELETE** – Captures DELETE statements
- **EXECUTE** – Captures EXECUTE statements

> **Note**   Additional database audit actions can be used. Descriptions of each are available in the following link:
>
> https://docs.microsoft.com/en-us/sql/relational-databases/
> security/auditing/sql-server-audit-action-groups-and-
> actions?view=sql-server-ver15#database-level-audit-actions

SQL Server Audit Examples

Here are some concrete examples of how you can implement the use cases I outlined in this chapter.

If you want to audit schema and permissions changes at the server and all databases the same way, implement a server audit specification with these actions:

- **AUDIT_CHANGE_GROUP**

- **SERVER_OBJECT_OWNERSHIP_CHANGE_GROUP**

- **SERVER_OBJECT_PERMISSION_CHANGE_GROUP**

- **SERVER_OPERATION_GROUP**

- **SERVER_PERMISSION_CHANGE_GROUP**

- **SERVER_PRINCIPAL_CHANGE_GROUP**

- **SERVER_ROLE_MEMBER_CHANGE_GROUP**

- **SERVER_STATE_CHANGE_GROUP**

- **LOGIN_CHANGE_PASSWORD_GROUP**

- **DATABASE_CHANGE_GROUP**

- **DATABASE_OBJECT_ACCESS_GROUP**

- **DATABASE_OBJECT_CHANGE_GROUP**

- **DATABASE_OBJECT_OWNERSHIP_CHANGE_GROUP**

- **DATABASE_OBJECT_PERMISSION_CHANGE_GROUP**

- **DATABASE_OWNERSHIP_CHANGE_GROUP**

- **DATABASE_PERMISSION_CHANGE_GROUP**

- **DATABASE_PRINCIPAL_CHANGE_GROUP**

- **DATABASE_ROLE_MEMBER_CHANGE_GROUP**

- **APPLICATION_ROLE_CHANGE_PASSWORD_GROUP**

- **DBCC_GROUP**

- **SCHEMA_OBJECT_CHANGE_GROUP**

- **SCHEMA_OBJECT_OWNERSHIP_CHANGE_GROUP**

- **SCHEMA_OBJECT_PERMISSION_CHANGE_GROUP**

If you want to audit schema and permissions changes at the server, but not any of the databases because you implement different database auditing on each database, implement a server audit specification with these actions:

- **AUDIT_CHANGE_GROUP**

- **SERVER_OBJECT_OWNERSHIP_CHANGE_GROUP**

- **SERVER_OBJECT_PERMISSION_CHANGE_GROUP**

- **SERVER_OPERATION_GROUP**

- **SERVER_PERMISSION_CHANGE_GROUP**

- **SERVER_PRINCIPAL_CHANGE_GROUP**

- **SERVER_ROLE_MEMBER_CHANGE_GROUP**

- **SERVER_STATE_CHANGE_GROUP**

- **LOGIN_CHANGE_PASSWORD_GROUP**

If you want to audit everything a specific user does, you will use a couple of additional audit actions. I like to keep the usage of these to a minimum unless you are filtering on a smaller subset of activities on your server. You will use all the actions that are listed earlier for auditing all the schema and permissions changes, and in addition, you will include these audit actions:

- **DATABASE_OBJECT_ACCESS_GROUP**

- **SCHEMA_OBJECT_ACCESS_GROUP**

If you want to audit everyone querying or modifying a table, you will need to use a database audited specification for this. You will use the following audit actions in this audit:

- **SELECT**

- **UPDATE**

- **INSERT**

- **DELETE**

- **EXECUTE**

If you want to audit everyone making schema and permissions changes at the server level and only a specific database, you will need a server audit specification and a database audit specification. Your server audit will include only server audit actions listed as follows:

- **AUDIT_CHANGE_GROUP**

- **SERVER_OBJECT_OWNERSHIP_CHANGE_GROUP**

- **SERVER_OBJECT_PERMISSION_CHANGE_GROUP**

- **SERVER_OPERATION_GROUP**

- **SERVER_PERMISSION_CHANGE_GROUP**

- **SERVER_PRINCIPAL_CHANGE_GROUP**

- **SERVER_ROLE_MEMBER_CHANGE_GROUP**

- **SERVER_STATE_CHANGE_GROUP**

- **LOGIN_CHANGE_PASSWORD_GROUP**

Your database audit for this case will include the following audit actions only on the database you want to audit:

- **DATABASE_CHANGE_GROUP**

- **DATABASE_OBJECT_ACCESS_GROUP**

- **DATABASE_OBJECT_CHANGE_GROUP**

- **DATABASE_OBJECT_OWNERSHIP_CHANGE_GROUP**

- **DATABASE_OBJECT_PERMISSION_CHANGE_GROUP**

- **DATABASE_OWNERSHIP_CHANGE_GROUP**

- **DATABASE_PERMISSION_CHANGE_GROUP**

- **DATABASE_PRINCIPAL_CHANGE_GROUP**

- **DATABASE_ROLE_MEMBER_CHANGE_GROUP**

- **APPLICATION_ROLE_CHANGE_PASSWORD_GROUP**

- **DBCC_GROUP**

- **SCHEMA_OBJECT_CHANGE_GROUP**

- **SCHEMA_OBJECT_OWNERSHIP_CHANGE_GROUP**

- **SCHEMA_OBJECT_PERMISSION_CHANGE_GROUP**

Multiple Audit Setups

If you need multiple different audits on the same server, there is a way to configure them such that you have little to no overlap in auditing. You may need some overlap depending on auditing requirements, though, but you want to avoid as much overlap as possible. Here are some audit specification setups that could work in conjunction with each other:

- **Auditing DDL and perms changes at the server level**

  - **Audit specification name** – Audit_DDLPerms

  - **Server audit specification name** – ServerAudit_DDLPerms

    For this audit, make sure to not include any audit actions that start with DATABASE or SCHEMA.

- **Audit everything a specific user does**

  - **Audit specification name** – Audit_user

    Make sure to filter the audit specification so it only captures actions made by the user account.

  - **Server audit specification name** – ServerAudit_user

    Make sure to audit all the database and server-level actions the same way and add in the DATABASE_OBJECT_ACCESS_GROUP and SCHEMA_OBJECT_ACCESS_GROUP actions.

- **Auditing schema and perms changes for a specific database**

  - **Audit specification name** – Audit_DatabaseChanges

  - **Database audit specification name** – DatabaseAudit_DatabaseChanges

    Make sure to add all the audit actions starting with DATABASE and SCHEMA into your database audit specification.

- **Audit everyone changing a table**

  - **Audit specification name** – Audit_tblChanges

  - **Database audit specification name** – DatabaseAudit_tblChanges

Make sure to use the audit action types of INSERT, UPDATE, DELETE, SELECT, and/or EXECUTE.

In the next chapter, you will learn how to set up and configure these audits in SQL Server Management Studio.

## CHAPTER 4

Implementing SQL Server Audit via the GUI

To make SQL Server auditing work, you need two or three components depending on what you want to audit. Chapter 3, "What Is SQL Server Audit?", covered what each of these components are and the audit categories and groups associated with them. In this chapter, you will learn how to set up the audit in SQL Server Management Studio (SSMS).

Setting Up the Audit

For a quick recap, to make SQL Server auditing work, you need two or three things depending on what you want to audit.

- **You're required to create an audit.** This will determine where you store audit data, how much audit data to keep, and several other settings associated with auditing.

- **You will also need one server and/or one database audit to collect audit data.** The server and database audits must be associated with an audit. Each audit can have one server and one database audit per database. These server and database audits are not dependent on each other. The server audit specification is generally good for auditing server-level changes and/or all the databases at the same time. The database audit specification is good for auditing one database or a subset of activities in one database.

Figure 4-1 shows how to create an audit in SSMS by right-clicking Audits under the Security section.

© Josephine Bush 2022
J. Bush, *Practical Database Auditing for Microsoft SQL Server and Azure SQL*,
https://doi.org/10.1007/978-1-4842-8634-0_4

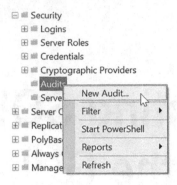

Figure 4-1. *Creating an audit*

By choosing New Audit, you will get a dialog box to choose the options of your audit as shown in Figure 4-2.

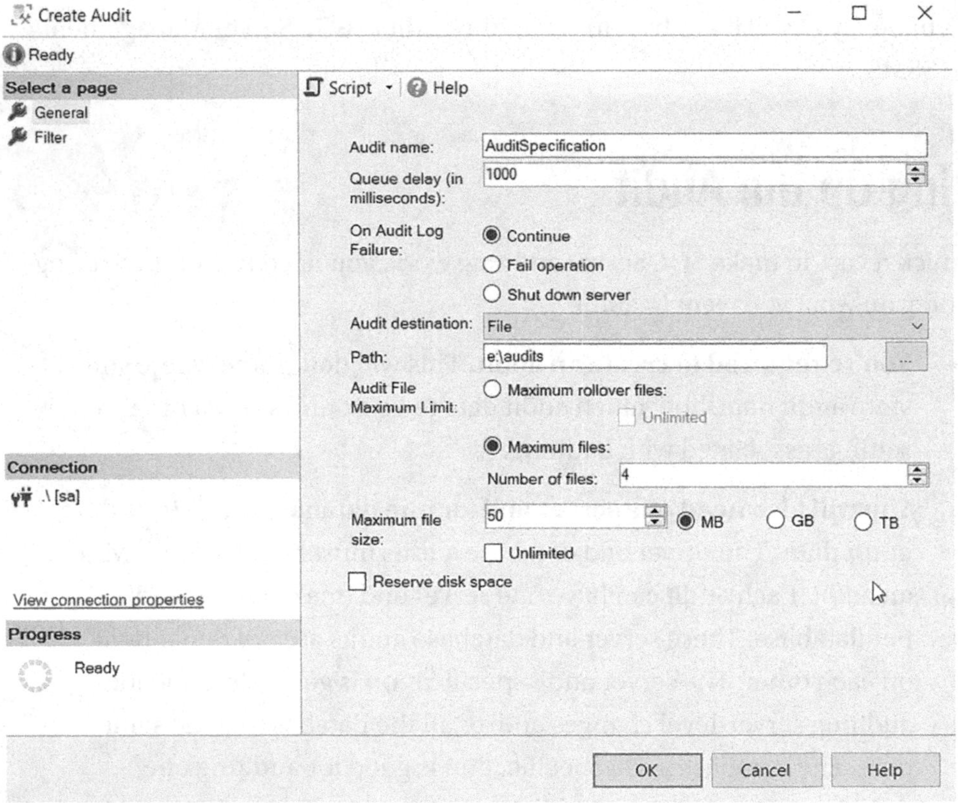

Figure 4-2. *Configuring an audit dialog box*

Here are some suggestions on how to configure your audit:

- **Audit name** – I tend to name it AuditSpecification or AuditSpecification_servername. This is entirely up to you based on how descriptive you want to name it. You can create multiple audits, though, so it may make sense to make it a more descriptive name if you plan to add additional audits.

- **Queue delay** – This is the wait time in milliseconds before it audits. You can set this to 0, 1000, or something greater than 1000. I leave it at 1000.

- **On audit log failure**

  - **Continue** – If the audit can't capture the statement, it keeps auditing. You might miss a statement here and there, but I doubt that happens often, if at all.

  - **Fail operation** – If it can't audit, it's going to cause the statement to fail. The user or application executing that statement will get an error.

  - **Shutdown server** – If it can't audit, it's going to do what it says, it's going to shut down the server. All users and applications will no longer have access to the server.

  I choose Continue on this option. I think Fail operation and Shutdown server are too drastic. I'll have people screaming at me that there's something wrong with the server if I don't choose Continue. You may want to choose Fail operation or Shutdown server if auditing is of the utmost importance like in a legal or financial database.

- **Audit destination**

  - **File** – I always write to the file choice because it's easiest for me. I don't have a lot of auditing restrictions. Yes, the auditors want to know what happened, but they don't think that we're going in there secretly deleting audit files and not reporting on audit data.

- **Application log** – I could see storing audit data in the application log if you have a log scraping application like Splunk that reads all the logs and gathers them in a central repository.

- **Security log** – This has more restrictions than writing to the application log, but the same concept applies. This is the most secure option for storing audit data because it's the least likely to have anyone tamper with it.

- **Path** – If you chose File for Audit Destination, you need to choose a path. Make sure don't put audit files on the C drive. Even though we're going to limit the audit file sizes in the next steps, you don't want it accidentally filling up the C drive. I don't recommend putting audit files on data drives or log drives either. We have an E drive for applications where I work; that's a great place for audit files to go.

- **Maximum files** – 4

- **Maximum file size** – 50 MB

  I never let the audit collect unlimited files and unlimited file sizes. This makes it difficult to query them. I've found 4 files of 50 MB each is good for my needs when collecting permissions and schema changes. Your number and sizing of files depend on your needs.

- **Reserve disk space** – Since my files are quite small, I never check that.

Caution   Don't set SQL Server Audit to collect unlimited files or allow unlimited file sizes. They will be gigantic and next to impossible to query.

If you want to store your audit data in the application log, you will set up your audit like in the screenshot in Figure 4-3.

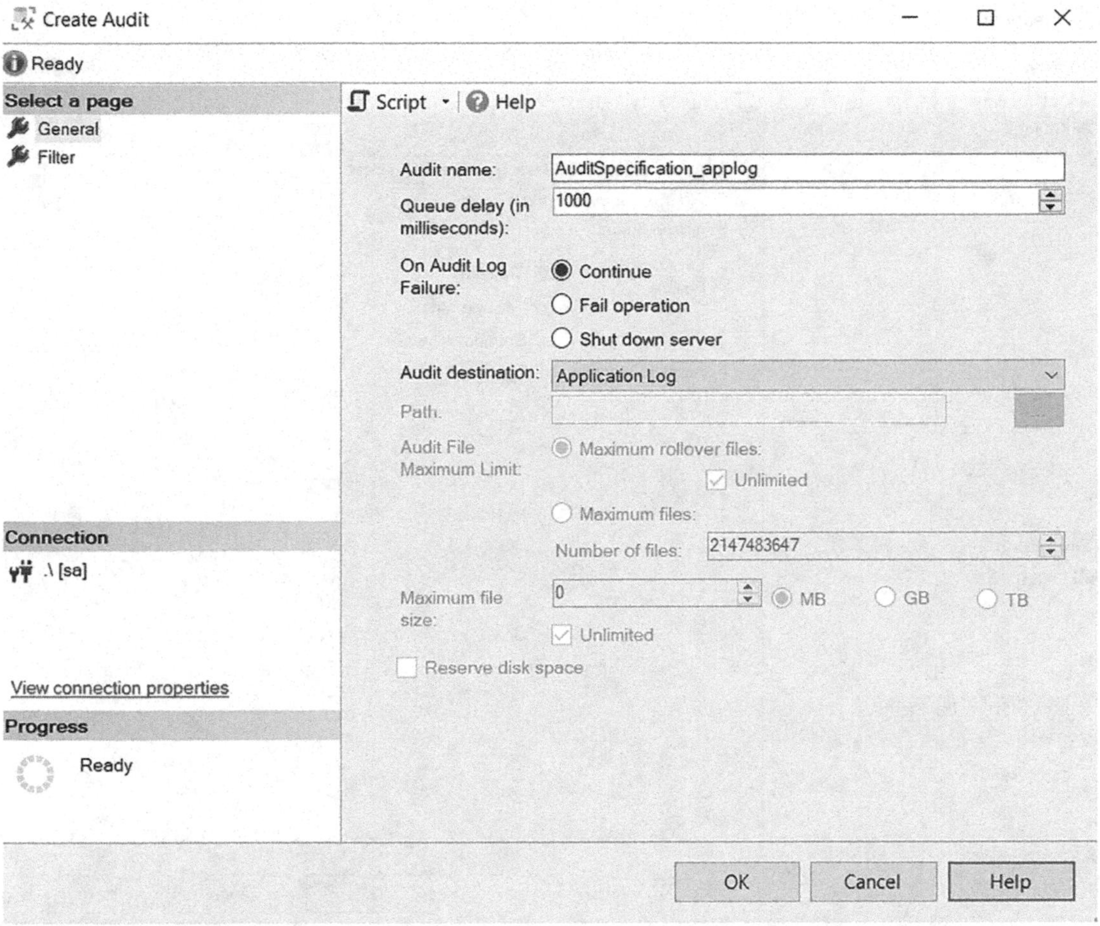

Figure 4-3. *Configuring an audit that writes to the application log*

The same goes for the security log, but instead, you choose Security Log from the Audit destination drop-down as shown in Figure 4-4.

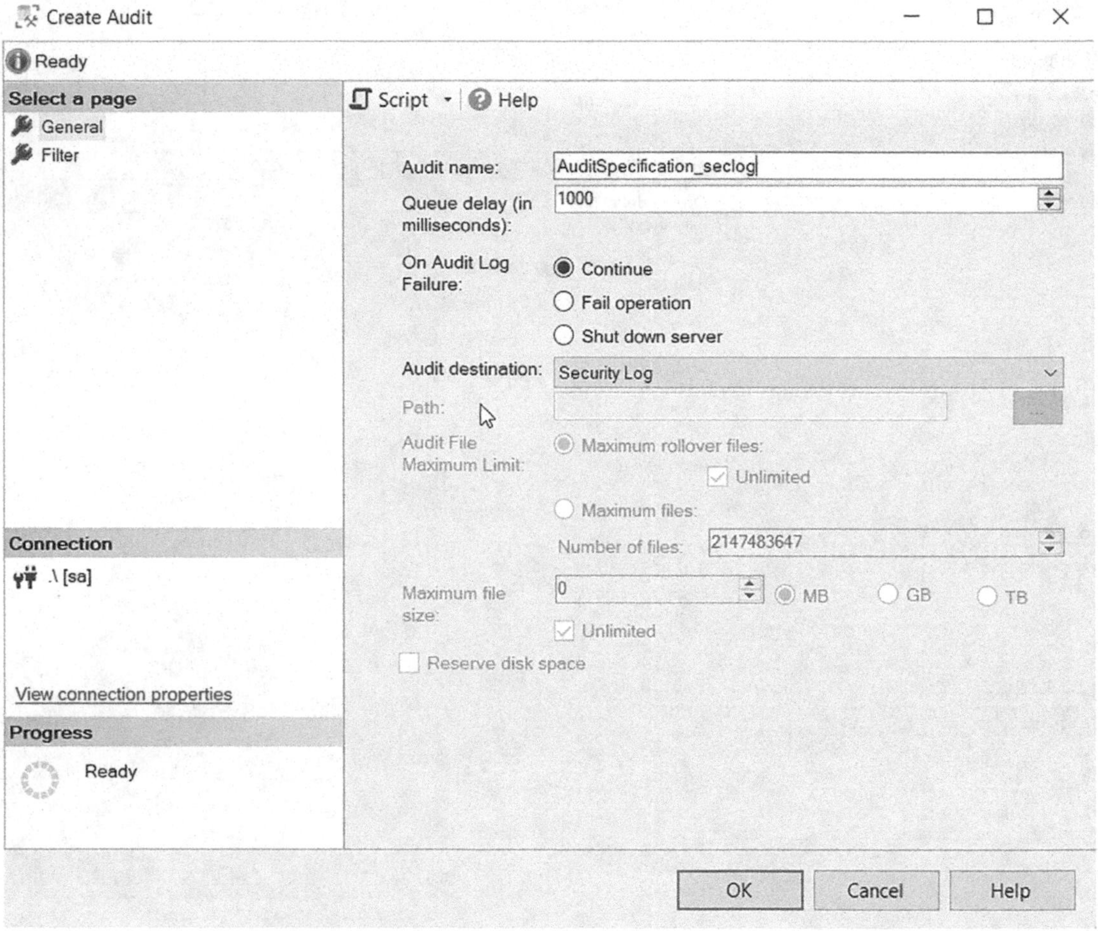

Figure 4-4. *Configuring an audit that writes to the security log*

Note   All audits are disabled when initially created.

Once your audit is created, you will need to enable it. You can right-click it and choose Enable Audit as shown in Figure 4-5. It won't collect any data if you don't enable it.

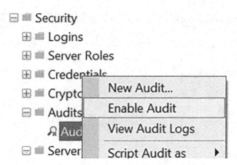

Figure 4-5. *Enabling audit*

You will get an error when you try to enable the audit that's configured to use the security log as shown in Figure 4-6.

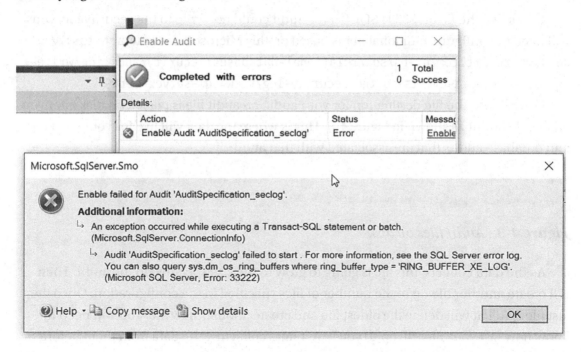

Figure 4-6. *Error when creating audit that writes to the security log*

The SQL Server Logs will give you additional information about the error as shown in Figure 4-7.

	2/11/2022 4:25:13 ...	spid66	SQL Server Audit could not write to the security log.
	2/11/2022 4:25:13 ...	spid66	Error: 33204, Severity: 17, State: 1.
	2/11/2022 4:25:13 ...	spid66	Audit: Server Audit: 65541, State changed from: START_FAILED to: TARGET_CREATION_FAILED
	2/11/2022 4:25:13 ...	spid66	Audit: Server Audit: 65541, Initialized and Assigned State: START_FAILED

Selected row details:
Date   2/11/2022 4:25:13 PM
Log   SQL Server (Current - 2/9/2022 1:52:00 PM)

Source   spid66

Message
SQL Server Audit could not write to the security log.

Figure 4-7. Additional information about the error when creating an audit that writes to the security log

To resolve the Error: 33204 SQL Server Audit could not write to the security log, you will need to configure additional items based on this Microsoft document: `https://docs.microsoft.com/en-us/sql/relational-databases/security/auditing/write-sql-server-audit-events-to-the-security-log?view=sql-server-ver15`

If you chose the file destination for your audit, an audit file is placed on disk after you enable the audit as shown in Figure 4-8. This is where the data will live for your server and database audits that are associated with that audit.

Name	Date modified	Type	Size
AuditSpecification_D0B8D5A4-96BE-468F-A58F-41CCC3BC9E57_0_132576453114750...	2/12/2021 4:15 PM	SQLAUDIT File	0 KB

Figure 4-8. Audit files on disk

As the data collects, this file is going to grow to the size specified in the audit. Then it'll create another file up to the number of files specified in the configuration. Once the last file is full, it will delete the oldest file and create another new file. You will need to know how fast your files fill up so you won't miss collecting the data from them before they are deleted.

Setting Up the Server Audit Specification

The first of two optional audits is the server audit. You set this up under the security section of the server. Right-click to create a new one as shown in Figure 4-9.

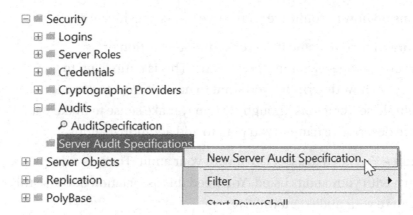

Figure 4-9. *Creating a server audit specification*

This will bring up a dialog box to configure your server audit specification as shown in Figure 4-10.

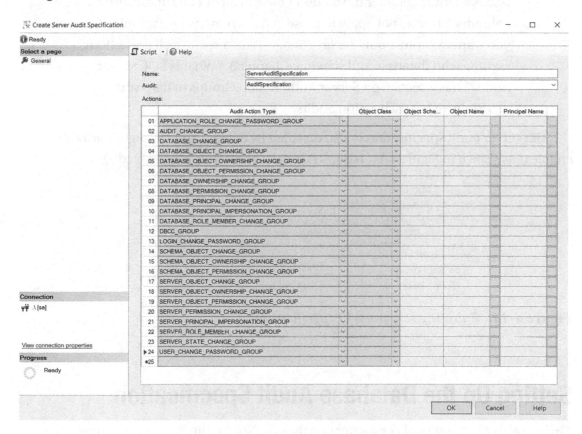

Figure 4-10. *Configuring server audit specification*

Suggestions on how to configure your server audit specification:

- **Name** – I tend to name it ServerAuditSpecification or ServerAuditSpecification_servername. This is entirely up to you based on how descriptive you want to name it. You can create multiple server audits, though, so it may make sense to make it a more descriptive name if you plan to add additional audits.

- **Audit** – You need to associate it with your audit. There is a drop-down with your audits listed. You need this association because this is where your audit data will live.

- **Actions** – I'm capturing permissions and schema changes at the server level and in all the databases on the server. I'm also capturing if someone changes a password, changes an audit, or if someone issues a DBCC command. You don't have to fill out any of the other columns. They do not apply to these action types. As an example, if you want to capture only server changes, you'd remove all the actions starting with database and schema. Chapter 3, "What Is SQL Server Audit?", has a section on Server Audit Action Groups to help you determine what each action audits.

The server audit specification is also disabled by default. You can right-click to enable it as shown in Figure 4-11. It doesn't collect any data if it's disabled.

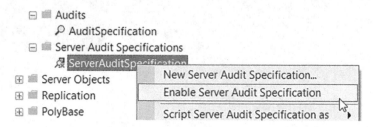

Figure 4-11. *Enabling server audit specification*

Setting Up the Database Audit Specification

The second of two optional components is the database audit. You have to go into each database's security section, and then right-click as shown in Figure 4-12.

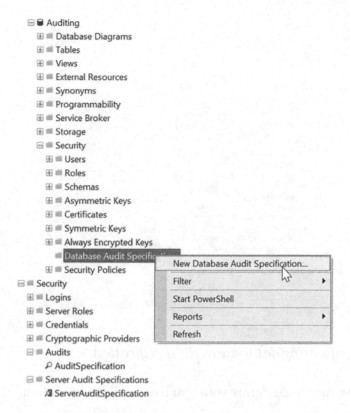

Figure 4-12. *Creating database audit specification*

This brings up a dialog box to configure the database audit specification as shown in Figure 4-13.

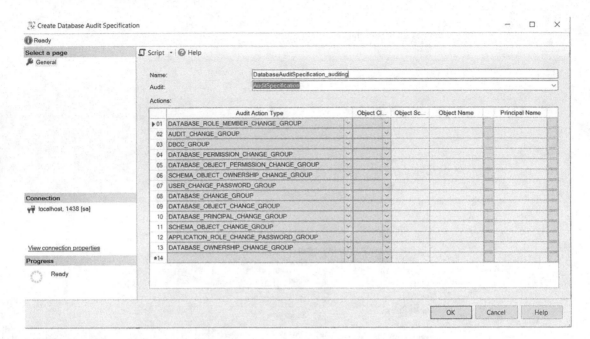

Figure 4-13. *Configuring database audit specification*

Suggestions on how to configure your database audit specification:

- **Name** – I always name it underscore database name because it helps
  identify what database it's auditing like DatabaseAuditSpecification_
  Auditing. This is entirely up to you based on how descriptive you
  want to name it. You can create multiple audits, though, so it may
  make sense to make it a more descriptive name if you plan to add
  additional audits. One thing to note is that if you don't put the name
  of the database in the name of the database audit, you won't be able
  to easily query the system views that store the audit information.
  Those views are very helpful if you've named your audits
  descriptively. Querying the system views will be covered in more
  detail in Chapter 5, "Implementing SQL Server Audit via SQL Scripts."

- **Audit** – You need to associate it with your audit. There is a drop-
  down with your audits listed. You need this association because this
  is where your audit data will live.

- **Actions** – I'm capturing permissions and schema changes at the database level. Chapter 3, "What Is SQL Server Audit?", has a section on Database Audit Action Groups to help you determine what each action audits. **Don't use this if you're already getting permissions and schema changes at the server audit level. This will produce duplicate audit records.**

Where the database audit shines is if you want to audit objects. With a database audit, you can audit things like insert, update, delete, select, and execute statements on objects in the current database, like tables, views, and stored procedures. You can also audit an entire schema or database. These action types do require you to fill in all the additional columns for the audit actions depending on the object class as shown in Figure 4-14.

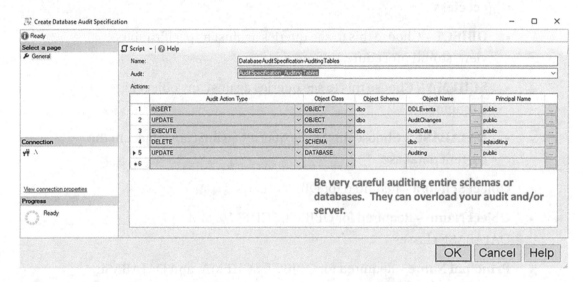

Figure 4-14. *Configuring a database audit specification to capture DML actions*

Suggestions on how to configure your database audit specification when auditing specific objects, schemas, or databases:

- **Name** – I always name it underscore something descriptive to its purpose because it helps identify what it's auditing.

- **Audit** – You need to associate it with your audit. There is a drop-down with your audits listed. You need this association because this is where your audit data will live.

- **Audit Action Type** – Chapter 3, "What Is SQL Server Audit?", has a section on Database Audit Action Groups to help you determine what each action audits.

    - **INSERT** – Audits who inserts to a table, schema, or database

    - **UPDATE** – Audits who updates a table, schema, or database

    - **EXECUTE** – Audits who executes on a stored procedure, schema, or database

    - **SELECT** – Audits who selects from a table, view, function, schema, or database

    - **DELETE** – Audits who deletes from a table, schema, or database

- **Object class**

    - **OBJECT –** Choose this to see queries against a specific table, view, stored procedure, or function.

    - **SCHEMA** – Choose this to see queries against any object in a schema.

    - **DATABASE** – Choose this to see queries against any object in the current database.

- **Object Schema** – Required for OBJECT class

- **Object Name** – Required for OBJECT, SCHEMA, and DATABASE classes

- **Principal Name** – Required for OBJECT, SCHEMA, and DATABASE classes Use public if you want to audit everyone. If you want to audit multiple users, you need one line for each user.

Once you create the database audit, it's also disabled by default. You can right-click to enable it as shown in Figure 4-15. It won't collect data when it's disabled.

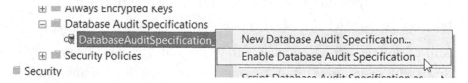

Figure 4-15. *Enabling database audit specification*

Adding Multiple Audits

If you try to add another server audit to an existing audit that already has a server audit, it will fail with an error that states the audit already exists as shown in Figure 4-16. This means you can't add another server audit to it.

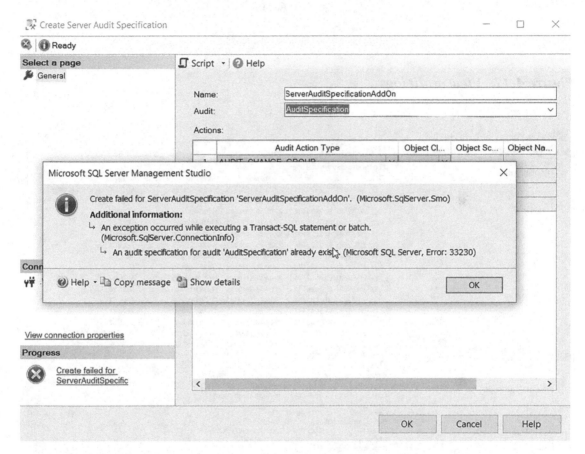

Figure 4-16. *Error when trying to add a second server audit specification to an audit*

That doesn't stop you from having multiple server and database audits because you can have multiple audits. Chapter 3, "What Is SQL Server Audit?", has a section on multiple audit setups and gives you some example scenarios you can follow.

Querying Audit Logs

You can query the audit via SSMS by right-clicking the audit as shown in Figure 4-17.

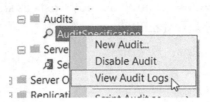

Figure 4-17. *View audit logs*

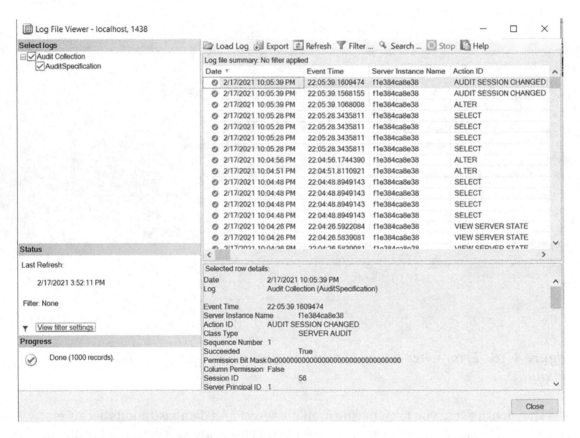

Figure 4-18. *Audit log results*

A dialog box pops up with the 1000 most recent events, as shown in Figure 4-18. There may be nothing listed because nothing auditable happened yet. There may be a lot of auditing data because there's a bunch of stuff happening in the background that you didn't realize was happening. SQL Server has a lot of internal processes that may be collected by your audit. There is a way to filter audit data before it collects, which will be covered soon.

If you stored your audit logs in the application or security log, you will get a different view on the Log File Viewer, which instead queries the audit data from the application or security log as shown in Figure 4-19.

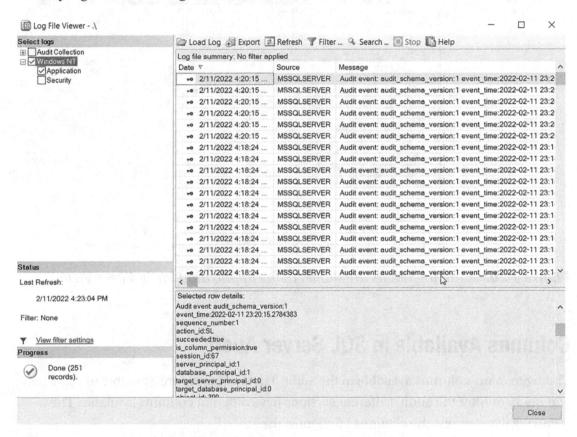

Figure 4-19. *Audit log results stored in the application log*

If you stored your audit logs in the application or security log, you can also view them from the Event Viewer on Windows as shown in Figure 4-20.

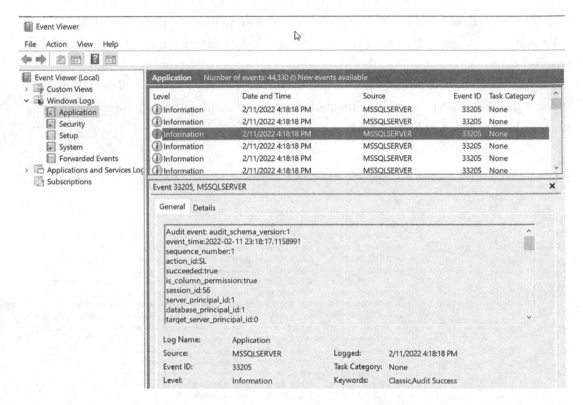

Figure 4-20. *Audit log results are shown in the application log in Event Viewer*

Columns Available in SQL Server Audit

There are many columns available in the audit. These columns are available to you when
you query or filter the audit. Different versions have different columns available. The
following list contains the columns I find most useful:

- **SQL Server 2012/2014/2016**

  - event_time

  - action_id

  - succeeded

  - server_principal_name

  - server_instance_name

  - database_name

- schema_name

- object_name

- statement

- file_name

- **SQL Server 2017 – All columns in 2016 and earlier, plus these additional columns**

  - client_ip

  - application_name

- **SQL Server 2019 – All columns in 2017 and earlier, plus this additional column**

  - host_name

Note   There are a lot more columns than those in the previous list and every version adds new columns. The following links provide more information on the columns available in the audit data depending on the location you chose to store your audit.

https://docs.microsoft.com/en-us/sql/relational-databases/security/auditing/sql-server-audit-records?view=sql-server-ver15

https://docs.microsoft.com/en-us/sql/relational-databases/system-functions/sys-fn-get-audit-file-transact-sql?view=sql-server-ver15

Filtering SQL Server Audits

You can use the audit dialog box to filter as shown in Figure 4-21.

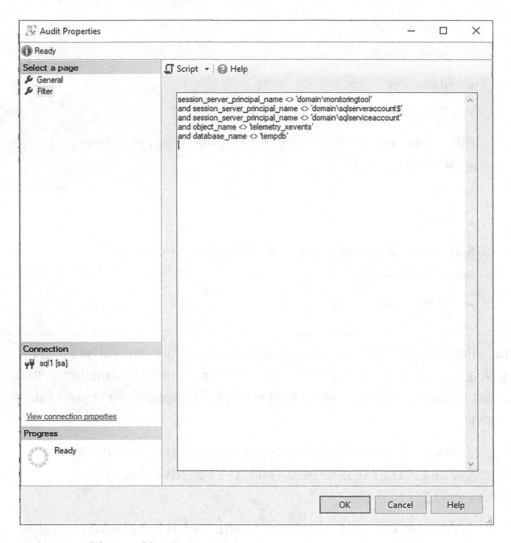

Figure 4-21. *Adding a filter to an audit*

You can filter on any column that's available in the audit collection. This way, you can filter out things like monitoring tools or service accounts. SQL Server has a servername$ account that does all kinds of stuff in the background. These types of accounts can fill up your auditing files fast making it hard to find the things you wanted to audit. For filtering, use the name of the column and what you don't want it equal to or what you want it equal to. For example, if you wanted to audit only sa, you can filter on that here. This is like a WHERE clause in a SQL statement, so you can do anything you can do in a where clause, except you don't use the WHERE keyword.

Tip   If you want to audit on a version of SQL Server that doesn't have the column you need, like client_ip or host_name, you can try to use extended events for that instead. Chapter 7, "Implementing Extended Events via the GUI," covers this information.

Deleting Audits

To delete an audit, you right-click the audit as shown in Figure 4-22.

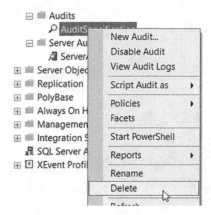

Figure 4-22. *Deleting an audit*

You will get a dialog box, and what's very nice about this dialog box is you can choose to disable it with a checkbox as shown in Figure 4-23. You need to disable an audit before you can delete it.

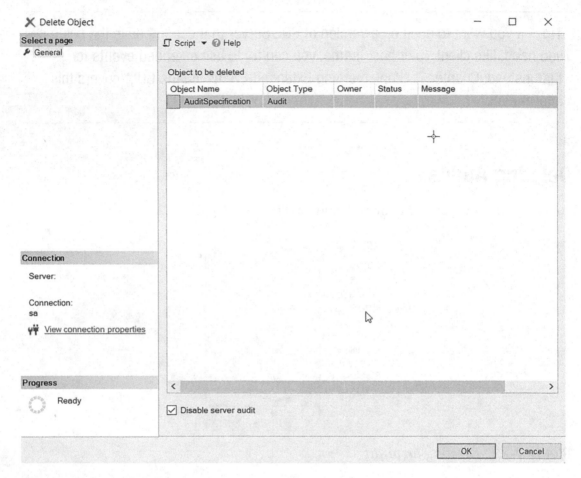

Figure 4-23. *Disabling the audit before deleting it*

When you delete the audit, the files remain on disk. I deleted the audit and thought the files were gone, too. No, the files are still there. This is in case you need them later for auditing purposes. You must go manually delete them.

When deleting audits, you can orphan your server and database audits. The server and database audits will stay there and seem fine, but no data will collect because the audit is gone. Figure 4-24 shows you server and database audits are still in place even though there is no audit.

Figure 4-24. *Audit is gone, but server and database audits seem fine*

If you go into the server or database audits, they will have a blank audit as shown in Figure 4-25.

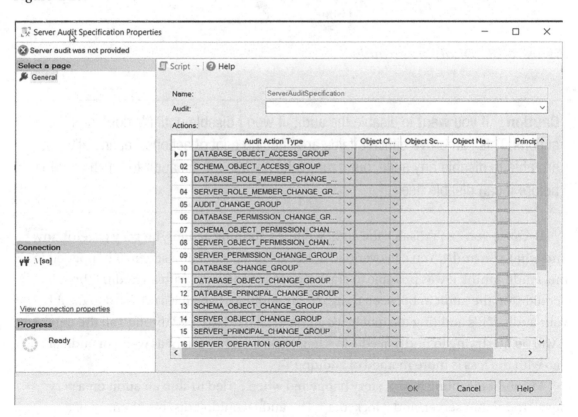

Figure 4-25. *Server audit specification is missing the audit*

There is a message at the top left of Figure 4-25 telling you "Server audit was not provided" and it needs that to collect data.

Even if you recreate the audit with the same name, the server and database audits don't automatically associate with the new audit. The server and database audits rely on the GUID of the audit. There is a way to recreate an audit with the same GUID. This is covered in Chapter 5, "Implementing SQL Server Audit Via SQL Scripts."

Disabling Audits

You can disable the audit by right-clicking it and choosing disable in the GUI as shown in Figure 4-26.

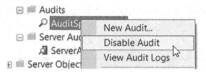

Figure 4-26. *Disabling an audit*

Caution   If you want to disable the audit, it won't disable until it's done auditing actions. This can prove difficult if you are auditing a lot of actions. Technically, you are able to disable any audit, but it may take a while for the audit to finish auditing before it can disable itself.

Because you can't disable the audit while it's auditing actions, **be very careful how and what you audit.** You can overload or freeze up a production server. It happened to me. I didn't think it was possible to crash a production server with an audit. I thought I could stop the audit in between things it was auditing. Even if it's not hard to disable your audit, if it's auditing too much, it's going to be hard to weed through all the data. It will be like trying to find a needle in a haystack, then you might as well not audit at all. I go with the less is more method of auditing.

My audit disabling horror story happened when I tried to stop an audit on a very busy production server, and it locked up. The audit wouldn't disable, then, all of a sudden, queries couldn't complete, then I couldn't even get into the server via SSMS. I had to restart the service and caused a production outage. Thankfully, a very short outage. Technically, that should not happen, though.

> **Note**   Always enable the dedicated administrator connection (DAC) in SQL Server. This way, you can always connect via DAC if you encounter connection issues. To learn more, visit `https://docs.microsoft.com/en-us/sql/database-engine/configure-windows/diagnostic-connection-for-database-administrators?view=sql-server-ver15#connecting-with-dac`

You should get a lock request timeout period exceeded error as shown in Figure 4-27.

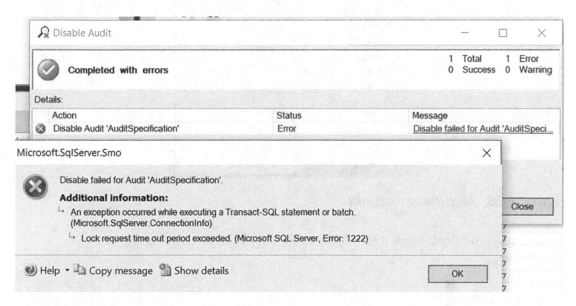

Figure 4-27. *Error disabling audit*

I couldn't get it to crash in 2019 because I couldn't mimic that load. The auditing doesn't care about long-running statements because it captures the statement and waits for the next one. The issue is when you audit statements that just keep coming one after the other and the audit never has a chance to disable in between statements. I was on a SQL Server 2014 when my horror story happened, so it may be the nature of the version I was on or how busy the server was. I also had very specific PCI auditing requirements, so I couldn't minimize the auditing as I've shown in this chapter.

Modifying Audits

Once an audit is created, you can modify it by right-clicking it and choosing Properties as shown in Figure 4-28.

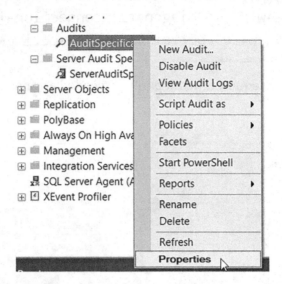

Figure 4-28. *Modifying an audit*

You can't modify it while it's enabled as shown by the error in Figure 4-29.

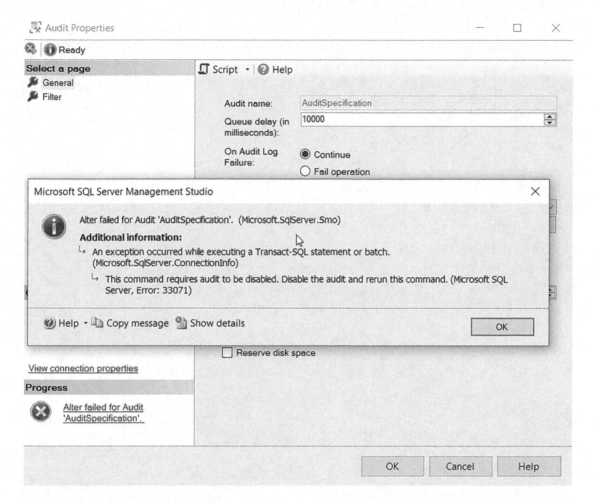

Figure 4-29. *Error modifying audit while it's enabled*

The only thing you can't modify is the name. You must delete it and recreate it to change the name.

In the next chapter, you will learn how to make your life easier by scripting out the audits you want to place on your servers. It's much easier than all of this clicking and right-clicking.

CHAPTER 5

Implementing SQL Server Audit via SQL Scripts

To make SQL Server auditing work, you need two or three components depending on what you want to audit. Chapter 3, "What Is SQL Server Audit?", covered what each of these components are and the audit categories and groups associated with them. In this chapter, you will learn how to set up the audit with SQL scripts. Chapter 4, "Implementing SQL Server Audit via the GUI," covered how to set up SQL Server Audit via the GUI in SSMS. In this chapter, you will learn how to set up SQL Server Audit via scripts.

Scripting Existing Specifications

An easy way for you to learn how to script audits is to script out existing audits. You can right-click any of the specifications created in Chapter 4, "Implementing SQL Server Audit via the GUI," and choose Script Audit as, then CREATE To, then New Query Editor Window, as shown in Figure 5-1.

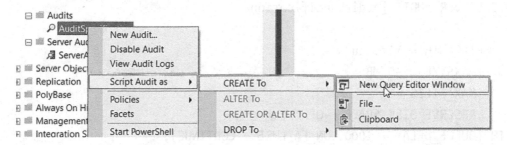

Figure 5-1. *Scripting out existing audit*

J. Bush, *Practical Database Auditing for Microsoft SQL Server and Azure SQL,*
https://doi.org/10.1007/978-1-4842-8634-0_5

This will bring a script version of your audit into a tab in SSMS. The scripts will be covered in this chapter, so you will have a better understanding of how you can create, modify, and delete them.

Setting Up the Audit

For a quick recap, to make SQL Server auditing work, you need two or three things depending on what you want to audit:

- **You're required to create an audit.** This will determine where you store audit data, how much audit data to keep, and several other settings associated with auditing.

- **You will also need one server and/or one database audit per database to collect audit data.** The server and database audits must be associated with an audit. Each audit can have one server and one database audit. These server and database audits are not dependent on each other. The server audit specification is generally good for auditing server-level changes and/or all the databases at the same time. The database audit specification is good for auditing one database or a subset of activities in one database.

Listing 5-1 shows how to create an audit via script.

Listing 5-1. Creating an audit

```
USE [master];
CREATE SERVER AUDIT [AuditSpecification]
TO FILE
(      FILEPATH = N'e:\audits\'
       ,MAXSIZE = 50 MB
       ,MAX_FILES = 4
       ,RESERVE_DISK_SPACE = OFF
) WITH (QUEUE_DELAY = 1000, ON_FAILURE = CONTINUE);
ALTER SERVER AUDIT [AuditSpecification] WITH (STATE = ON);
```

Let's look at each of the pieces of the script in Listing 5-1:

- **Database context** – USE [master];

  All audits are created in the master database.

- **Audit name** – CREATE SERVER AUDIT [AuditSpecification]

  I tend to name it AuditSpecification or AuditSpecification_ servername. This is entirely up to you based on how descriptive you want to name it. You can create multiple audits, though, so it may make sense to make it a more descriptive name if you plan to add additional audits.

- **Audit destination**

  - TO FILE – I always write to the file choice because it's easiest for me. I don't have a lot of auditing restrictions. Yes, the auditors want to know what happened, but they don't think that we're going in there secretly deleting audit files and not reporting on audit data.

  - TO APPLICATION_LOG – I could see storing audit data in the application log if you have a log scraping application like Splunk that reads all the logs and gathers them in a central repository. This has different options, much fewer options, to configure than TO FILE. An example is provided in the next section.

  - TO SECURITY_LOG – This has more restrictions than writing to the application log, but the same concept applies. This is the most secure option for storing audit data because it's the least likely to have anyone tamper with it. This has different options, much fewer options, to configure than TO FILE. An example is provided in the next section.

- **Queue delay** – QUEUE_DELAY = 1000

  This is the wait time in milliseconds before it audits. You can set this to 0, 1000, or something greater than 1000. I leave it at 1000.

- **On audit log failure** – ON_FAILURE = CONTINUE

- **CONTINUE** – If the audit can't capture the statement, it keeps auditing. No statements will fail because of this option. You might miss a statement here and there, but I doubt that happens often, if at all.

- **FAIL_OPERATION** – If it can't audit, it's going to cause the statement to fail. The user or application executing that statement will get an error.

- **SHUTDOWN** – If it can't audit, it's going to do what it says; it's going to shut down the server. All users and applications will no longer have access to the server.

I choose Continue on this option. I think Fail operation and Shutdown server are too drastic. I'll have people screaming at me that there's something wrong with the server if I don't choose Continue. You may want to choose Fail operation or Shutdown server if auditing is of the utmost importance like in a legal or financial database.

- **Path** – `FILEPATH = N'e:\audits\'`

If you chose File for Audit Destination, you need to choose a path. Make sure don't put audit files on the C drive. Even though we're going to limit the audit file sizes in the next steps, you don't want it accidentally filling up the C drive. I don't recommend putting audit files on data drives or log drives either. We have an E drive for applications where I work; that's a great place for audit files to go.

- **Maximum files** – `MAX_FILES = 4`

- **Maximum file size** – `MAXSIZE = 50 MB`

I never let the audit collect unlimited files and unlimited file sizes. This makes it difficult to query them. I've found 4 files of 50 MB each is good for my needs when collecting permissions and schema changes. Your number and sizing of files depend on your needs.

- **Reserve disk space** – `RESERVE_DISK_SPACE = OFF`

Since my files are quite small, I leave this set to OFF.

- **Enabling your audit** – ALTER SERVER AUDIT [AuditSpecification] WITH (STATE = ON)

  You will need to enable it, so it will collect audit data.

Caution   Don't set SQL Server Audit to collect unlimited files or allow unlimited file sizes. They will be gigantic and next to impossible to query.

If you want to store your audit data in the application log, you will set up your audit as shown in Listing 5-2.

Listing 5-2. Configuring an audit that writes to the application log

```
USE [master];
CREATE SERVER AUDIT [AuditSpecification]
TO APPLICATION_LOG
WITH (QUEUE_DELAY = 1000, ON_FAILURE = CONTINUE);
ALTER SERVER AUDIT [AuditSpecification] WITH (STATE = ON);
```

If you want to store your audit data in the security log, you will set up your audit as shown in Listing 5-3.

Listing 5-3. Configuring an audit that writes to the security log

```
USE [master];
CREATE SERVER AUDIT [AuditSpecification]
TO SECURITY_LOG
WITH (QUEUE_DELAY = 1000, ON_FAILURE = CONTINUE);
ALTER SERVER AUDIT [AuditSpecification] WITH (STATE = ON);
```

You will get an error when you try to enable the audit that's configured to use the security log as shown in Listing 5-4.

Listing 5-4. Error when creating audit that writes to the security log

```
Msg 33222, Level 16, State 1, Line 7
Audit 'AuditSpecification3' failed to start. For more information, see the
SQL Server error log.
```

The SQL Server Logs will give you additional information about the error as shown in Figure 5-2.

	2/11/2022 4:25:13 ...	spid66	SQL Server Audit could not write to the security log.
	2/11/2022 4:25:13 ...	spid66	Error: 33204, Severity: 17, State: 1.
	2/11/2022 4:25:13 ...	spid66	Audit: Server Audit: 65541, State changed from: START_FAILED to: TARGET_CREATION_FAILED
	2/11/2022 4:25:13 ...	spid66	Audit: Server Audit: 65541, Initialized and Assigned State: START_FAILED

Selected row details:
Date   2/11/2022 4:25:13 PM
Log   SQL Server (Current - 2/9/2022 1:52:00 PM)

Source   spid66

Message
SQL Server Audit could not write to the security log.

Figure 5-2. *Additional information about the error when creating an audit that writes to the security log*

To resolve the Error: 33204 SQL Server Audit could not write to the security log, you will need to configure additional items based on this Microsoft document:
`https://docs.microsoft.com/en-us/sql/relational-databases/security/auditing/write-sql-server-audit-events-to-the-security-log?view=sql-server-ver15`

If you chose the file destination for your audit, an audit file is placed on disk after you enable the audit as shown in Figure 5-3. This is where the data will live for your server and database audits that are associated with that audit.

Name	Date modified	Type	Size
AuditSpecification_D0B8D5A4-96BE-468F-A58F-41CCC3BC9E57_0_132576453114750...	2/12/2021 4:15 PM	SQLAUDIT File	0 KB

Figure 5-3. *Audit files on disk*

As the data collects, this file is going to grow to the size specified in the audit. Then it'll create another file up to the number of files specified in the configuration. Once the last file is full, it will delete the oldest file and create another new file. You will need to know how fast your files fill up so you won't miss collecting the data from them before they are deleted.

Setting Up the Server Audit Specification

The first of two optional audits is the server audit specification. Listing 5-5 shows how to create a server audit specification via script.

Listing 5-5. Creating a server audit specification

```
USE [master];
CREATE SERVER AUDIT SPECIFICATION [ServerAuditSpecification]
FOR SERVER AUDIT [AuditSpecification]
ADD (DATABASE_OBJECT_ACCESS_GROUP),
ADD (SCHEMA_OBJECT_ACCESS_GROUP),
ADD (DATABASE_ROLE_MEMBER_CHANGE_GROUP),
ADD (SERVER_ROLE_MEMBER_CHANGE_GROUP),
ADD (AUDIT_CHANGE_GROUP),
ADD (DBCC_GROUP),
ADD (DATABASE_PERMISSION_CHANGE_GROUP),
ADD (SCHEMA_OBJECT_PERMISSION_CHANGE_GROUP),
ADD (SERVER_OBJECT_PERMISSION_CHANGE_GROUP),
ADD (SERVER_PERMISSION_CHANGE_GROUP),
ADD (DATABASE_CHANGE_GROUP),
ADD (DATABASE_OBJECT_CHANGE_GROUP),
ADD (DATABASE_PRINCIPAL_CHANGE_GROUP),
ADD (SCHEMA_OBJECT_CHANGE_GROUP),
ADD (SERVER_OBJECT_CHANGE_GROUP),
ADD (SERVER_PRINCIPAL_CHANGE_GROUP),
ADD (SERVER_OPERATION_GROUP),
ADD (APPLICATION_ROLE_CHANGE_PASSWORD_GROUP),
ADD (LOGIN_CHANGE_PASSWORD_GROUP),
ADD (SERVER_STATE_CHANGE_GROUP),
ADD (DATABASE_OWNERSHIP_CHANGE_GROUP),
ADD (SCHEMA_OBJECT_OWNERSHIP_CHANGE_GROUP),
ADD (SERVER_OBJECT_OWNERSHIP_CHANGE_GROUP),
ADD (USER_CHANGE_PASSWORD_GROUP)
WITH (STATE = ON);
```

Suggestions on how to configure your server audit specification:

71

- **Database context** – `USE [master];`

  All server audit specifications are created in the master database.

- **Name** – `CREATE SERVER AUDIT SPECIFICATION [ServerAuditSpecification]`

  I tend to name it ServerAuditSpecification or ServerAuditSpecification_servername. This is entirely up to you based on how descriptive you want to name it. You can create multiple server audits, though, so it may make sense to make it a more descriptive name if you plan to add additional audits.

- **Audit** – `FOR SERVER AUDIT [AuditSpecification]`

  You need to associate it with your audit. You need this association because this is where your audit data will live.

- **Actions** – `ADD (AUDIT_ACTIONS)`

  I'm capturing permissions and schema changes at the server level and in all the databases on the server. I'm also capturing if someone changes a password, changes an audit, or if someone issues a DBCC command. Chapter 3, "What Is SQL Server Audit?", has a section on Server Audit Action Groups to help you determine what each action audits.

- **Enabling your audit** – `WITH (STATE = ON);`

  You will need to enable it, so it will collect audit data.

Setting Up the Database Audit Specification

The second of two optional components is the database audit. Listing 5-6 shows how to create a database audit specification via script.

Listing 5-6. Creating a database audit specification

```
USE [dbname];
CREATE DATABASE AUDIT SPECIFICATION [DatabaseAuditSpecification_dbname]
FOR SERVER AUDIT [AuditSpecification]
```

```
ADD (DATABASE_ROLE_MEMBER_CHANGE_GROUP),
ADD (AUDIT_CHANGE_GROUP),
ADD (DBCC_GROUP),
ADD (DATABASE_PERMISSION_CHANGE_GROUP),
ADD (DATABASE_OBJECT_PERMISSION_CHANGE_GROUP),
ADD (SCHEMA_OBJECT_PERMISSION_CHANGE_GROUP),
ADD (DATABASE_CHANGE_GROUP),
ADD (DATABASE_OBJECT_CHANGE_GROUP),
ADD (DATABASE_PRINCIPAL_CHANGE_GROUP),
ADD (SCHEMA_OBJECT_CHANGE_GROUP),
ADD (APPLICATION_ROLE_CHANGE_PASSWORD_GROUP),
ADD (DATABASE_OWNERSHIP_CHANGE_GROUP),
ADD (DATABASE_OBJECT_OWNERSHIP_CHANGE_GROUP),
ADD (SCHEMA_OBJECT_OWNERSHIP_CHANGE_GROUP),
ADD (USER_CHANGE_PASSWORD_GROUP)
WITH (STATE = ON);
```

Suggestions on how to configure your database audit specification:

- **Database context** – USE [dbname];

  All database audit specifications are created in the database you want
  to audit.

- **Name** – CREATE DATABASE AUDIT SPECIFICATION
  [DatabaseAuditSpecification_dbname]

  I always name it underscore database name because it helps identify
  what database it's auditing like DatabaseAuditSpecification_Auditing.
  This is entirely up to you based on how descriptive you want to name
  it. You can create multiple audits, though, so it may make sense to
  make it a more descriptive name if you plan to add additional audits.
  One thing to note is that if you don't put the name of the database
  in the name of the database audit, you won't be able to easily query
  the system tables that store the audit information. Those tables are
  very helpful if you've named your audits descriptively. Querying the
  system tables will be covered in more detail in this chapter.

- **Audit** – FOR SERVER AUDIT [AuditSpecification]

You need to associate it with your audit. You need this association because this is where your audit data will live.

- **Actions** – `ADD (AUDIT_ACTIONS)`

  I'm capturing permissions and schema changes at the database level. Chapter 3, "What Is SQL Server Audit?", has a section on Database Audit Action Groups to help you determine what each action audits. **Don't use this if you're already getting permissions and schema changes at the server audit level. This will produce duplicate audit records.**

- **Enabling your audit** – `WITH (STATE = ON);`

  You will need to enable it, so it will collect audit data.

Where the database audit shines is if you want to audit objects. With a database audit, you can audit things like insert, update, delete, select, and execute statements on objects in the current database, like tables, views, and stored procedures. You can also audit an entire schema or database. Listing 5-7 shows how to create a database audit specification to audit DML actions via script.

Listing 5-7. Creating a database audit specification to audit DML actions

```
USE [Auditing];
CREATE DATABASE AUDIT SPECIFICATION [DatabaseAuditSpecification_
AuditingTables]
FOR SERVER AUDIT [AuditSpecification_AuditingTables]
ADD (INSERT ON OBJECT::[dbo].[testing] BY [public]),
ADD (EXECUTE ON OBJECT::[dbo].[SelectTestingTable] BY [public]),
ADD (SELECT ON OBJECT::[dbo].[TestingTop10] BY [public]),
ADD (DELETE ON SCHEMA::[dbo] BY [auditing]),
ADD (UPDATE ON DATABASE::[Auditing] BY [public])
WITH (STATE = ON);
```

Suggestions on how to configure your database audit specification when auditing specific objects, schemas, or databases:

- **Database context** – `USE [dbname];`

All database audit specifications are created in the database you want to audit.

- **Name** – `CREATE DATABASE AUDIT SPECIFICATION [DatabaseAuditSpecification_AuditingTables]`

  I always name it underscore something descriptive to its purpose because it helps identify what it's auditing.

- **Audit** – `FOR SERVER AUDIT [AuditSpecification_AuditingTables]`

  You need to associate it with your audit. You need this association because this is where your audit data will live. I tend to create a separate audit for these types of audits because I don't want this audit data stored along with permissions and schema changes.

- **Audit Action Type** – Chapter 3, "What Is SQL Server Audit?", has a section on Database Audit Action Groups to help you determine what each action audits.

  - **INSERT** – `ADD (INSERT ON OBJECT::[dbo].[testing] BY [public])`

    Audits who inserts to a table, schema, or database. In this case, it's capturing inserts on the object dbo.testing by public. Public, in this case, means anyone who inserts to this table. If you want to audit one user, you can change that to a specific user. If you want to audit more than one user, you need to add one line for each user like so:

    `ADD (INSERT ON OBJECT::[dbo].[testing] BY [user1]),`

    `ADD (INSERT ON OBJECT::[dbo].[testing] BY [user2])`

  - **UPDATE** – `ADD (UPDATE ON DATABASE::[Auditing] BY [public])`

    Audits who updates a table, schema, or database. In this case, it's capturing updates on the entire auditing database by anyone who updates it. **Be very careful auditing entire schemas or databases. They can overload your audit and/or server.**

- **EXECUTE** – ADD (EXECUTE ON OBJECT::[dbo].
  [SelectTestingTable] BY [public])

  Audits who executes a single stored procedure, schema, or
  database. In this case, it's capturing anyone who executes the
  dbo.SelectTestingTable stored procedure.

- **SELECT** – ADD (SELECT ON OBJECT::[dbo].[TestingTop10] BY
  [public])

  Audits who selects from a table, view, function, schema, or
  database. In this case, it's capturing anyone who selects from the
  dbo.TestingTop10 object.

- **DELETE** – ADD (DELETE ON SCHEMA::[dbo] BY [auditing])

  Audits who deletes from a table, schema, or database. In this
  case, it's capturing deletes on the entire dbo schema in the
  auditing database by anyone who deletes. **Be very careful
  auditing entire schemas or databases. They can overload your
  audit and/or server.**

Note   You can use INSERT, EXECUTE, UPDATE, SELECT, and DELETE on an
OBJECT, SCHEMA, or DATABASE.

Querying System Views

You can query system views to see the settings of your audits. This can make it easier to
see the audit settings without having to go in via the GUI.

Listing 5-8 gives you the query to get a listing of the audits and their settings.

Listing 5-8. Querying system view to list audits

```
USE master;
SELECT * FROM sys.server_file_audits;
```

Figure 5-4 shows you a cross-section of results from the sys.server_file_audits view.

	audit_id	name	type_desc	queue_delay	max_file_size	max_files	log_file_path	log_file_name
1	65536	AuditSpecification	FILE	1000	50	4	C:\audits\	AuditSpecification_A39B90EF

Figure 5-4. *System view results listing audits*

Tip   To get a description of all the columns in the sys.server_file_audits table, visit `https://docs.microsoft.com/en-us/sql/relational-databases/ system-catalog-views/sys-server-file-audits-transact- sql?view=sql-server-ver15`

Listing 5-9 gives you the query to get a listing of the server audit specifications and their settings.

Listing 5-9. Querying system view to list server audit specifications

```
USE master;
SELECT
        sas.name as ServerAuditSpecName,
        sfa.name as AuditSpecName,
        sasd.audit_action_name,
        sas.is_state_enabled
FROM sys.server_audit_specifications sas
LEFT JOIN sys.server_audit_specification_details sasd
ON sas.server_specification_id = sasd.server_specification_id
LEFT JOIN sys.server_file_audits sfa
ON sas.audit_guid = sfa.audit_guid;
```

Figure 5-5 shows you a cross-section of results from the query in Listing 5-9.

	ServerAuditSpecName	AuditSpecName	audit_action_name	is_state_enabled
1	ServerAuditSpecification	AuditSpecification	DATABASE_OBJECT_ACCESS_GROUP	1
2	ServerAuditSpecification	AuditSpecification	SCHEMA_OBJECT_ACCESS_GROUP	1
3	ServerAuditSpecification	AuditSpecification	DATABASE_ROLE_MEMBER_CHANGE_GROUP	1
4	ServerAuditSpecification	AuditSpecification	SERVER_ROLE_MEMBER_CHANGE_GROUP	1
5	ServerAuditSpecification	AuditSpecification	AUDIT_CHANGE_GROUP	1

Figure 5-5. *System view results listing server audit specifications*

Tip   To get a description of all the columns in the server audit system views, visit
https://docs.microsoft.com/en-us/sql/relational-databases/
system-catalog-views/sys-server-audit-specifications-
transact-sql?view=sql-server-ver15

https://docs.microsoft.com/en-us/sql/relational-databases/
system-catalog-views/sys-server-audit-specification-details-
transact-sql?view=sql-server-ver15

Listing 5-10 gives you the query to get a listing of the database audit specifications
and their settings.

Listing 5-10. Querying system view to list database audit specifications

```
USE dbname;
SELECT
        das.name,
        sfa.name,
        dasd.audit_action_name,
        das.is_state_enabled
FROM sys.server_file_audits sfa
LEFT JOIN sys.database_audit_specifications das
ON sfa.audit_guid = das.audit_guid
LEFT JOIN sys.database_audit_specification_details dasd
ON das.database_specification_id = dasd.database_specification_id;
```

Figure 5-6 shows you a cross-section of results from the query in Listing 5-10.

	name	name	audit_action_name	is_state_enabled
1	DatabaseAuditSpecification_Auditing	AuditSpecification	DATABASE_ROLE_MEMBER_CHANGE_GROUP	1
2	DatabaseAuditSpecification_Auditing	AuditSpecification	AUDIT_CHANGE_GROUP	1
3	DatabaseAuditSpecification_Auditing	AuditSpecification	DBCC_GROUP	1
4	DatabaseAuditSpecification_Auditing	AuditSpecification	DATABASE_PERMISSION_CHANGE_GROUP	1
5	DatabaseAuditSpecification_Auditing	AuditSpecification	DATABASE_OBJECT_PERMISSION_CHANGE_GROUP	1
6	DatabaseAuditSpecification_Auditing	AuditSpecification	SCHEMA_OBJECT_PERMISSION_CHANGE_GROUP	1
7	DatabaseAuditSpecification_Auditing	AuditSpecification	DATABASE_CHANGE_GROUP	1
8	DatabaseAuditSpecification_Auditing	AuditSpecification	DATABASE_OBJECT_CHANGE_GROUP	1
9	DatabaseAuditSpecification_Auditing	AuditSpecification	DATABASE_PRINCIPAL_CHANGE_GROUP	1

Figure 5-6. *System view results listing database audit specifications*

Tip   To get a description of all the columns in the database audit system views, visit `https://docs.microsoft.com/en-us/sql/relational-databases/ system-catalog-views/sys-database-audit-specifications- transact-sql?view=sql-server-ver15`

`https://docs.microsoft.com/en-us/sql/relational-databases/ system-catalog-views/sys-database-audit-specification- details-transact-sql?view=sql-server-ver15`

Adding Multiple Audits

If you try to add another server audit to an existing audit that already has a server audit, it will fail with an error that states the audit already exists as shown in Figure 5-7. This means you can't add another server audit to it.

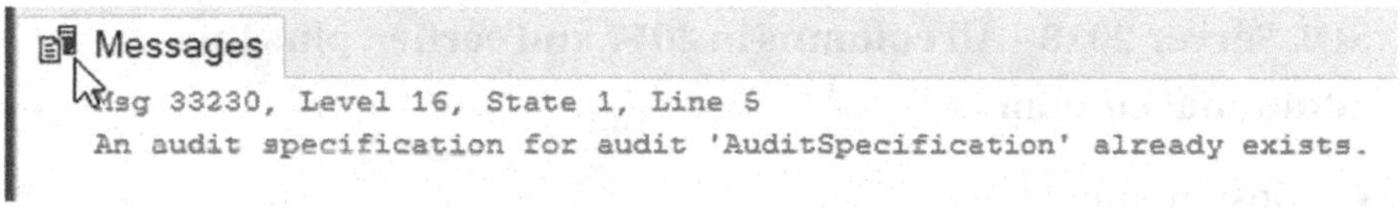

Figure 5-7. *Error when trying to add a second server audit specification to an audit*

That doesn't stop you from having multiple server and database audits because you can have multiple audits. Chapter 3, "What Is SQL Server Audit?", has a section on multiple audit setups and gives you some example scenarios you can follow.

Columns Available in SQL Server Audit

There are many columns available in the audit. These columns are available to you when you query or filter the audit. Different versions have different columns available. The following list contains the columns I find most useful:

- **SQL Server 2012/2014/2016**

  - event_time

  - action_id

- succeeded

- server_principal_name

- server_instance_name

- database_name

- schema_name

- object_name

- statement

- file_name

- **SQL Server 2017 – All columns in 2016 and earlier, plus these additional columns**

  - client_ip

  - application_name

- **SQL Server 2019 – All columns in 2017 and earlier, plus this additional column**

  - host_name

Note   There are a lot more columns than those in the previous list and every version adds new columns. The following links provide more information on the columns available in the audit data depending on the location you chose to store your audit.

https://docs.microsoft.com/en-us/sql/relational-databases/
security/auditing/sql-server-audit-records?view=sql-
server-ver15

https://docs.microsoft.com/en-us/sql/relational-databases/
system-functions/sys-fn-get-audit-file-transact-sql?view=sql-
server-ver15

Querying Audit Logs

You can query the audit files with a SQL Server system function, sys.fn_get_audit_file. This will give you a lot of different information about your audit and its associated metadata. Listing 5-11 gives you a query to get the most relevant columns of the audit returned for the last four hours.

Listing 5-11. Query audit logs

```
USE master;
SELECT DISTINCT
        event_time,
        aa.name as audit_action,
        statement,
        succeeded,
        database_name,
        server_instance_name,
        schema_name,
        session_server_principal_name,
        server_principal_name,
        object_Name,
        file_name,
        client_ip,
        application_name,
        host_name,
        file_name
FROM sys.fn_get_audit_file ('E:\audits\*.sqlaudit',default,default) af
INNER JOIN sys.dm_audit_actions aa
ON aa.action_id = af.action_id
WHERE event_time > DATEADD(HOUR, -4, GETDATE())
ORDER BY event_time DESC;
```

Figure 5-8 shows you a cross-section of the results from the query in Listing 5-11.

	event_time	audit_action	statement	succeeded	database_name
1	2022-03-17 21:49:00.8681610	ADD MEMBER	ALTER ROLE [db_datareader] ADD MEMBER [testingaudit]	1	Auditing
2	2022-03-17 21:49:00.8580276	CREATE	CREATE USER [testingaudit] FOR LOGIN [testingaudit]	1	Auditing
3	2022-03-17 21:29:09.8486870	CREATE	CREATE DATABASE AUDIT SPECIFICATION [DatabaseAuditSpeci...	1	Auditing

Figure 5-8. Audit query results

Tip   Find out more about sys.fn_get_audit_file by visiting `https://docs.microsoft.com/en-us/sql/relational-databases/system-functions/sys-fn-get-audit-file-transact-sql?view=sql-server-ver15`

Find out more about sys.dm_audit_actions by visiting `https://docs.microsoft.com/en-us/sql/relational-databases/system-dynamic-management-views/sys-dm-audit-actions-transact-sql?view=sql-server-ver15`

There may be nothing listed because nothing auditable happened yet. There may be a lot of auditing data because there's a bunch of stuff happening in the background that you didn't realize was happening. SQL Server has a lot of internal processes that may be collected by your audit. There is a way to filter audit data before it collects, which will be covered soon.

Note   SQL Server Audit data is stored in UTC time zone.

If you stored your audit logs in the application or security log, you will need to view those with the Log File Viewer or Windows Event Viewer, which instead queries the audit data from the application or security log. This is covered in more detail in Chapter 4, "Implementing SQL Server Audit via the GUI."

Filtering SQL Server Audits

You can filter on any column that's available in the audit collection. This way, you can filter out things like monitoring tools or service accounts. SQL Server has a servername$ account that does all kinds of stuff in the background. These types of accounts can fill up your auditing files fast, making it hard to find the things you wanted to audit. For filtering, use the name of the column and what you don't want it equal to or what you want it equal to. For example, if you wanted to audit only sa, you can filter on that here. This is like a WHERE clause in a SQL statement, so you can do anything you can do in a WHERE clause using the columns that are available in the audit.

Listing 5-12 uses a WHERE clause to add a filter to the audit.

Listing 5-12. Adding a WHERE clause to filter an audit

```
USE [master];
CREATE SERVER AUDIT [Audit_AuditingUser]
TO FILE
(FILEPATH = N'E:\sqlaudit\auditinguser\'
,MAXSIZE = 100 MB
,MAX_FILES = 4
,RESERVE_DISK_SPACE = OFF
) WITH (QUEUE_DELAY = 1000, ON_FAILURE = CONTINUE)
        WHERE ([server_principal_name]='auditing'
        AND [schema_name]<>'sys')
ALTER SERVER AUDIT [Audit_AuditingUser] WITH (STATE = ON);
```

In Listing 5-12, the WHERE clause will filter such that only the auditing database is audited and it will filter out the sys schema.

Tip   If you want to audit on a version of SQL Server that doesn't have the columns you need like client_ip or host_name, you can try using extended events for that instead. Chapter 7, "Implementing Extended Events via the GUI," covers this information.

Deleting Audits

To delete an audit, you can execute the query in Listing 5-13.

Listing 5-13. Deleting an audit

```
USE [master];
DROP SERVER AUDIT [AuditSpecification];
```

The query in Listing 5-13 will produce an error if the audit isn't disabled first, as shown in Figure 5-9.

📑 **Messages**

```
Msg 33071, Level 16, State 1, Line 2
This command requires audit to be disabled. Disable the audit and rerun this command.
```

Figure 5-9. *Error deleting an audit while it's enabled*

When you delete the audit, the files remain on disk. I deleted the audit and thought the files were gone, too. No, the files are still there. This is in case you need them later for auditing purposes. You must go manually delete them.

When deleting audits, you can orphan your server and database audits. The server and database audits will stay there and seem fine, but no data will collect because the audit is gone. Figure 5-10 shows you server and database audits are still in place even though there is no audit.

Figure 5-10. *Audit is gone, but server and database audits seem fine*

If you go into the server or database audits via the GUI, they will have a blank audit as shown in Figure 5-11.

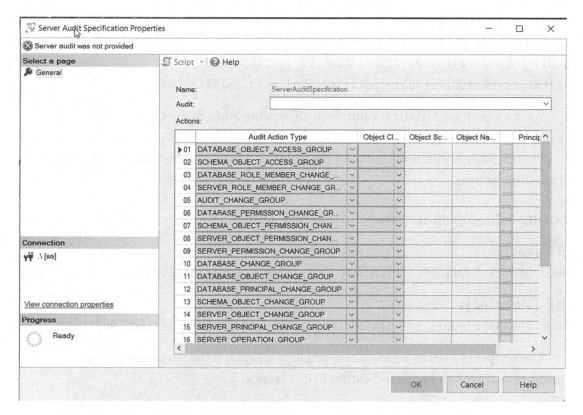

Figure 5-11. *Server audit specification is missing the audit*

There is a message at the top left of Figure 5-11 telling you "Server audit was not provided" and it needs that to collect data.

Even if you recreate the audit with the same name, the server and database audits don't automatically associate with the new audit. The server and database audits rely on the GUID of the audit. There is a way to recreate an audit with the same GUID as shown in Listing 5-14.

Listing 5-14. Recreating audit with the same GUID

```
USE [master];
CREATE SERVER AUDIT [AuditSpecification]
TO FILE
(       FILEPATH = N'C:\audits\'
        ,MAXSIZE = 50 MB
        ,MAX_FILES = 4
```

```
        ,RESERVE_DISK_SPACE = OFF
) WITH (QUEUE_DELAY = 1000, ON_FAILURE = CONTINUE,
AUDIT_GUID = 'a39b90ef-dc26-486b-b297-1571161dfda1')
ALTER SERVER AUDIT [AuditSpecification] WITH (STATE = ON);
```

You can get the GUID by scripting out an existing audit in the GUI as discussed earlier in this chapter.

There's slightly different syntax for deleting server and database audits. Listing 5-15 show these scripts.

Listing 5-15. Deleting server and database audits

```
USE [master];
DROP SERVER AUDIT SPECIFICATION [ServerAuditSpecification];

USE [Auditing];
DROP DATABASE AUDIT SPECIFICATION [DatabaseAuditSpecification_Auditing];
```

The scripts in Listing 5-15 will also produce an error if the specifications aren't disabled as shown in Figure 5-9 earlier in this section.

Disabling Audits

You can disable the audits via script as shown in Listing 5-16.

Listing 5-16. Disabling an audit

```
USE master;
ALTER SERVER AUDIT AuditSpecification
WITH (STATE = OFF);

USE master;
ALTER SERVER AUDIT SPECIFICATION [ServerAuditSpecification]
WITH (STATE = OFF);

USE Auditing;
ALTER DATABASE AUDIT SPECIFICATION [DatabaseAuditSpecification_Auditing]
WITH (STATE = OFF);
```

Listing 5-16 shows the different variations for disabling the server and database audit specifications.

Caution   If you want to disable the audit, it won't disable until it's done auditing actions. This can prove difficult if you are auditing a lot of actions. Technically, you are able to disable any audit, but it may take a while for the audit to finish auditing before it can disable itself.

Modifying Audits

Once an audit is created, you can modify it by executing an ALTER statement on it. You will need to disable it first. The only thing you can't change is the name of the audit. To change the name, you need to delete and recreate it. Listing 5-17 shows the script you can use to modify an audit.

Listing 5-17. Modifying an audit

```
USE [master];
ALTER SERVER AUDIT [AuditSpecification] WITH (STATE = OFF);
ALTER SERVER AUDIT [AuditSpecification]
TO FILE
(       MAXSIZE = 25 MB
        ,MAX_FILES = 3
)ALTER SERVER AUDIT [AuditSpecification] WITH (STATE = ON);
```

You can also modify server and database audits similarly, but they require a slightly different syntax. Listing 5-18 shows this syntax. Like the audit, you will need to disable the audit before making changes, and then reenable it when done.

Listing 5-18. Modifying a server or database audit

```
USE Auditing;
ALTER DATABASE AUDIT SPECIFICATION [DatabaseAuditSpecification_Auditing]
WITH (STATE = OFF);
ALTER DATABASE AUDIT SPECIFICATION [DatabaseAuditSpecification_Auditing]
ADD (TRANSACTION_GROUP),
```

```
ADD (SUCCESSFUL_DATABASE_AUTHENTICATION_GROUP);
ALTER DATABASE AUDIT SPECIFICATION [DatabaseAuditSpecification_Auditing]
WITH (STATE = ON);

USE master;
ALTER SERVER AUDIT SPECIFICATION [ServerAuditSpecification]
WITH (STATE = OFF);
ALTER SERVER AUDIT SPECIFICATION [ServerAuditSpecification]
ADD (LOGOUT_GROUP),
ADD (FULLTEXT_GROUP);
ALTER SERVER AUDIT SPECIFICATION [ServerAuditSpecification]
WITH (STATE = ON);
```

In the next chapter, you will learn about extended events and how you can use them to audit actions on your SQL Server.

CHAPTER 6

What Is Extended Events?

Extended events, abbreviated as XEvents, is a built-in auditing and monitoring functionality available via SQL Server Management Studio GUI or SQL scripts. You can set up and configure it to capture pretty much anything that happens on SQL Server. It's quite flexible and fairly easy to set up.

Extended events was intended as a replacement for Profiler, which was supposed to be deprecated in some future SQL Server version. Profiler is a way to create a trace that can capture everything happening on your SQL Server.

Extended events was first introduced in SQL Server 2008. In SQL Server 2012, a graphical interface was added for ease of use. It's available in every edition of SQL Server. It doesn't have restrictions based on edition like SQL Server Audit.

Extended Events Default Sessions

When you look at extended events in SSMS, you will see that there are some there already. These come with SQL Server by default and the SQL Server engine uses them. You may see different default sessions based on your version of SQL Server. Figure 6-1 shows you an example of the default sessions you may see.

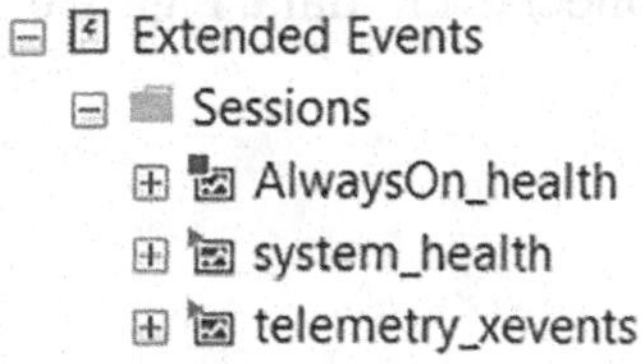

Figure 6-1. *Default extended event sessions*

system_health uses the ring buffer to store the information it's collecting and uses an event file. More information about extended events storage locations will be covered in Chapter 7, "Implementing Extended Events via the GUI." AlwaysOn_health is disabled

89

© Josephine Bush 2022
J. Bush, *Practical Database Auditing for Microsoft SQL Server and Azure SQL*,
https://doi.org/10.1007/978-1-4842-8634-0_6

by default unless you are using an availability group set up in SQL Server. system_ health and telemetry_xevents, in 2016 version and later, mainly gather information on errors, deadlocks, and waits. Don't disable or change these extended events. They are needed by SQL Server. I've read that even if you delete telemetry_xevents, Microsoft has mechanisms to put it back in place within 60 seconds. You are not prevented from querying them if they are gathering what you already need. I'm not going to cover querying these default sessions because they don't collect the audit data. I will show you how to collect in Chapter 7, "Implementing Extended Events via the GUI."

Extended Event Components

To make extended events work, you need to configure a session. This session will collect the information you want to audit.

Note   You will need sysadmin permissions to set up extended events via the SSMS GUI. If you create them via scripts, you need ALTER ANY EVENT permissions. If you only need to query them, you will need VIEW SERVER STATE.

Here are the components you need to use to configure a session.

Extended Events Templates

Extended events comes with many different templates from which to choose. This allows for easier configuration, especially if you aren't comfortable using or don't know exactly what you need to configure to collect event data. Figure 6-2 shows a list of the templates available by default.

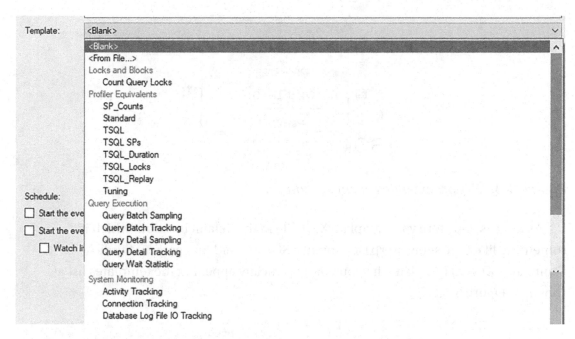

Figure 6-2. *Default templates available with extended events*

When you choose a template while creating an extended event in the GUI, you will get a description of what each template does as shown in Figure 6-3.

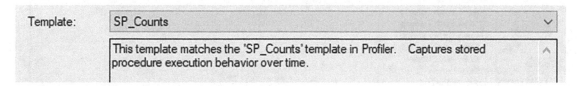

Figure 6-3. *Default templates description*

For auditing with extended events, we won't be using the templates, but they are useful for understanding how events can be captured.

You can create a custom template by exporting a session. If you know you will want to use a custom extended event session over and over, it may make sense to add it as a template. You can export a session by right-clicking on it in SSMS and choosing Export Session as shown in Figure 6-4.

Figure 6-4. *Export extended event session*

As long as you store your template XML file in the default location, which is something like C:\Users\[user]\Documents\SQL Server Management Studio\ Templates\XEventTemplates, it should automatically appear in the templates list as shown in Figure 6-5.

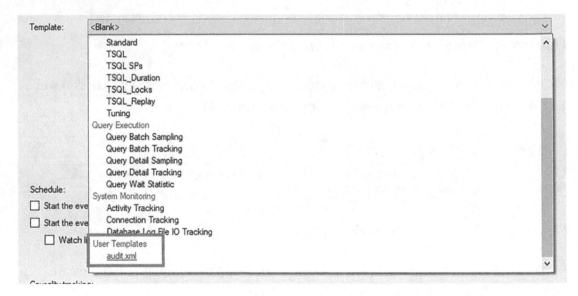

Figure 6-5. *User create templates*

If you don't see it listed under User Templates, you can choose <From File...> in the Template drop-down as shown in Figure 6-6.

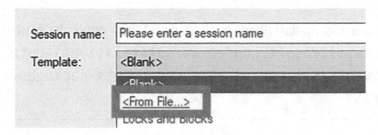

Figure 6-6. *Import a template*

Extended Events Event Library

The event library in extended events is quite extensive. It enables you to capture events happening in SQL Server.

A package is a container for extended event objects. There are many types of packages. Packages can include channels, categories, and events, all of which will be covered in this section. Figure 6-7 shows you the packages available in extended events.

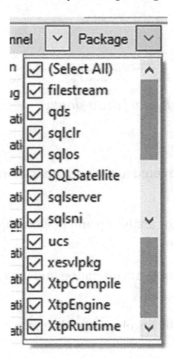

Figure 6-7. *Extended event package drop-down*

> **Note**   For more information about packages and their contents, please visit
> https://docs.microsoft.com/en-us/sql/relational-databases/
> extended-events/sql-server-extended-events-packages?view=sql-
> server-ver15

There are four channels of events helping to organize events in logical groupings.
Figure 6-8 shows you the channel drop-down that's part of the extended event setup. By
default, debug is unchecked.

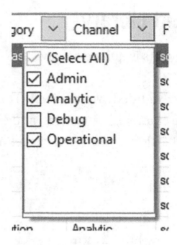

Figure 6-8. *Extended event channel drop-down*

The four channels of events are

- **Admin** – Primarily targeted to the end users, administrators, and support

- **Operational** – Used for analyzing and diagnosing a problem or occurrence

- **Analytic** – Describe program operation and are typically used in performance investigations

- **Debug** – Used solely by developers to diagnose a problem for debugging

There are many categories of events. Figure 6-9 shows you a cross-section of the
categories available in the extended event library.

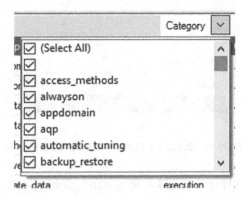

Figure 6-9. *Extended event category drop-down*

The events listed in the following are the events I recommend for auditing user actions. You can use other events if you choose, but these events I always use in my extended event audits:

- rpc_completed

- sql_batch_completed

You don't need to filter the category, channel, or package drop-downs to use these events. You can search for them in the search box shown in Figure 6-10. The event will be listed under Name.

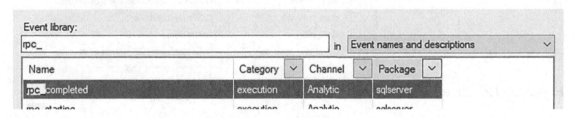

Figure 6-10. *Searching for an event in the event library*

Extended Events Global Fields and Predicates

For each of the events you select, you will need to choose global fields to capture event data. Global events are also known as actions. When you first select an event to include in your extended event session, it will default to 0 global fields shown in Figure 6-11. This doesn't mean it won't capture any information, though, because there are fields that are captured by default. Global fields give you more control over what you are capturing.

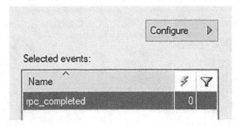

Figure 6-11. *Extended events selected events with no global fields*

You need to click the configure button to see the global fields for your selected event, which is shown in Figure 6-11.

After you click configure, you will be brought to a configuration screen where you can choose your global fields. Figure 6-12 shows you rpc_completed and its associated global fields.

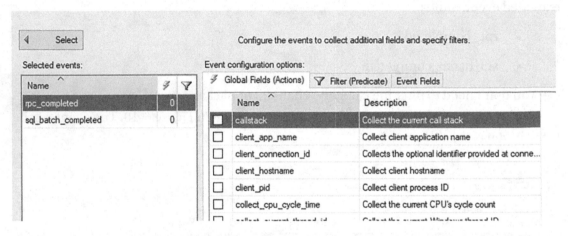

Figure 6-12. *Extended events rpc_completed without any global fields selected*

I recommend using these global fields to capture the information you will need for your event:

- client_app_name

- client_hostname

- database_name

- server_instance_name

- server_principal_name

- sql_text

Also note in Figure 6-12 there is a filter tab. Filter is also known as a predicate. This is where you can filter your extended events to capture only certain users, databases, schemas, objects, and many more. Once you have a filter on your selected event, it will show a checkmark under the filter symbol as shown in Figure 6-13. You will also see that the lightning bolt icon has six listed under it because I've chosen six global fields for each event.

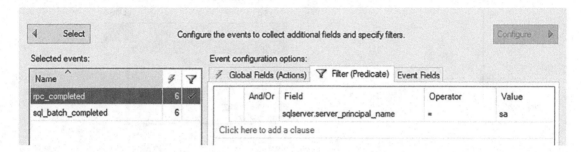

Figure 6-13. *Extended events rpc_completed with filter*

You will also need to add this filter to the sql_batch_completed event to ensure you are getting the same filter across all your events. You can filter on many different fields.

How to set up an extended event with these settings will be covered in Chapter 7, "Implementing Extended Events via the GUI."

Extended Events Targets

You need to select a target for your extended event. This target type will store your session data. This is set under the Data Storage page as shown in Figure 6-14.

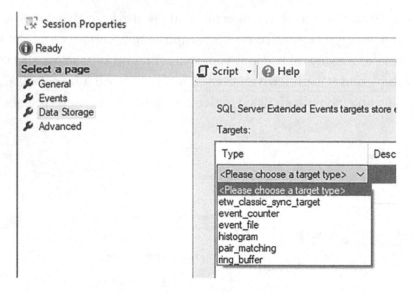

Figure 6-14. *Target options for extended events*

You have several choices for storage location. These locations will differ based on your version of SQL Server.

- **etw_classic_sync_target** – Interoperates with Event Tracing for Windows (ETW) to monitor system activity.

- **event_counter** – Counts how many times each specified event occurs.

- **event_file** – Writes event session output from buffer to a disk file.

- **histogram** – Fancier than the event_counter target.

- **pair_matching** – Detects start events that occur without a corresponding end event.

- **ring_buffer** – Good for quick and simple event testing. Holds data in memory on a first-in-first-out basis. When you stop the event session, the stored output is discarded.

Note   For more information about targets, please visit https://docs.microsoft.com/en-us/sql/relational-databases/extended-events/targets-for-extended-events-in-sql-server?view=sql-server-ver15

How to set up an extended event with event_file target will be covered in Chapter 7, "Implementing Extended Events via the GUI."

Extended Events Advanced Settings

There are some additional settings on the Advanced page of the extended event session setup. These can only be changed when you first set up your extended event. They can't be modified later. If you need to change them later, you need to drop and recreate your extended event. I never change these settings. If you decide to change these settings, be very careful since different settings can cause performance issues on your SQL Server. Figure 6-15 shows the settings from the Advanced page. These are the default settings.

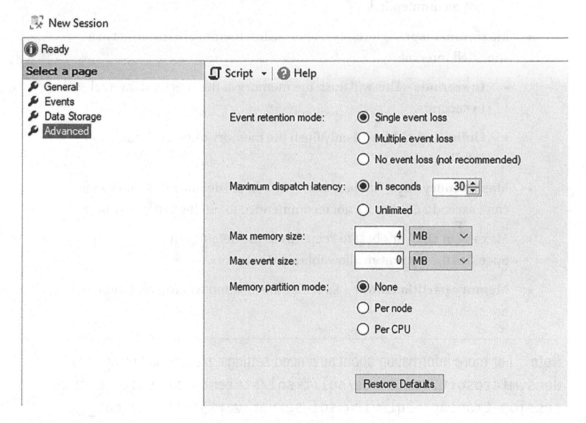

Figure 6-15. *Advanced options for extended events*

You have several advanced options. It's best to leave these on the default values, but here are some descriptions to understand what each means.

- **Event retention mode** – This will determine how SQL Server handles event loss. If the system is really busy, this will tell it whether it's acceptable to lose some or no event data.

  - **Single event loss** – This means SQL Server will lose one event if the system is too busy to audit with extended events at that time.

  - **Multiple event loss** – This means SQL Server will lose multiple events if the system is too busy to audit with extended events at that time.

  - **No event loss (not recommended)** – This won't lose any events, but can overload your system especially if it's busy. This is why it's not recommended.

- **Maximum dispatch latency** – This flushes memory to the target at a specified interval.

  - **In seconds** – This will flush the memory at the specified interval in seconds.

  - **Unlimited** – This will only flush the memory once the buffer is full.

- **Max memory sizes** – It's best to keep this at the default of 4 MB. The max can't exceed 2 GB, but it's not recommended to set this in the GB range.

- **Max event size** – It's best to keep this as the default value of 0. Specifies the maximum allowable size for events.

- **Memory partition mode** – Specifies the location where event buffers are created.

Note   For more information about advanced settings, please visit `https://docs.microsoft.com/en-us/sql/t-sql/statements/create-event-session-transact-sql?view=sql-server-ver15#with--event_session_options--n-`

Again, it's best to leave these advanced settings at the defaults to avoid issues with performance on your SQL Server.

Extended Events Use Cases

The following list takes you through some scenarios for auditing with extended events:

- **Audit everything a user does**

- Events to capture: rpc_completed and sql_batch_completed

- Global fields:

  - client_app_name

  - client_hostname

  - database_name

  - server_instance_name

  - server_principal_name

  - sql_text

  This requires a filter on server_principal_name for each of your selected events.

- **Audit everything happening in a specific database**

- Events to capture: rpc_completed and sql_batch_completed

- Global fields:

  - client_app_name

  - client_hostname

  - database_name

  - server_instance_name

  - server_principal_name

  - sql_text

  This requires a filter on database_name for each of your selected events, but be careful with this because it can create a lot of audit data. I usually only use this if I'm trying to figure out if a database is no longer used.

- **Audit everything happening on the database server**

  Events to capture: rpc_completed and sql_batch_completed

  Global fields:

  - client_app_name

  - client_hostname

  - database_name

  - server_instance_name

  - server_principal_name

  - sql_text

  This does not require a filter, but be careful with this because it can create a lot of audit data. I usually only do this if I'm trying to figure out if a SQL Server is no longer used.

- **Audit everyone using a stored procedure or table**

  Events to capture: rpc_completed

  Global fields:

  - client_app_name

  - client_hostname

  - database_name

  - server_instance_name

  - server_principal_name

  - sql_text

This requires a filter on object_name for each of your selected events.

In the next chapter, you will learn how to set up and configure extended events in SQL Server Management Studio. You also learn how to query extended events to find out what's happening on your database server.

## CHAPTER 7

Implementing Extended Events via the GUI

To make extended events work, you need to set up a session. Chapter 6, "What Is Extended Events?", covered the parts and pieces that comprise a session. In this chapter, you will learn how to set up an extended event in SQL Server Management Studio (SSMS).

Caution Just because you can audit everything, doesn't mean that you should. If you audit everything and anything, you will have a hard time weeding through it all, and you could cause performance issues on your system.

Setting Up an Extended Event via the New Session Wizard Option

The new session wizard will help to walk you through the setup of your extended event. Figure 7-1 shows how to create an extended event in SSMS by right-clicking Sessions under the Extended Events section in the Management section. During this setup, you will learn how to audit one user with extended events.

© Josephine Bush 2022
J. Bush, *Practical Database Auditing for Microsoft SQL Server and Azure SQL*,
https://doi.org/10.1007/978-1-4842-8634-0_7

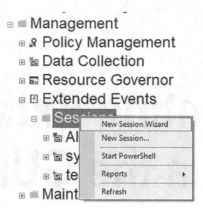

Figure 7-1. *Creating an extended event with the New Session Wizard*

Note   Not all extended event options are available in the New Session Wizard; most are, but not all. If you want to see all available options, use the New Session option instead.

By choosing New Session Wizard, you will get a dialog box that takes you step by step through filling out the details and options of your extended event as shown in Figure 7-2.

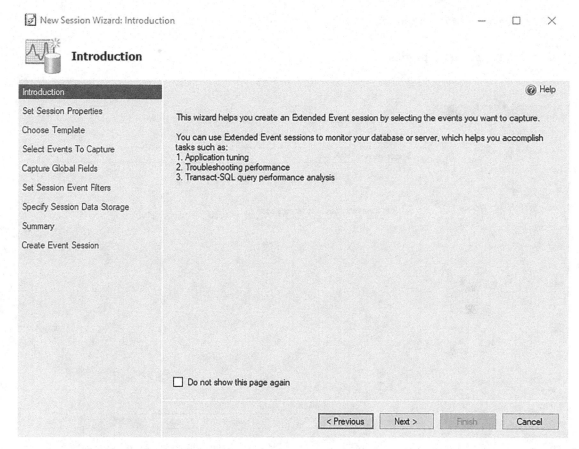

Figure 7-2. *New Session Wizard Introduction screen*

The Introduction screen gives you an overview of how you can use extended events. Clicking Next will bring you to the first configuration screen, Set Session Properties, shown in Figure 7-3. This screen requires you to name your extended event. You can also choose whether you want it to start the session at server startup. I recommend you check this box; otherwise, your extended event will be stopped on a restart, and you will have to manually start it.

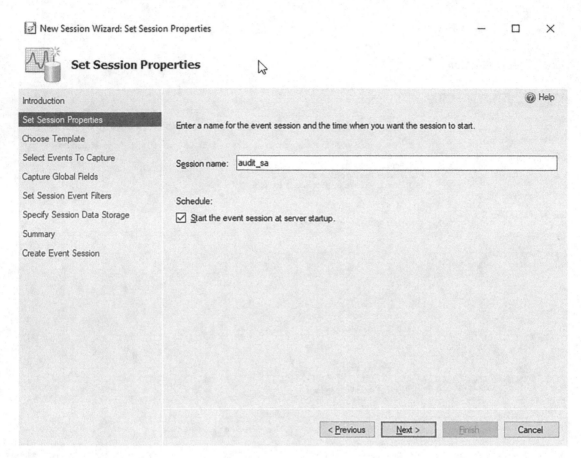

Figure 7-3. *New Session Wizard Set Session Properties screen*

After you click Next on the Set Session Properties screen, you will see the Choose Template screen as shown in Figure 7-4. I've chosen Do not use a template because I want to capture all the activity from one user, and most of these templates won't accomplish that. Chapter 6, "What Is Extended Events?", covers a bit more on templates.

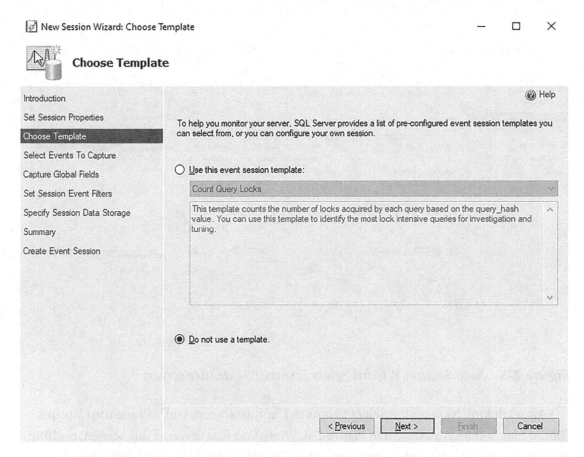

Figure 7-4. *New Session Wizard Choose Template screen*

After you click Next on the Choose Template screen, you will see the Select Events to Capture screen as shown in Figure 7-5. On this screen, you will choose rpc_completed and sql_batch_completed. These events are covered in more detail in Chapter 6, "What Is Extended Events?" You can search for each of these events in the Event Library text box. Select them, and then click the right arrow (>) to move them to the Selected events panel.

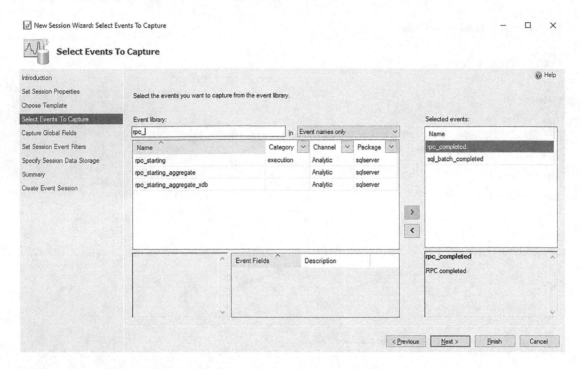

Figure 7-5. *New Session Wizard Select Events To Capture screen*

After clicking Next on the Select Events to Capture screen, you will see the Capture Global Fields screen as shown in Figure 7-6. When you first come to this screen, nothing will be checked. At this point, you must select the global fields you want to collect for each of your selected events.

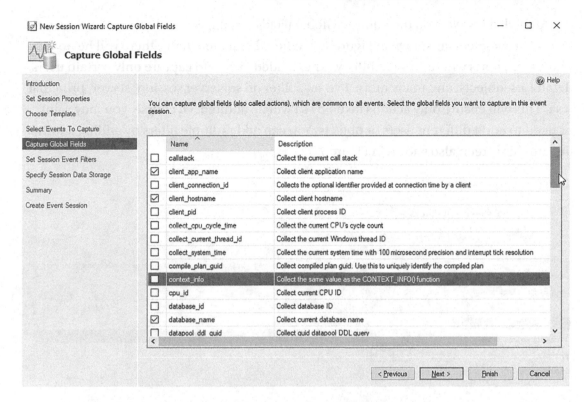

Figure 7-6. *New Session Wizard Capture Global Fields screen*

I recommend using these global fields to capture the information you will need for your event:

- client_app_name

- client_hostname

- database_name

- server_instance_name

- server_principal_name

- sql_text

These global fields are covered in more detail in Chapter 6, "What Is Extended Events?"

If you don't select any global fields, your extended event will still collect event data, but it may not include everything you may want to see associated with that event. This is why I like to select specific global fields to ensure I'm getting the global fields I need.

After clicking Next on the Capture Global Fields screen, you will see the Set Session Event Filters screen as shown in Figure 7-7. When this screen loads, there will be no filters set. This is where you can filter your extended events to capture only certain users, databases, objects, and many more. I've set a filter on sqlserver.session_server_principal = sa. This will ensure only actions taken by sa will be audited. Of course, you may want or need to audit different users or objects. You can add multiple filters by adding another line on this screen also shown in Figure 7-7.

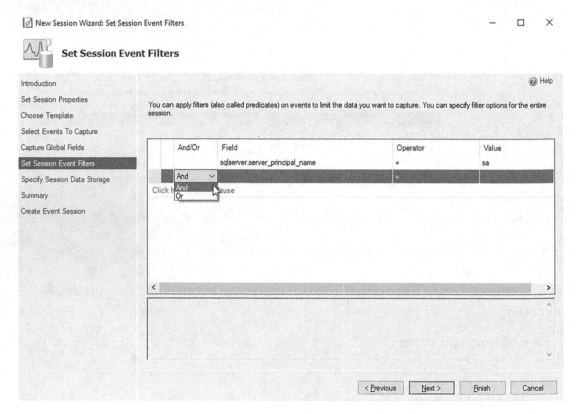

Figure 7-7. *New Session Wizard Set Session Event Filters screen*

If you want a different operator than equal (=), you can click the Operator drop-down and see all the different choices as shown in Figure 7-8. You can think of this like a WHERE clause in a SQL query.

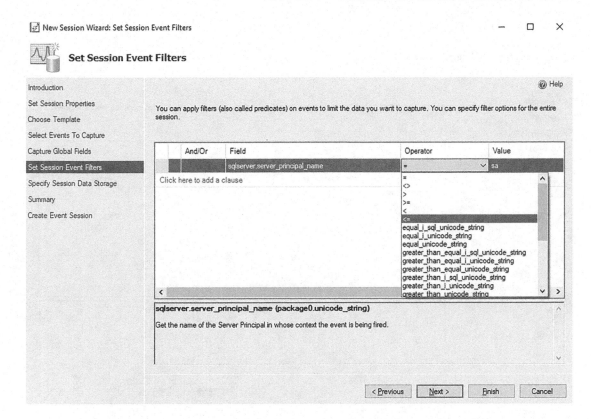

Figure 7-8. *New Session Wizard Set Session Event Filters Operator drop-down*

You can have multiple filters. For example, you could add another filter on sqlserver. database_name = master. This way, you are only auditing actions done by sa on the master database. This example is shown in Figure 7-9.

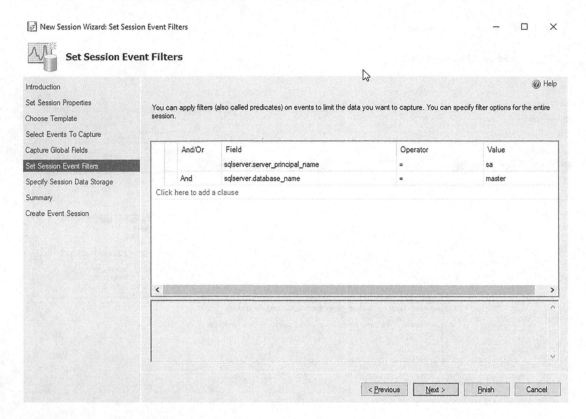

Figure 7-9. *New Session Wizard Set Session Event Filters multiple filters*

If you need to add or remove clauses, you can right-click them and choose your option from a pop-up menu as shown in Figure 7-10.

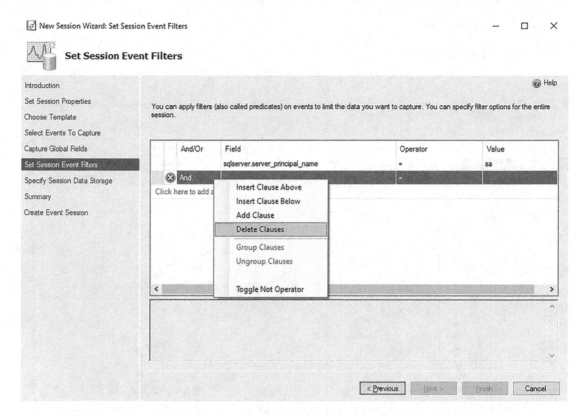

Figure 7-10. *New Session Wizard Set Session Event Filters modify filters*

If you choose Toggle Not Operator, the filter you set will be the opposite. For example, if you added sqlserver.database_name = master, but then chose Toggle Not Operator, it will get all databases except master as shown in Figure 7-11. The exclamation mark (!) shows this filter is toggled to not.

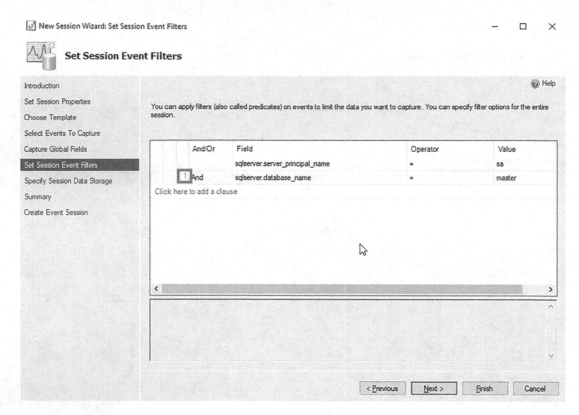

Figure 7-11. *New Session Wizard Set Session Event Filters Toggle Not Operator*

You can also group clauses together by selecting more than one row and choosing Group Clauses. These rows would then be connected by a bracket ([) as shown in Figure 7-12.

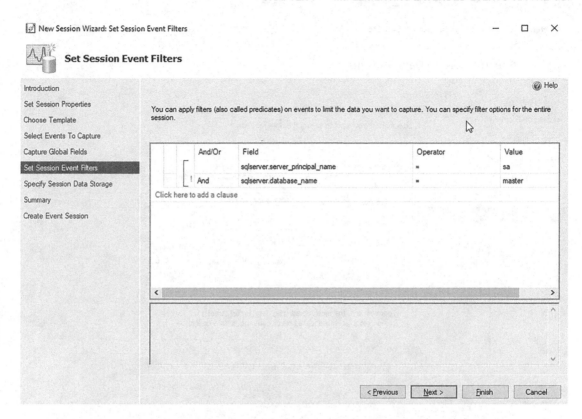

Figure 7-12. *New Session Wizard Set Session Event Filters Group Clauses*

After clicking Next on the Set Session Event Filters screen, you will see a Specify Session Data Storage screen. You will set your storage options here. This is where the New Session Wizard is more limited than the New Session dialog box setup. The New Session option is covered later in the chapter. There are only two options for storage in the New Session Wizard: file and ring buffer as shown in Figure 7-13. I tend to store events in a file, so that option is chosen.

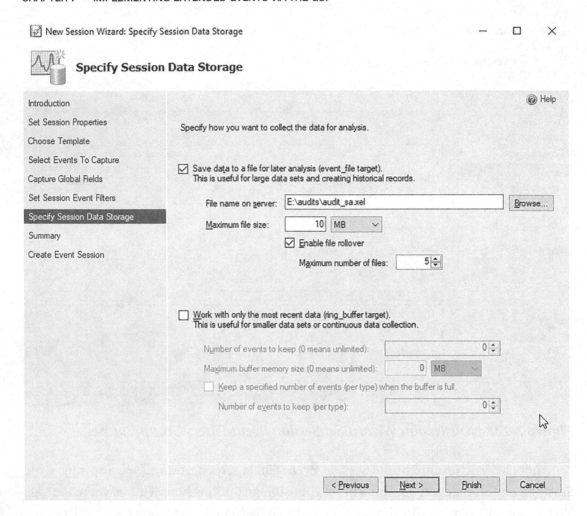

Figure 7-13. *New Session Wizard Specify Session Data Storage screen*

Here are some suggestions for file storage:

- Don't store the files on the C drive or other drives SQL Server is using for data and log files.

- Set the maximum file size to something small like 10 MB and enable file rollover of 5–10 files. If you set large file sizes with many rollover files, they will be next to impossible to query.

You can also store the data in the ring buffer or just the ring buffer. The ring buffer is more difficult to query because it's stored in XML. With a file, you have more control of how long the data will be around, whereas, with the ring buffer, you may lose data before you realize it because the ring buffer only stores a certain number of events and those events can come from more than just this extended event you are setting up.

After clicking Next on the Specify Session Data Storage screen, you will see the Summary screen. This will outline all the settings you've chosen. This screen also has a Script button, so you can script out all your settings. Figure 7-14 shows you the expanded view of the summary.

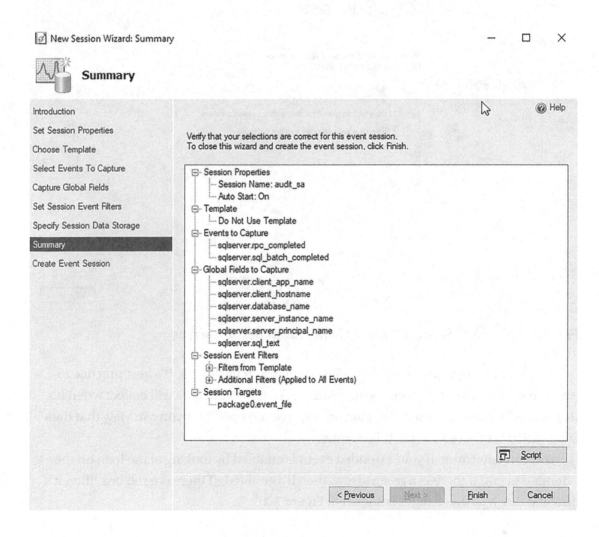

Figure 7-14. *New Session Wizard Summary*

To create the extended event, click Finish. The extended event will be set up and you will have the option to start it after creation and watch live data on screen as shown in Figure 7-15.

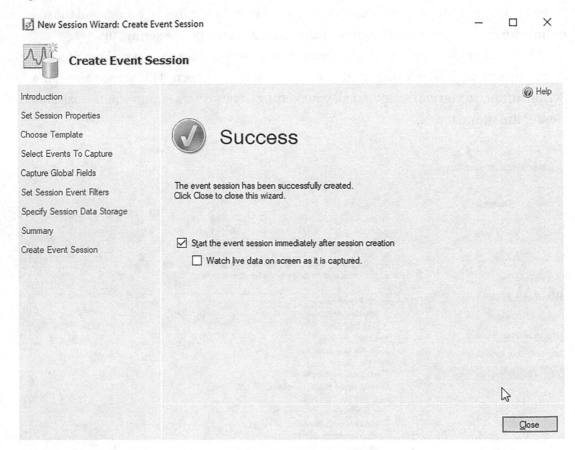

Figure 7-15. *New Session Wizard Create Event Session screen*

Each of these options in Figure 7-15 is not checked by default. It's best practice to start the session after creation. It's not required, but no event data will collect when it's stopped. Also, you can watch live data on screen at this point, or you can view that data later, which is covered later in this chapter.

You can determine if your extended event is enabled by looking at the icon on the extended event. If there is a green arrow, then it's enabled. If there is a red box, then it's disabled. Each of these states is shown in Figure 7-16.

Extended Events
  Sessions
    AlwaysOn_health
    audit_sa
    system_health
    telemetry_xevents

Figure 7-16. *Extended event state*

AlwaysOn_health is disabled and the rest of the extended events are enabled in Figure 7-16.

Setting Up an Extended Event via the New Session Option

The New Session dialog box will help you set up your extended event. Figure 7-17 shows how to create an extended event in SSMS by right-clicking New Session under the Extended Events section in the Management section. This option allows you to configure the full suite of extended event options. It's similar to the wizard. It doesn't step you through the configuration, but instead has all the pages for configuration in one easily accessed dialog box with a listing of pages on the left side. During this setup, you will learn how to audit one user with extended events.

Figure 7-17. *Creating an extended event with the New Session dialog box*

By choosing New Session, you will get a dialog box that has similar screens to the New Session Wizard. On the General screen as shown in Figure 7-18, you will

- Name it

- Choose a template (in this case, we will leave it blank)

- Decide on a schedule for starting

- Choose whether you want to watch live data after it's created

- Choose if you want causality tracking

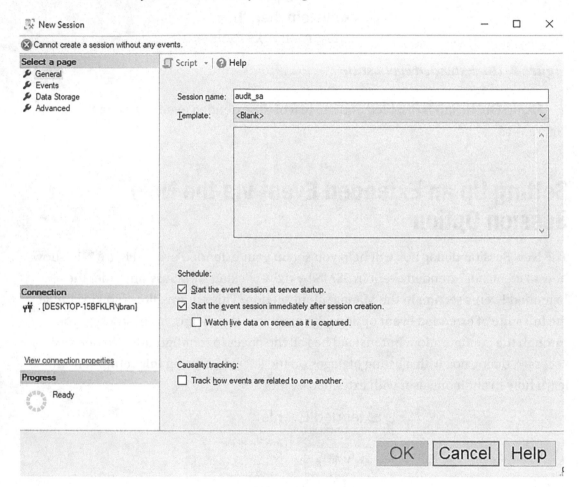

Figure 7-18. *New Session General page*

I don't use templates. I always choose to Start the session at server startup and Start the event session after creation. I never watch live data as it's captured because I can view it later, which will be covered in this chapter. I don't use causality tracking, but it can help you determine all the events associated with a query.

Once you have the General page configured, you can click on the Events page. This is where you will select your events like rpc_completed and sql_batch_completed, covered in more detail in Chapter 6, "What Is Extended Events?", as shown in Figure 7-19.

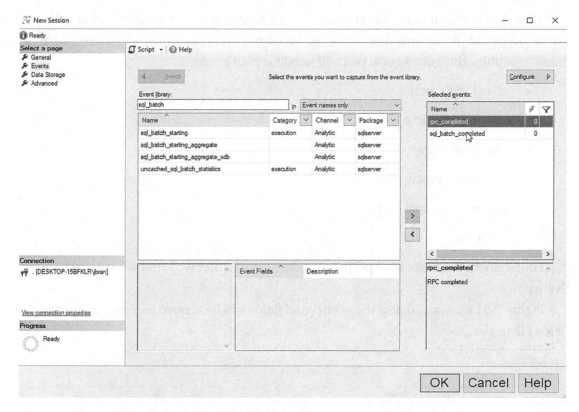

Figure 7-19. *New Session Events page*

Once you add your events to the Selected events, no Global Fields, also known as Actions, are configured for these events, yet. You can see that under the lightning bolt icon. It shows 0. To configure these, you must click Configure.

Since I'm recommending capturing the same fields for both events, select them both before clicking Configure as shown in Figure 7-20.

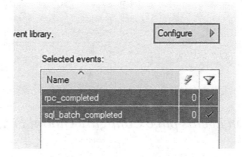

Figure 7-20. *Select both events to configure them the same*

After clicking Configure, you are brought to a configuration page with global fields. There are default fields included with each event, but I recommend using these global fields to capture the information you will need for your event:

- client_app_name

- client_hostname

- database_name

- server_instance_name

- server_principal_name

- sql_text

These global fields are covered in more detail in Chapter 6, "What Is Extended Events?"

Figure 7-21 shows you how the events and fields will look once you've selected the fields I listed earlier.

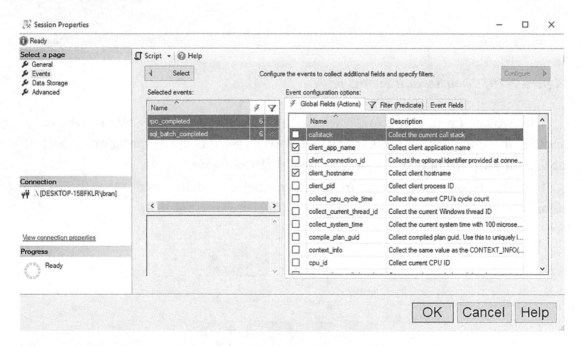

Figure 7-21. *New Session Events page Configure Global Fields*

You can see in Figure 7-21 that rpc_completed and sql_batch_completed both have six global fields.

There is a tab for Filter, also known as Predicate. Figure 7-22 shows you what it looks like when the filter is set. I've set a filter on sqlserver.server_principal_name = sa. Like with global fields, it's best to keep your filter the same for each event.

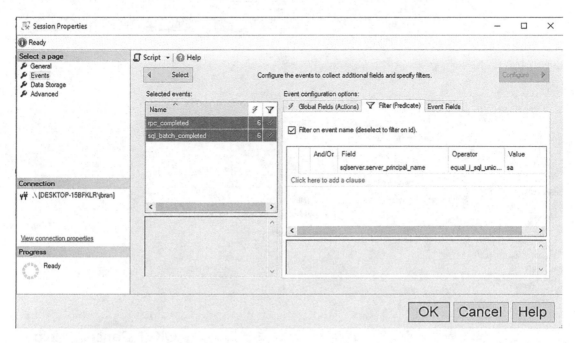

Figure 7-22. *New Session Events page filter*

If you needed to add more events to your selected events, you can click the Select button shown in Figure 7-22. This will take you back to the Event Library. If you are satisfied with your events and their global fields and filters, you can click the Data Storage page. This brings you to a page where you can configure your storage options. You have more storage options than in the New Session Wizard. These options are covered in more detail in Chapter 6, "What Is Extended Events?" Figure 7-23 shows you how I set up the storage for my extended events.

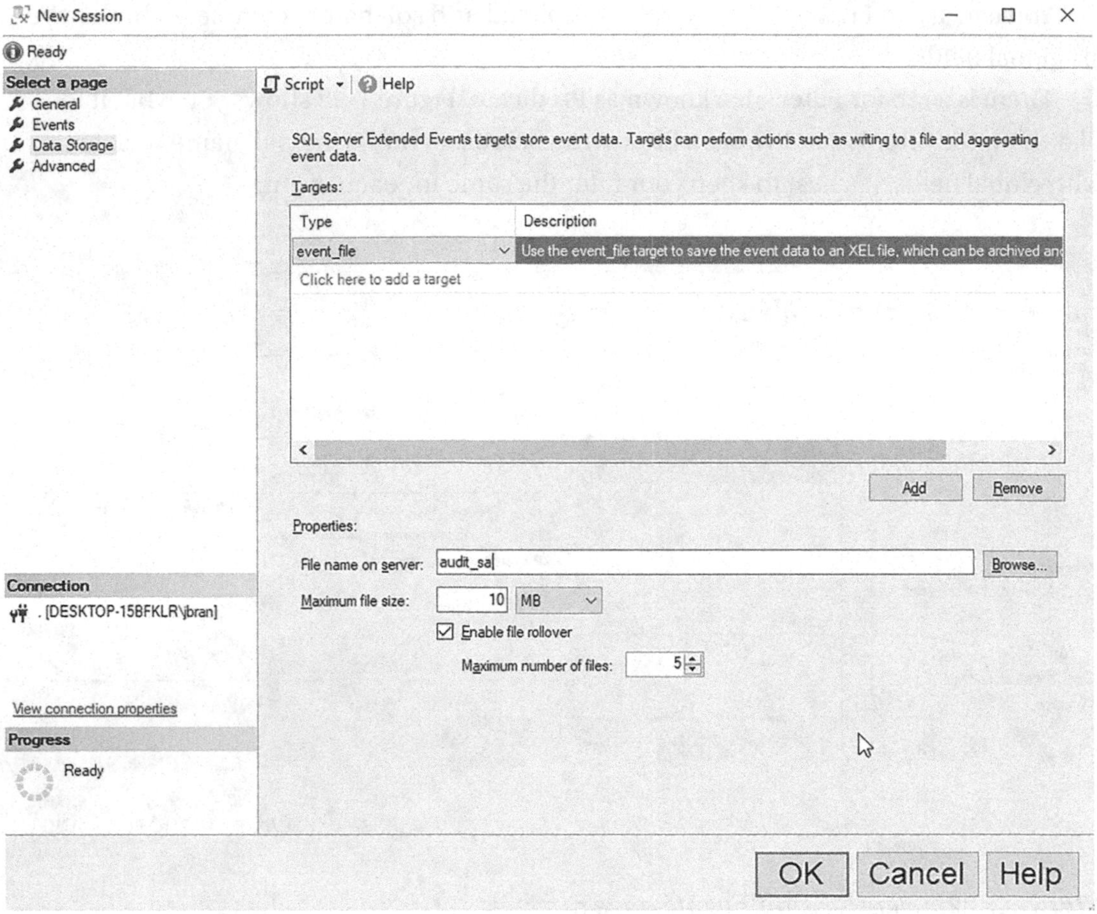

Figure 7-23. *New Session Data Storage page*

Here are some suggestions for file storage:

- Don't store the files on the C drive or other drives SQL Server is using for data and log files.

- Set the maximum file size to something small like 10 MB and enable file rollover of 5–10 files. If you set large file sizes with many rollover files, they will be next to impossible to query.

There is also an Advanced page. I suggest leaving that alone. There is more explanation of these options in Chapter 6, "What Is Extended Events?"

When you are satisfied with your session configuration, click the OK button, as shown in Figure 7-23, and the session will create.

Extended Event Files

If you chose the file destination for your extended event, the .xel file is placed on disk after you enable the extended event as shown in Figure 7-24. This is where the event data will live.

This PC > apps (E:) > audits			
Name	Date modified	Type	Size
audit_sa_0_132937560460800000.xel	4/6/2022 4:07 PM	Microsoft SQL Ser...	11 KB

Figure 7-24. *Extended event files on disk*

As the data collects, this file is going to grow to the size specified in the extended event. Then it'll create another file up to the number of files specified in the configuration. Once the last file is full, it will delete the oldest file and create another new file. You will need to know how fast your files fill up so you won't miss collecting the data from them before they are deleted.

Querying Extended Event Data

You can query the extended event via SSMS by right-clicking the extended event session as shown in Figure 7-25.

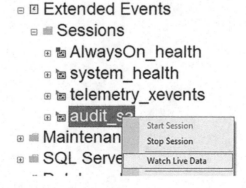

Figure 7-25. *View extended event data*

A new tab opens in the SSMS query window area as shown in Figure 7-26. Watch live data is always empty at first. It only displays events going forward, not those in the past. There may be nothing listed because nothing auditable happened yet. There may be a lot of auditing data because there's a bunch of stuff happening that you didn't realize was happening.

You can also expand the extended event and see the files inside of it, as shown in Figure 7-26. This will give you the same view as Watch Live Data, but for this specific file.

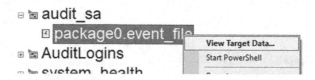

Figure 7-26. *View Target Data*

Figure 7-27 shows you a default view of the event data, but this might not be a great way to view the data.

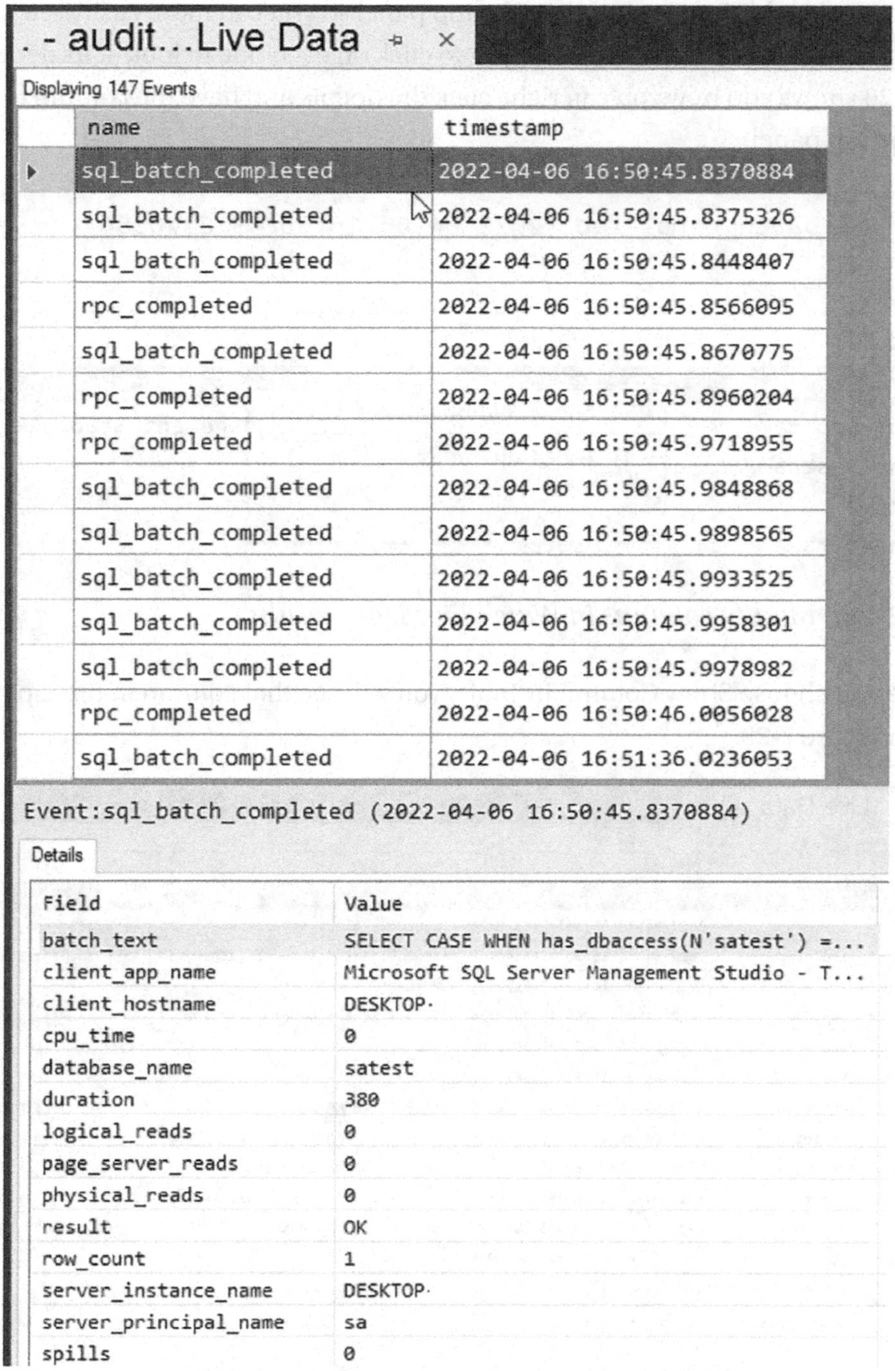

Figure 7-27. *Watch Live Data results*

You can add additional columns to the top panel so you can more easily see what each event captured instead of having to click on each one to look at its details. Figure 7-28 shows you how you can right-click the details and have the column load as part of the top panel.

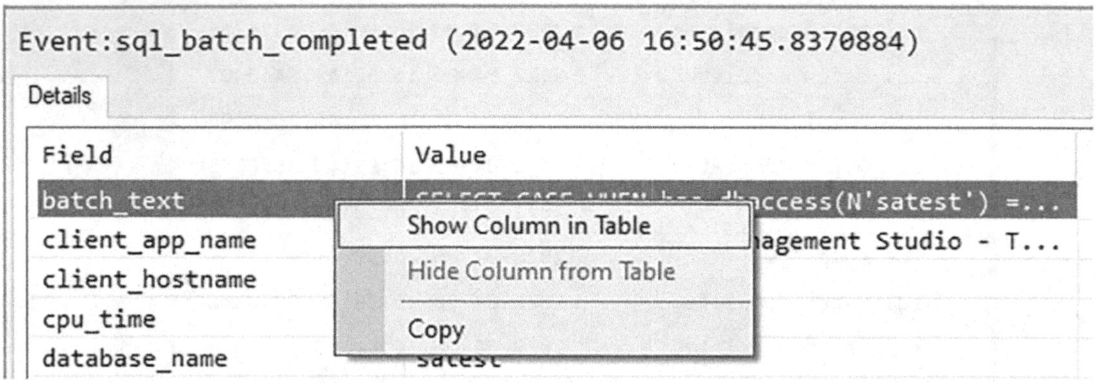

Figure 7-28. *Modify columns in Watch Live Data results*

Once you choose Show Column in Table, you will see that column in the top panel as shown in Figure 7-29.

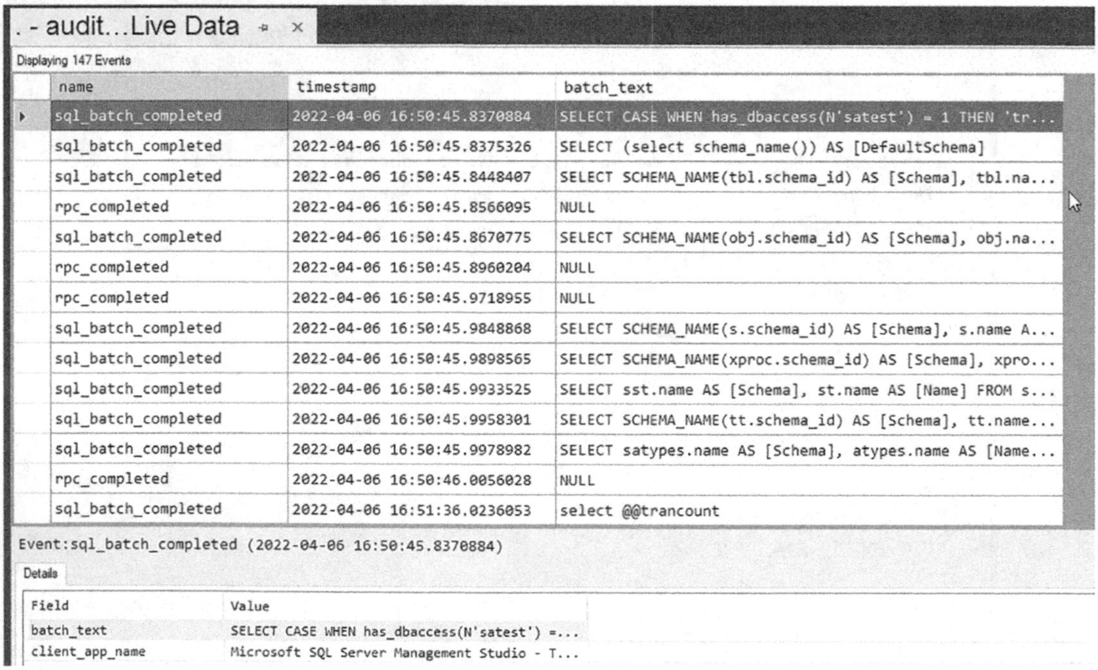

Figure 7-29. *Modified columns in Watch Live Data results*

You can also add or remove other columns in Watch Live Data as shown in
Figure 7-30.

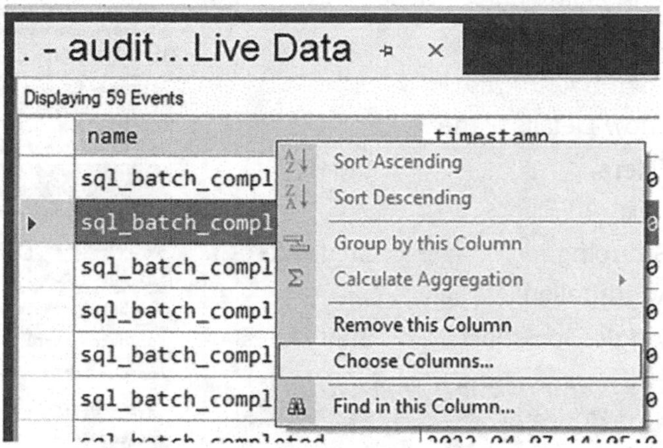

Figure 7-30. *Watch Live Data tab and add or remove columns*

When you have the Watch Live Data tab open, you will have access to a new menu
item in SSMS, Extended Events. In particular, this menu makes it easy to export the data
with the Export to option as shown in Figure 7-31.

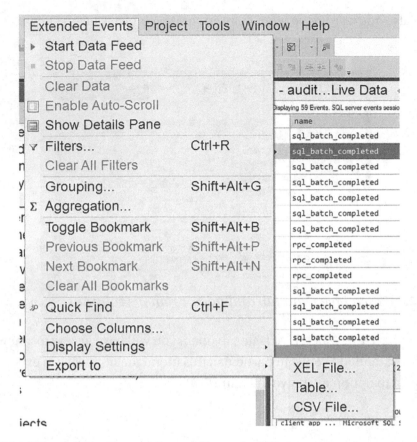

Figure 7-31. *Watch Live Data tab and Extended Events menu item*

You can filter on a value by right-clicking on it and choosing Filter by this Value as shown in Figure 7-32.

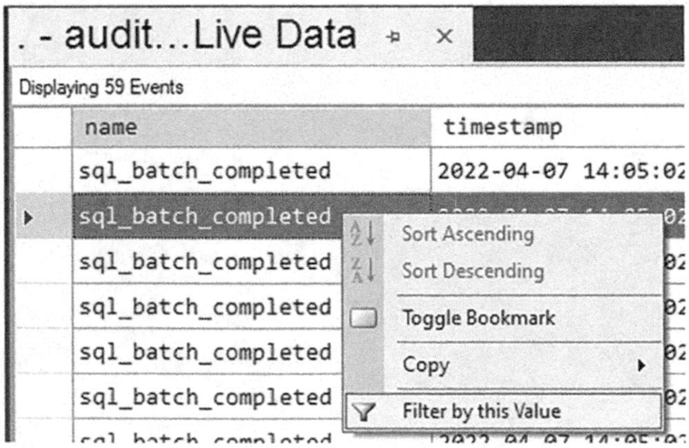

Figure 7-32. *Filtering values in Watch Live Data results*

Filter by this Value will bring up a dialog box for you to set your filter options. It will add the value you chose when you clicked Filter by this Value as shown in Figure 7-33. You can also set other filters in this dialog box as needed.

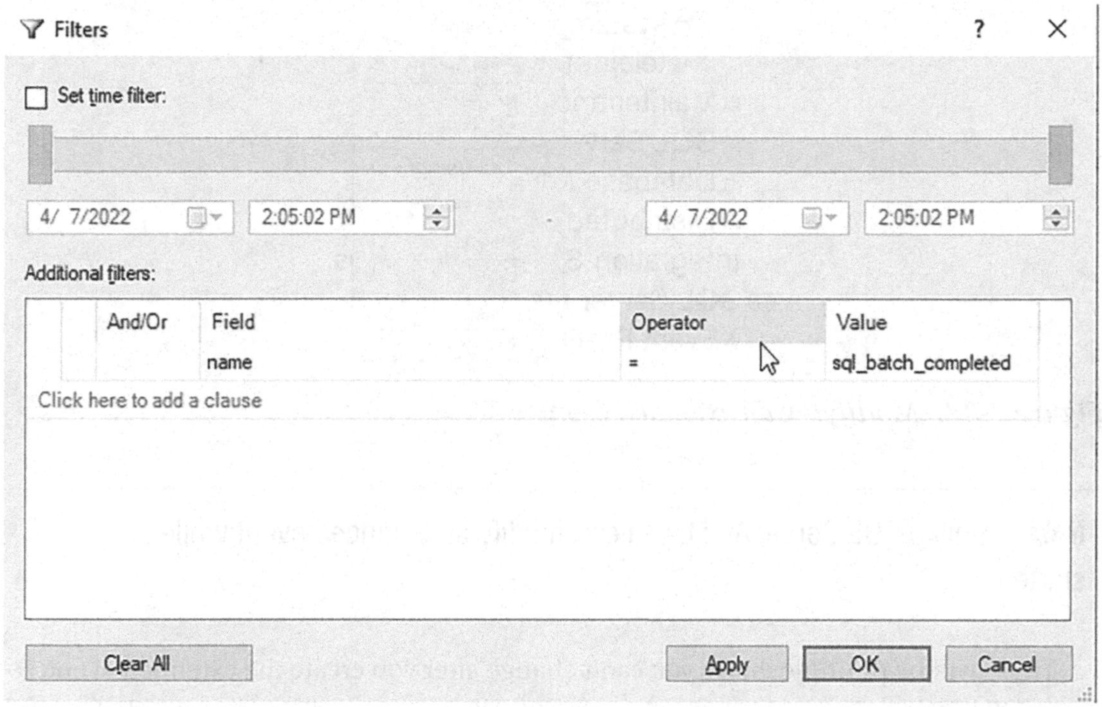

Figure 7-33. *Filtering values dialog box in Watch Live Data results*

If you find you are filtering a lot of event data when you watch live data, you will want to modify your extended event session's properties so the event data is filtered before being captured into your .xel event file, if you are using the file target. You may have seen that SQL Server does a lot in the background to support the actions being taken by a user. This is a good time to discuss modifying your extended event because you may need to tweak some of the settings and add additional filters to limit event data.

Modifying Extended Events

Once an extended event is created, you can modify it by right-clicking on the session and choosing Properties as shown in Figure 7-34. You can modify an extended event when it's started or stopped.

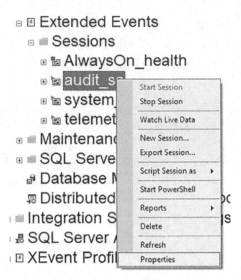

Figure 7-34. *Modifying an extended event*

Note   Unlike SQL Server Audit, you can modify an extended event while it's started.

There will be multiple things you can't change after you create the extended event, so those will be grayed out as shown in Figure 7-35. When you modify your extended event, the dialog box will look just like the New Session dialog box.

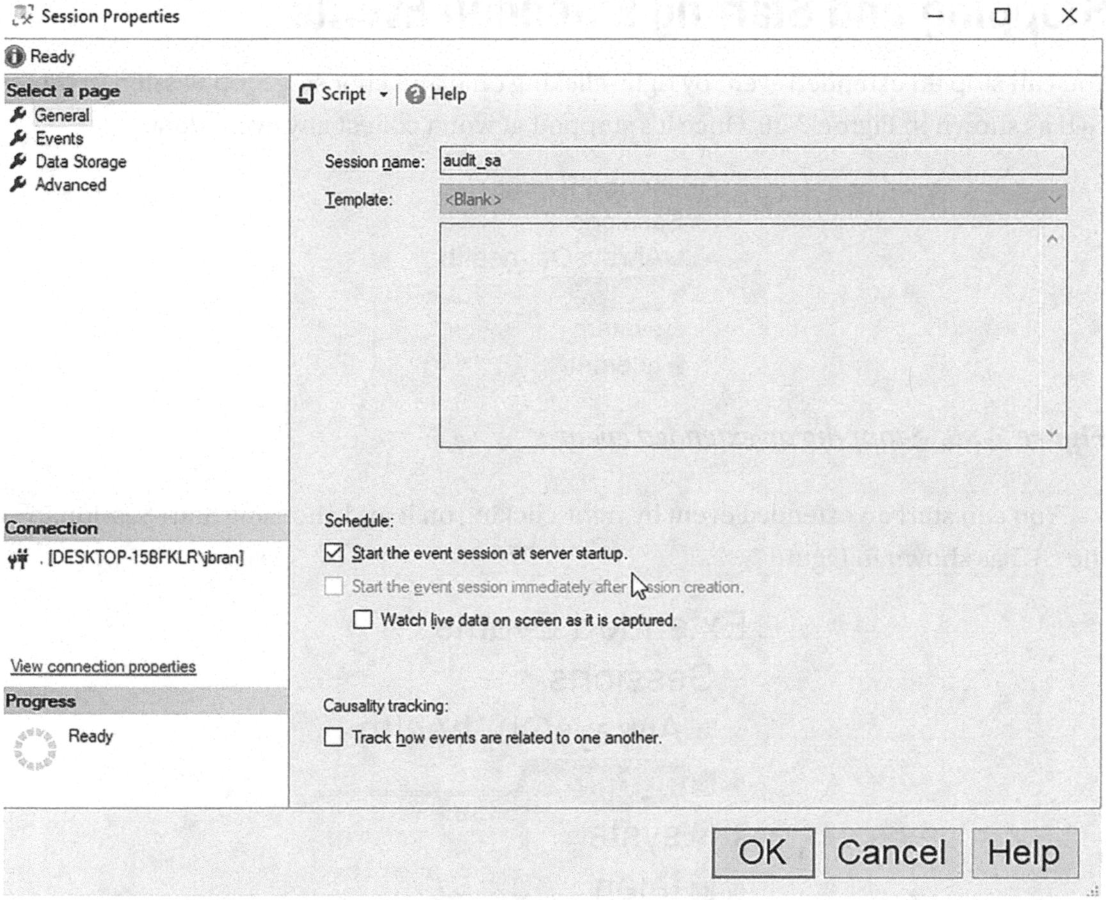

Figure 7-35. *Modifying an extended event dialog box*

You can't change these items after creation:

- Session name

- Template

- Start immediately after creation (since you aren't creating, but modifying)

- Advanced settings

If you need to change any of these items, you will have to delete and recreate your extended event.

Stopping and Starting Extended Events

You can stop an extended event by right-clicking on it and choosing Stop Session in the GUI as shown in Figure 7-36. Once it's stopped, it won't collect any event data.

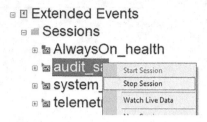

Figure 7-36. *Stopping an extended event*

You can start an extended event by right-clicking on it and choosing Start Session in the GUI as shown in Figure 7-37.

Figure 7-37. *Starting an extended event*

Note   Unlike SQL Server Audit, you can stop an extended event even if it's auditing events.

Deleting Extended Events

To delete an extended event, you can right-click the session and choose Delete as shown in Figure 7-38.

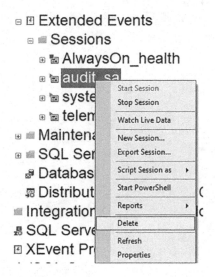

Figure 7-38. *Deleting an extended event*

You will get a dialog box as shown in Figure 7-39. Clicking the OK button in this dialog box will delete the extended event.

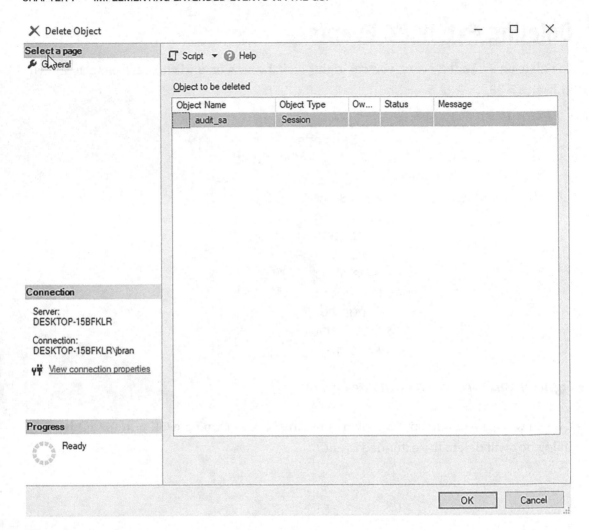

Figure 7-39. *Deleting extended event dialog box*

When you delete the extended event, the files remain on disk. I deleted the extended event and thought the files were gone, too. No, the files are still there. This is in case you need them later for auditing purposes. You must go manually delete them.

In the next chapter, you will learn how to make your life easier by scripting out the extended events you want to place on your servers.

## CHAPTER 8

Implementing Extended Events via SQL Scripts

To make extended events work, you need to set up a session. Chapter 6, "What Is Extended Events?", covered the parts and pieces that comprise a session. Chapter 7, "Implementing Extended Events via the GUI," covered how to set up a session in the GUI. In this chapter, you will learn how to set up an extended event session with SQL scripts.

Caution   Just because you can audit everything, doesn't mean that you should. If you audit everything and anything, you will have a hard time weeding through it all, and you could cause performance issues on your system.

Scripting Existing Extended Events

An easy way for you to learn how to script extended events is to script out existing ones. You can right-click on the session created in Chapter 7, "Implementing Extended Events via the GUI," choose Script Session as, then CREATE To, and then New Query Editor Window as shown in Figure 8-1.

© Josephine Bush 2022

J. Bush, *Practical Database Auditing for Microsoft SQL Server and Azure SQL,*
https://doi.org/10.1007/978-1-4842-8634-0_8

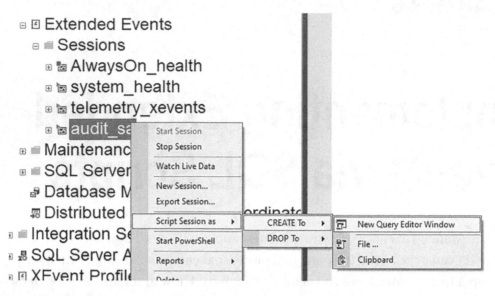

Figure 8-1. *Scripting out existing extended event session*

This will bring a script version of your extended event into a tab in SSMS. How to create the scripts will be covered in this chapter, so you will have a better understanding of how you can create, modify, and delete extended event sessions via script.

Setting Up an Extended Event

Listing 8-1 shows how to create an audit specification via script.

Listing 8-1. Creating an extended event

```
CREATE EVENT SESSION [audit_sa] ON SERVER
ADD EVENT sqlserver.rpc_completed(
    ACTION(sqlserver.client_app_name,
        sqlserver.client_hostname,
        sqlserver.database_name,
        sqlserver.server_instance_name,
        sqlserver.server_principal_name,
        sqlserver.sql_text)
    WHERE ([sqlserver].[server_principal_name]=N'sa')),
ADD EVENT sqlserver.sql_batch_completed(
```

```
    ACTION(sqlserver.client_app_name,
            sqlserver.client_hostname,
            sqlserver.database_name,
            sqlserver.server_instance_name,
            sqlserver.server_principal_name,
            sqlserver.sql_text)
    WHERE ([sqlserver].[server_principal_name]=N'sa'))
ADD TARGET package0.event_file(
SET filename=N'e:\audits\audit_sa',
            max_file_size=(10),
            max_rollover_files=(5))
WITH (STARTUP_STATE=ON);

ALTER EVENT SESSION [audit_sa] ON SERVER
STATE=START;
```

Let's look at each of the pieces of the script in Listing 8-1:

- **Extended event name**

  `CREATE EVENT SESSION [audit_sa] ON SERVER`

  I tend to name it something descriptive with audit at the front, so I know what it's auditing, if possible.

- **Auditing events**

  `ADD EVENT sqlserver.rpc_completed`

  `ADD EVENT sqlserver.sql_batch_completed`

  You can add many different types of events here. These are the two I use for auditing. There is a longer description of these in Chapter 6, "What Is Extended Events?"

- **Auditing event actions (global fields)**

  `ACTION(sqlserver.client_app_name,sqlserver.client_`
  `hostname,sqlserver.database_name,sqlserver.server_instance_`
  `name,sqlserver.server_principal_name,sqlserver.sql_text)`

You can add many different types of actions here. These are the actions I use for auditing events. There is a longer description of these in Chapter 6, "What Is Extended Events?" Each event needs actions associated with it to ensure you see the information you need. You can leave off these actions, but then you are left with default fields for your events, which may or may not be useful to you.

- **Filtering events**

```
WHERE ([sqlserver].[server_principal_name]=N'sa'))
```

Filtering is a very important part of auditing. You will want to filter your auditing data before it's written to a file; otherwise, you can get overloaded by too much auditing data. I tend to filter on a user or a database. You need to be careful auditing an entire database. I usually only do this if I'm trying to determine if the database is being used at all, so there will most likely be very little audit data.

- **Writing events out to disk**

```
filename=N'e:\audits\audit_sa',max_file_size=(10) ,max_
rollover_files=(5))
```

There are many different options for writing your event data out from your extended event. These are covered in more detail in Chapter 6, "What Is Extended Events?" This script is writing events out to disk. This will write to e:\audits\audit_sa with a max file size of 10 MB and 5 rollover files. This means you will get a total of 50 MB of storage for your events. Here are some suggestions for file storage:

- Don't store the files on the C drive or other drives SQL Server is using for data and log files.

- Set the maximum file size to something small like 10 MB and enable file rollover of 5–10 files. If you set large file sizes with many rollover files, they will be next to impossible to query.

Caution   If you have large files and many rollover files, they can get gigantic and be next to impossible to query.

- **Advanced options**

  ```
  WITH (STARTUP_STATE=ON);
  ```

  There are more options you can set in advanced options, but I prefer to not change any of those settings. Changing these settings can cause performance issues on your database server. The advanced options are covered in more detail in Chapter 6, "What Is Extended Events?" The only advanced option I set is STARTUP_STATE=ON, which means the extended event will start again after any restart of SQL Server.

- **Starting your extended event session**

  ```
  ALTER EVENT SESSION [audit_sa] ON SERVER

  STATE=START;
  ```

  When an extended event session is stopped, it doesn't collect any data. This is why I always start it after creating it.

Querying System Tables and Views

You can query a system view to see what events and actions are available to use. Listing 8-2 shows these queries.

Listing 8-2. Querying system tables to list extended events available events and actions

```
SELECT name, description
FROM sys.dm_xe_objects
WHERE object_type ='Event'
ORDER BY name
SELECT name, description
FROM sys.dm_xe_objects
WHERE object_type ='Action'
ORDER BY name
```

sys.dm_xe_objects, with a filter on 'Event', will list the events you can use in your extended event session. A cross-section of the query results from Listing 8-2 are shown in Figure 8-2. There over 1800 events available in SQL Server 2019. The number of events available to you depends on your version of SQL Server.

	name	description
1	adaptive_join_query	Occurs when a query using at least one adaptive j...
2	adaptive_join_skipped	Adaptive join is not possible in some scenarios.
3	add_file_in_database	Occurs when a file is being added to the database ...
4	add_new_file_operation_error	Error during AddFileRedo
5	add_xact_outcome	XEvent used to indicate that transaction outcome i...
6	additional_memory_grant	Occurs when a query tries to get more memory gra...
7	adr_cleanup_test_deallocated_pages	For ADR cleanup test to record the deallocated pa...
8	adr_sweep_aborted_transactions_snapshot_done	The ADR sweep has snapshotted the list of aborte...
9	adr_sweep_for_skip_pages_started	The ADR sweep for skipped pages in ADR started.
10	ae_deferred_databases_add	XEvent used to indicate that database is added to ...
11	ae_deferred_databases_remove	XEvent used to indicate that database is removed f...
12	after_changestatetx_event	Fires after transaction changes state.
13	after_natively_compiled_proc_entry_removal_on...	Fired after the procedure cache entry is flushed wh...

Figure 8-2. *Extended events listing of events*

sys.dm_xe_objects, with a filter on 'Event', will list the actions you can use in your extended event session. A cross-section of the query results from Listing 8-2 are shown in Figure 8-3. There 68 actions available in SQL Server 2019. The number of actions available to you depends on your version of SQL Server.

	name	description
1	attach_activity_id	Attach an activity ID to an event
2	attach_activity_id_xfer	Attach an activity ID transfer to an event
3	callstack	Collect the current call stack
4	client_app_name	Collect client application name
5	client_connection_id	Collects the optional identifier provided at connectio...
6	client_hostname	Collect client hostname
7	client_pid	Collect client process ID
8	collect_cpu_cycle_time	Collect the current CPU's cycle count
9	collect_current_thread_id	Collect the current Windows thread ID
10	collect_system_time	Collect the current system time with 100 microsecon...
11	compile_plan_guid	Collect compiled plan guid. Use this to uniquely iden...
12	context_info	Collect the same value as the CONTEXT_INFO() fun...

Figure 8-3. *Extended events listing of actions*

You can also query system views to see the settings of your extended events sessions. This can make it easier to see the settings without having to go in via the GUI prompts.

Listing 8-3 gives you the query to get a listing of the extended events and some of their settings. There are more columns included in sys.server_event_sessions, but they are advanced settings that I recommend you never change.

Listing 8-3. Querying system table to list extended events

```
SELECT event_session_id, name, startup_state
FROM sys.server_event_sessions;
```

Figure 8-4 shows you the results from the sys.server_event_sessions query. You may have a different list of extended events depending on your version of SQL Server.

	event_session_id	name	startup_state
1	65536	system_health	1
2	65537	AlwaysOn_health	0
3	70044	telemetry_xevents	1
4	70049	audit_sa	1

Figure 8-4. *Extended events listing*

Once you get the event_session_id for the audit_sa extended event from the query in Listing 8-3, you can place it into the WHERE clause in the queries in Listings 8-4, 8-5, and 8-6.

Listing 8-4. Querying system tables to list extended events details

```
SELECT es.name AS ExtendedEventName,
            se.name AS EventName,
            sa.name AS GlobalFieldName,
            se.predicate AS Filter
FROM sys.server_event_session_events se
INNER JOIN sys.server_event_sessions es
ON se.event_session_id = es.event_session_id
INNER JOIN sys.server_event_session_actions sa
ON sa.event_session_id = es.event_session_id
AND sa.event_id = se.event_id
WHERE es.event_session_id = 70049;
```

Listing 8-4 returns the results for the extended event session's settings configured events, global fields, and filters. Figure 8-5 shows you what the query in Listing 8-4 returns.

	ExtendedEventName	EventName	GlobalFieldName	Filter
1	audit_sa	rpc_completed	client_app_name	([sqlserver].[server_principal_name]=N'sa')
2	audit_sa	rpc_completed	client_hostname	([sqlserver].[server_principal_name]=N'sa')
3	audit_sa	rpc_completed	database_name	([sqlserver].[server_principal_name]=N'sa')
4	audit_sa	rpc_completed	server_instance_name	([sqlserver].[server_principal_name]=N'sa')
5	audit_sa	rpc_completed	server_principal_name	([sqlserver].[server_principal_name]=N'sa')
6	audit_sa	rpc_completed	sql_text	([sqlserver].[server_principal_name]=N'sa')
7	audit_sa	sql_batch_completed	client_app_name	([sqlserver].[server_principal_name]=N'sa')
8	audit_sa	sql_batch_completed	client_hostname	([sqlserver].[server_principal_name]=N'sa')
9	audit_sa	sql_batch_completed	database_name	([sqlserver].[server_principal_name]=N'sa')
10	audit_sa	sql_batch_completed	server_instance_name	([sqlserver].[server_principal_name]=N'sa')
11	audit_sa	sql_batch_completed	server_principal_name	([sqlserver].[server_principal_name]=N'sa')
12	audit_sa	sql_batch_completed	sql_text	([sqlserver].[server_principal_name]=N'sa')

Figure 8-5. *Extended events details about events and their global fields and filters*

Figure 8-5 shows you that the extended event named audit_sa has two events associated with it. Those events each have six global fields associated with them. Also, each event has a filter to only capture events if the event action was done by the sa user.

Listing 8-5 shows you how to query the target for the extended event.

Listing 8-5. Querying system tables to list extended event target

```
SELECT es.name AS ExtendedEventName,
       st.name AS TargetLocation
FROM sys.server_event_session_targets st
INNER JOIN sys.server_event_sessions es
ON st.event_session_id = es.event_session_id
WHERE es.event_session_id = 70049;
```

Figure 8-6 shows you what the query in Listing 8-5 returns.

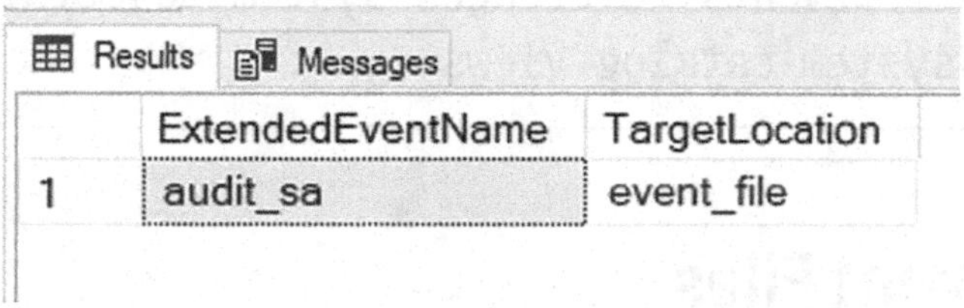

Figure 8-6. *Extended events target*

Figure 8-6 shows you that the extended event named audit_sa has a target location of event_file.

Listing 8-6 shows you how to query additional settings for the extended event like filename and max file size.

Listing 8-6. Querying system tables to list extended events settings

```
SELECT es.name AS ExtendedEventName,
          sf.name AS SettingName,
          sf.value AS SettingValue
FROM sys.server_event_session_fields sf
INNER JOIN sys.server_event_sessions es
ON sf.event_session_id = es.event_session_id
WHERE es.event_session_id = 70049;
```

Figure 8-7 shows you what the query in Listing 8-4 returns.

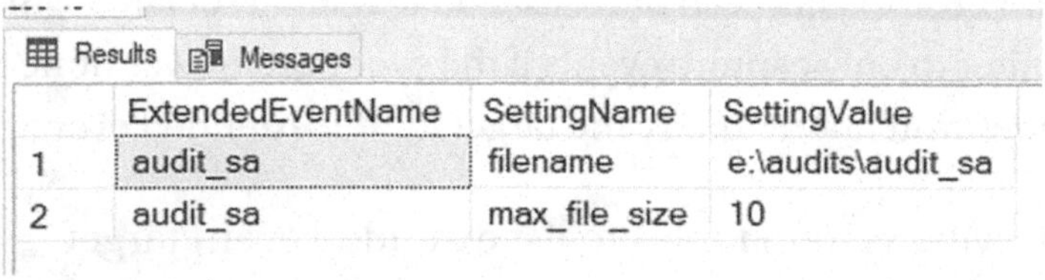

	ExtendedEventName	SettingName	SettingValue
1	audit_sa	filename	e:\audits\audit_sa
2	audit_sa	max_file_size	10

***Figure 8-7.** Extended events additional settings*

Figure 8-7 shows you that the extended event named audit_sa has two settings in the system views. filename shows where the file is stored. max_file_size shows it's set to 10 MB.

Tip To get a description of all the columns in the extended event system views, visit `https://docs.microsoft.com/en-us/sql/relational-databases/extended-events/xevents-references-system-objects?view=sql-server-ver15#system-catalog-views`

Extended Event Files

If you chose the file destination for your extended event, the .xel file is placed on disk after you enable the extended event as shown in Figure 8-8. This is where the event data will live.

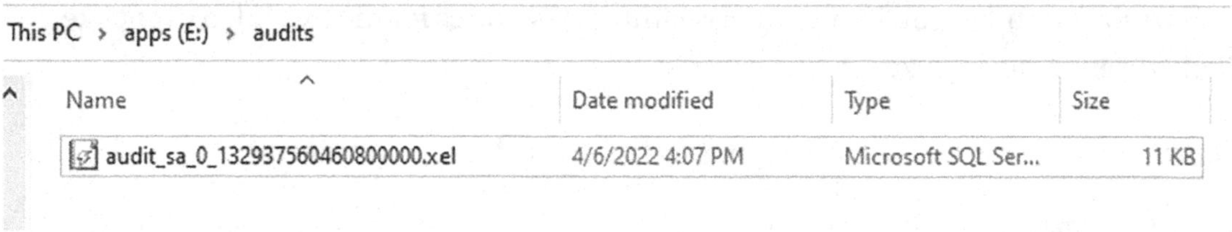

Name	Date modified	Type	Size
audit_sa_0_132937560460800000.xel	4/6/2022 4:07 PM	Microsoft SQL Ser...	11 KB

***Figure 8-8.** Extended event files on disk*

As the data collects, this file is going to grow to the size specified in the extended event. Then it'll create another file up to the number of files specified in the configuration. Once the last file is full, it will delete the oldest file and create another new file. You will need to know how fast your files fill up so you won't miss collecting the data from them before they are deleted.

Querying Extended Event Data

You can query your extended event session with a SQL Server system function, sys. fn_xe_file_target_read_file. This will give you a lot of different information about your extended event and its associated metadata. Listing 8-7 gives you a query to get the most relevant columns of the audit returned for the last hour. There are a lot more fields in the XML, but they would need to be parsed similarly as how I've parsed the fields out in Listing 8-7.

Listing 8-7. Query extended event session

```
SELECT n.value('(@timestamp)[1]', 'datetime') as timestamp,
       n.value('(action[@name="sql_text"]/value)[1]', 'nvarchar(max)')
as [sql],
       n.value('(action[@name="client_hostname"]/value)[1]',
'nvarchar(50)') as [client_hostname],
       n.value('(action[@name="server_principal_name"]/value)[1]',
'nvarchar(50)') as [user],
       n.value('(action[@name="database_name"]/value)[1]', 'nvarchar(50)')
as [database_name],
       n.value('(action[@name="client_app_name"]/value)[1]',
'nvarchar(50)') as [client_app_name]
FROM (SELECT CAST(event_data as XML) as event_data
FROM sys.fn_xe_file_target_read_file('e:\audits\audit_sa*.xel', NULL, NULL,
NULL)) ed
CROSS APPLY ed.event_data.nodes('event') as q(n)
WHERE n.value('(@timestamp)[1]', 'datetime')
       >= DATEADD(HOUR, -1, GETDATE())
ORDER BY timestamp DESC;
```

Figure 8-9 shows you a cross-section of the results from the query in Listing 8-6.

	timestamp	sql	client_hostname	user	database_name	client_app_name
1	2022-04-14 21:06:50.500	/****** Script for SelectTopNRows comm...	DESKTOP-15	sa	MagicWandServices	Microsoft SQL Server Management Studio - Query
2	2022-04-14 21:06:50.367	SELECT @@SPID;	DESKTOP-15	sa	MagicWandServices	Microsoft SQL Server Management Studio - Query
3	2022-04-14 21:06:50.250	DECLARE @edition sysname; SET @e...	DESKTOP-15	sa	MagicWandServices	Microsoft SQL Server Management Studio - Query
4	2022-04-14 21:06:50.220	select @@spid; select SERVERPROPE...	DESKTOP-15	sa	MagicWandServices	Microsoft SQL Server Management Studio - Query
5	2022-04-14 21:06:50.220	SET ROWCOUNT 0 SET TEXTSIZE 21...	DESKTOP-15	sa	MagicWandServices	Microsoft SQL Server Management Studio - Query
6	2022-04-14 21:06:49.647	declare @HkeyLocal nvarchar(18...	DESKTOP-15	sa	MagicWandServices	Microsoft SQL Server Management Studio
7	2022-04-14 21:06:49.610	select SERVERPROPERTY(N'serverna...	DESKTOP-15	sa	MagicWandServices	Microsoft SQL Server Management Studio
8	2022-04-14 21:06:49.607	(@_msparam_0 nvarchar(4000),@_ms...	DESKTOP-15	sa	MagicWandServices	Microsoft SQL Server Management Studio
9	2022-04-14 21:06:49.570	use [MagicWandServices]	DESKTOP-15	sa	MagicWandServices	Microsoft SQL Server Management Studio
10	2022-04-14 21:06:47.857	(@_msparam_0 nvarchar(4000),@_ms...	DESKTOP-15	sa	MagicWandServices	Microsoft SQL Server Management Studio
11	2022-04-14 21:06:47.800	use [MagicWandServices]	DESKTOP-15	sa	MagicWandServices	Microsoft SQL Server Management Studio
12	2022-04-14 21:06:47.797	DECLARE @edition sysname; SET @e...	DESKTOP-15	sa	master	Microsoft SQL Server Management Studio
13	2022-04-14 21:06:47.797	SET LOCK_TIMEOUT 10000	DESKTOP-15	sa	master	Microsoft SQL Server Management Studio

Figure 8-9. *Extended event query results*

Tip   Find out more about sys.fn_xe_file_target_read_file by visiting
`https://docs.microsoft.com/en-us/sql/relational-databases/`
`system-functions/sys-fn-xe-file-target-read-file-transact-`
`sql?view=sql-server-ver15`

There may be nothing listed because nothing auditable happened yet. There may be a lot of auditing data because there's a bunch of stuff happening in the background that you didn't realize was happening. SQL Server has a lot of internal processes that may be collected by your extended event. It's important to filter as much out in the session setup as possible to avoid excessive amounts of event data.

Note   Extended event data is stored in UTC time zone.

Modifying Extended Events

Once an extended event is created, you can alter it to changing its settings. You can modify an extended event when it's started or stopped. Listing 8-8 shows you how to modify your extended event session to add an event.

Listing 8-8. Modifying an extended event

```
ALTER EVENT SESSION [audit_sa] ON SERVER
ADD EVENT sqlserver.sql_transaction(
    ACTION(
            sqlserver.client_app_name,
            sqlserver.client_hostname,
            sqlserver.database_name,
            sqlserver.server_instance_name,
            sqlserver.server_principal_name,
            sqlserver.sql_text)
    WHERE ([sqlserver].[server_principal_name]=N'sa'));
```

Note   Unlike SQL Server Audit, you can modify an extended event while it's started.

You can't change these items after creation:

- Session name

- Template

- Start immediately after creation (since you aren't creating, but modifying)

- Advanced settings

If you need to change any of these items, you will have to delete and recreate your extended event.

Tip   For more information on altering an extended event, visit https://docs.microsoft.com/en-us/sql/t-sql/statements/alter-event-session-transact-sql?view=sql-server-ver15

Stopping and Starting Extended Events

You can stop an extended event by executing the query in Listing 8-9. Once it's stopped, it won't collect any event data.

Listing 8-9. Stopping an extended event

```
ALTER EVENT SESSION [audit_sa]
ON SERVER STATE = STOP;
```

You can start an extended event by executing the query in Listing 8-10.

Listing 8-10. Starting an extended event

```
ALTER EVENT SESSION [audit_sa]
ON SERVER STATE = START;
```

Note   Unlike SQL Server Audit, you can stop an extended event even if it's auditing events.

Deleting Extended Events

To delete an extended event, you can execute the query shown in Listing 8-11.

Listing 8-11. Deleting an extended event

```
DROP EVENT SESSION [audit_sa] ON SERVER;
```

When you delete the extended event, the files remain on disk. I deleted the extended event and thought the files were gone, too. No, the files are still there. This is in case you need them later for auditing purposes. You must go manually delete them.

In the next chapter, you will learn how to track configuration changes from the SQL Server Log. This will be particularly useful to you if you are using SQL Server Audit to audit changes. SQL Server Audit isn't good at capturing configuration changes made, so collecting them from the SQL Server Log can help you track these changes.

## CHAPTER 9

Tracking SQL Server Configuration Changes

This chapter will outline the ways you can view configuration changes in SQL Server. You will want and need to capture these changes since they can have a large impact on your database server.

Configuration changes can include enabling SQL Agent or Database Mail. They can also include things like changing max and min memory. There are a lot of different configuration settings. Most server configuration options are available via SSMS. Some of you can only access with sp_configure.

Tip To see a list of configuration options, visit `https://docs.microsoft.com/en-us/sql/database-engine/configure-windows/server-configuration-options-sql-server?view=sql-server-ver15#configuration-options-table`

Configuration Changes History in SSMS

To see the configuration changes history in SSMS, right-click on the server connection. Then navigate to Reports ➤ Standard Reports ➤ Configuration Changes History as shown in Figure 9-1.

© Josephine Bush 2022
J. Bush, *Practical Database Auditing for Microsoft SQL Server and Azure SQL*,
https://doi.org/10.1007/978-1-4842-8634-0_9

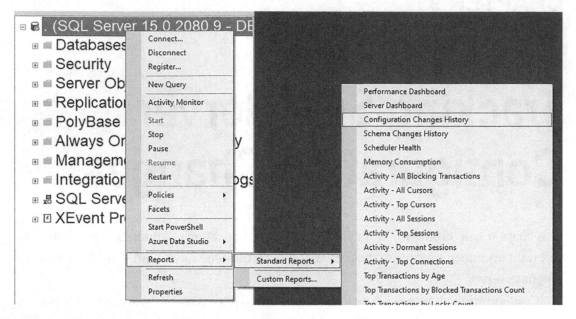

Figure 9-1. *Configuration Changes History navigation*

Once the Configuration Changes History Report opens, you will see any recent changes. The screenshot in 9-2 shows you this report. It's important to note that you may not see ten days of history as I have in my report. This will depend on how much is written to the default trace and how fast those files roll over. The default trace is enabled by default in SQL Server. It collects a log of activity including configuration changes. I don't recommend querying it, though, because this feature will be removed in a future version of SQL Server, per Microsoft.

Configu...15BFKLR

Configuration Changes History   SQL Server
on | 5BFKLR at 4/24/2022 11:35:30 AM

This report provides a history of all sp_configure and Trace Flag changes recorded by the Default Trace.

Configuration Changes History (Since 4/14/2022 3:30:01 PM).
Shows changes in server configuration and flags.

Configuration Option	Old Value	New Value	Time	User
max server memory (MB)	5666	5667	4/24/2022 11:28:49 AM	I5BFKLR\jbran
max server memory (MB)	5748	5666	4/14/2022 3:30:01 PM	sa

Figure 9-2. *Configuration Changes History report*

Figure 9-2 shows that max server memory (MB) was changed to 5666 by sa. It also shows it was changed to 5667 by another user. This report is useful to have a quick look at recent changes, but it's not a great way to track changes in the long term.

Querying Configuration Changes in the SQL Server Logs

You can also see configuration changes in the SQL Server Log. To access this log, right-click SQL Server Logs under Management. Then choose View ➤ SQL Server Log as shown in Figure 9-3.

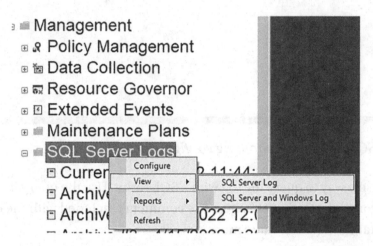

Figure 9-3. *SQL Server Log navigation*

Figure 9-4 shows the log with the last memory configuration change. The availability of this information depends on how long it takes your log to fill up and how many log files you are keeping.

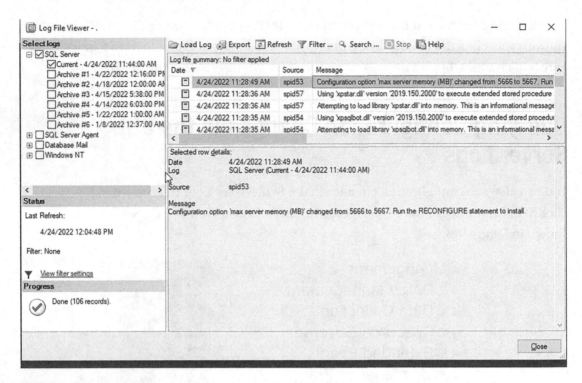

Figure 9-4. *SQL Server Log showing configuration change*

There is also a way to query the log with a SQL script. Use the query in Listing 9-1 to query the log for configuration changes. The comments included with the query help you to understand what each value means.

Listing 9-1. Querying the log for configuration changes

```
USE master;
EXEC sys.xp_readerrorlog
0, --0 = current log file, 1 = archive file #1, etc
1, --1 or NULL = error log, 2 = SQL Agent log
N'Configuration option', --String you want to find
NULL, --String you can set to further refine results
NULL, --Start time
NULL, --End time
N'asc'; --orders results asc = ascending, desc = descending
```

Figure 9-5 shows the query results from Listing 9-1. I made an additional configuration change. This way, you can see that configuration changes come through with "Configuration option" at the beginning of the Text.

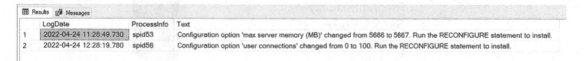

Figure 9-5. *SQL Server Log query results*

This query will only get one log file at a time. There is a way to loop through them, but a better way to capture them is with SQL Server Audit.

Using SQL Server Audit to Capture Configuration Changes

To understand how to set up SQL Server Audit, please read Chapter 4, "Implementing SQL Server Audit via the GUI." This will show you how to create an audit that the database audit will use in this section.

To audit configuration changes, you will need to audit the stored procedure, sp_configure. This stored procedure is in the master database. When you use SSMS GUI to make changes, this stored procedure gets called. You can also call it yourself from a query window.

To audit sp_configure, you need to set up a database audit on master. To do this, right-click Database Audit Specifications under Security in the master database as shown in Figure 9-6.

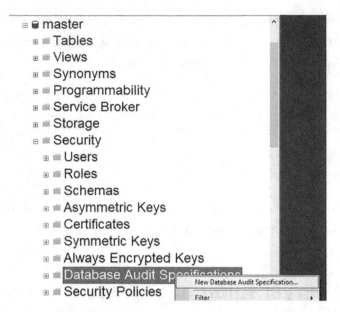

Figure 9-6. *Menu for database audit specification in the master database*

This will bring up a dialog box, and you need to fill out the options as shown in Figure 9-7.

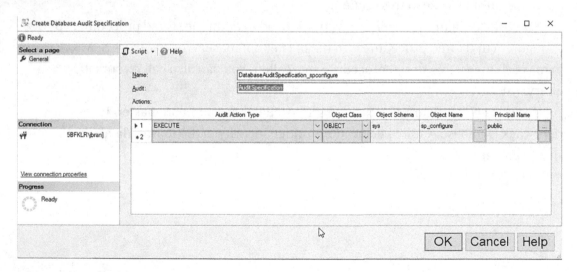

Figure 9-7. *Set up database audit specification in the master database*

Note   I've associated this database audit specification with the audit that also has my server audit specification. That server audit specification captures changes to permissions and objects on SQL Server. This is covered in Chapter 4, "Implementing SQL Server Audit via the GUI." By associating the sp_configure database audit with the audit that has my server audit, I can ensure I capture all the server changes in one audit.

To configure the database audit specification in master, you will need these pieces:

- **Name** – DatabaseAuditSpecification_spconfigure. I like to name this specific to what I'm auditing.

- **Audit** – You need to associate it with your audit. There is a drop-down with your audit listed. You need this association because this is where your audit data will live. This audit setup is covered in Chapter 4, "Implementing SQL Server Audit via the GUI."

- **Audit Action Type** – Chapter 3, "What Is SQL Server Audit?", has a section on Database Audit Action Groups to help you determine what each action audits. In this case, we are only using EXECUTE. This audits who executes a stored procedure or executes on an entire schema or database.

- **Object Class** – Here you will choose OBJECT. There are other options covered in more detail in Chapter 4, "Implementing SQL Server Audit via the GUI." Choose OBJECT to see queries using a specific table, view, stored procedure, or function.

- **Object Schema** – Required for OBJECT class, in this case, sys.

- **Object Name** – Required for OBJECT, SCHEMA, and DATABASE classes. In this case, sp_configure.

- **Principal Name** – Required for OBJECT, SCHEMA, and DATABASE classes. Use public if you want to audit everyone. If you want to audit multiple users, you need one line for each user. I'm using public here because I want to capture anytime anyone makes a configuration change.

Note   All audits are disabled when created. Make sure to enable it, so it collects audit data.

You can also set up the database audit specification with a script, as shown in Listing 9-2. This was covered in Chapter 5, "Implement SQL Server Audit via SQL Scripts."

Listing 9-2. Creating a database audit specification with SQL script

```
USE [master];
CREATE DATABASE AUDIT SPECIFICATION [DatabaseAuditSpecification_
spconfigure]
FOR SERVER AUDIT [AuditSpecification]
ADD (EXECUTE ON OBJECT::[sys].[sp_configure] BY [public])
WITH (STATE = ON);
```

There is a way to query the audit via the GUI, which was covered in Chapter 4, "Implementing SQL Server Audit via the GUI." Instead, let's query the audit data with a SQL script. This was covered in Chapter 5, "Implementing SQL Server Audit via SQL Scripts." First, make a configuration change, and then execute the script in Listing 9-3.

Listing 9-3. Querying the audit with a SQL script

```
USE master;
SELECT DISTINCT
        event_time,
        aa.name as audit_action,
        statement,
        succeeded,
        database_name,
        server_instance_name,
        schema_name,
        session_server_principal_name,
        server_principal_name,
        object_Name,
        file_name,
```

```
       client_ip,
       application_name,
       host_name,
       file_name
FROM sys.fn_get_audit_file ('E:\audits\*.sqlaudit',default,default) af
INNER JOIN sys.dm_audit_actions aa
ON aa.action_id = af.action_id
WHERE event_time > DATEADD(HOUR, -4, GETDATE())
ORDER BY event_time DESC;
```

Figure 9-8 shows you the results of the query in Listing 9-3. Make sure you make a configuration change. The database audit won't pick up changes from before it was created. Even if you make a change via the SSMS GUI, it will still use sp_configure, so it shows up that way in the audit.

	event_time	audit_action	statement	succeeded	database_name
1	2022-04-24 19:03:51.3038436	EXECUTE	EXEC sys.sp_configure N'max server memory (MB)', N'5688'	1	master

Figure 9-8. *Set up database audit specification in the master database*

In the next chapter, you will learn about the additional SQL Server auditing options like Common Criteria compliance, C2 audit trace, change data capture, successful/failed logins, and DDL triggers.

Additional SQL Server Auditing and Tracking Methods

In this chapter, you will learn about additional SQL Server auditing options. I don't use most of these very much, if at all. They can cause performance issues or create so much data you can't weed through it all. I want to show you these options to help you make an informed decision on whether to use them at all. Depending on your use cases, they may prove valuable when used with caution.

Common Criteria Compliance

If you don't have an auditor requiring you to turn this on, leave it off. It can be very impactful to server performance. Even if an auditor thinks you need it, have a conversation with them. Explain the implications of turning it.

I will only briefly mention C2 audit mode here because C2 will be removed in a future version of SQL Server. Microsoft says to use Common Criteria compliance.

Common Criteria compliance was developed by the European Union. It's an internationally recognized set of guidelines for security. The SQL Server functionality is only available in Enterprise and Datacenter editions.

© Josephine Bush 2022
J. Bush, *Practical Database Auditing for Microsoft SQL Server and Azure SQL*,
https://doi.org/10.1007/978-1-4842-8634-0_10

With Common Criteria compliance

- Memory allocation is overwritten with a known pattern of bits before being reallocated to a new resource. This can cause slow performance.

- Login auditing is enabled. The login statistics can be viewed by querying the sys.dm_exec_sessions view.

- Table-level DENY takes precedence over a column-level GRANT.

To enable Common Criteria compliance, right-click the server connection and choose Properties as shown in Figure 10-1.

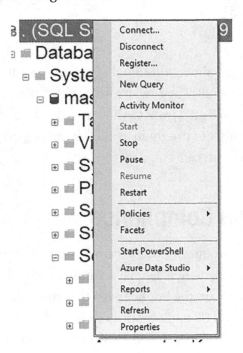

Figure 10-1. *Opening server properties*

Once the properties dialog box opens, click the Security page. Then check the Enable Common Criteria compliance box as shown in Figure 10-2.

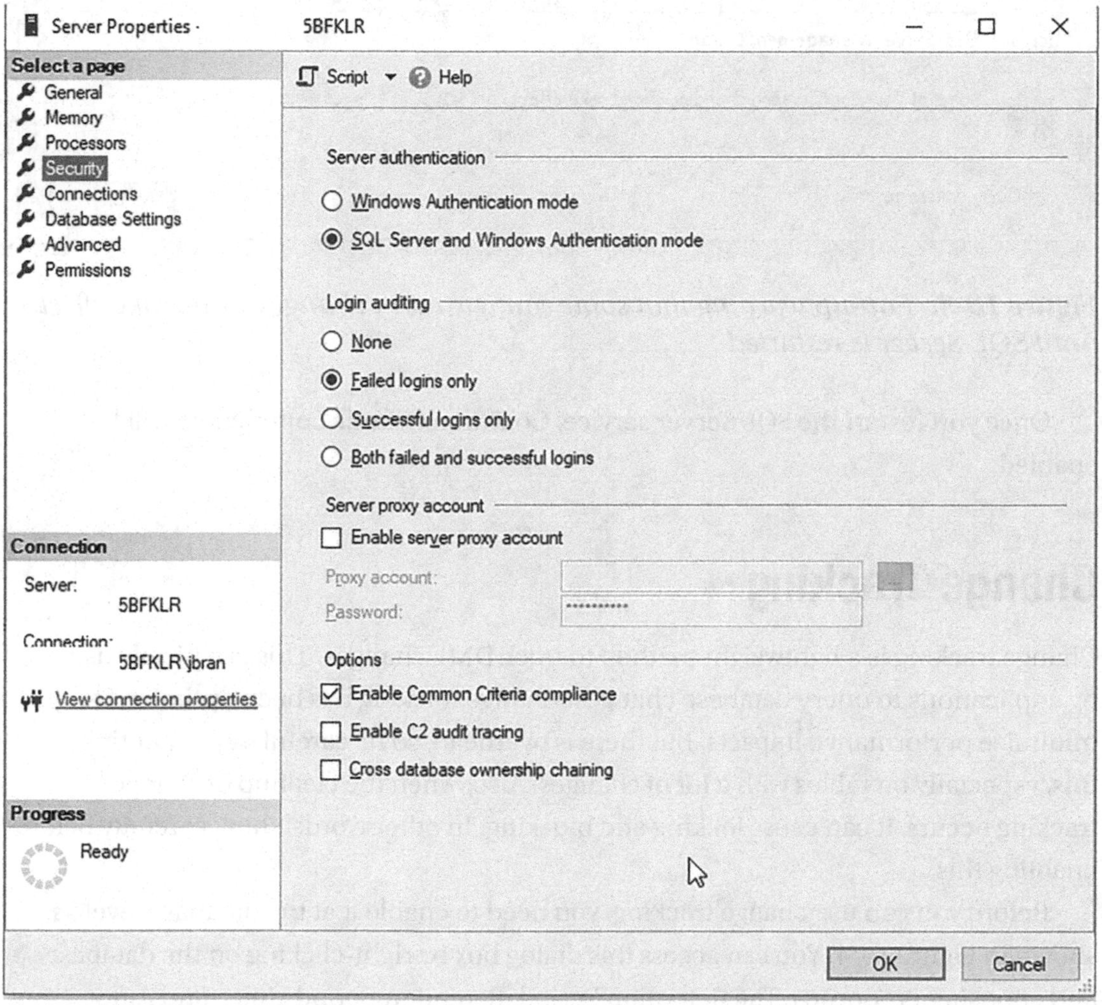

Figure 10-2. *Checking Enable Common Criteria compliance box*

When you click OK on the dialog box, you will receive a pop-up message warning you that you need to restart SQL Server as shown in Figure 10-3.

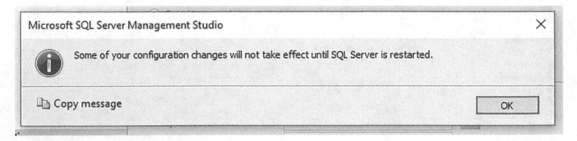

Figure 10-3. *Pop-up warning that some configuration changes won't take effect until SQL Server is restarted*

Once you restart the SQL Server service, Common Criteria compliance will be enabled.

Change Tracking

Change tracking is a lightweight method to track DML changes. This is typically used by applications to query database changes. Change tracking has been optimized to minimize performance impacts, but there is overhead, so be careful implementing this, especially on tables with a lot of changes. Also, when the cleanup of change tracking occurs, it can cause locking and blocking. In other words, think carefully before enabling this.

Before you can use change tracking, you need to enable it at the database level as shown in Figure 10-4. You can access this dialog box by right-clicking on the database and choosing Properties. The Retention Period, Retention Period Units, and Auto Cleanup options are left as is with the default values.

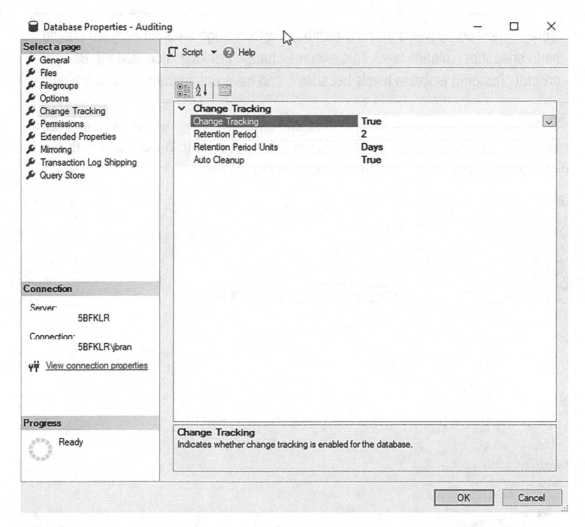

Figure 10-4. *Enabling change tracking at the database level*

You can also enable change tracking with a SQL script as shown in Listing 10-1.

Listing 10-1. Enabling change tracking at the database level

```
USE [master];
ALTER DATABASE [YourDBName] SET CHANGE_TRACKING = ON
(CHANGE_RETENTION = 2 DAYS, AUTO_CLEANUP = ON);
```

Note   Microsoft advises that any database with change tracking enabled should be in snapshot isolation level. This ensures change tracking is consistent. Be careful changing isolation levels because it can have unintended consequences.

Once change tracking is enabled at the database level, you must enable it for each table you want to track. Figure 10-5 shows you how to enable it. You can access this dialog box by right-clicking on the table and choosing Properties.

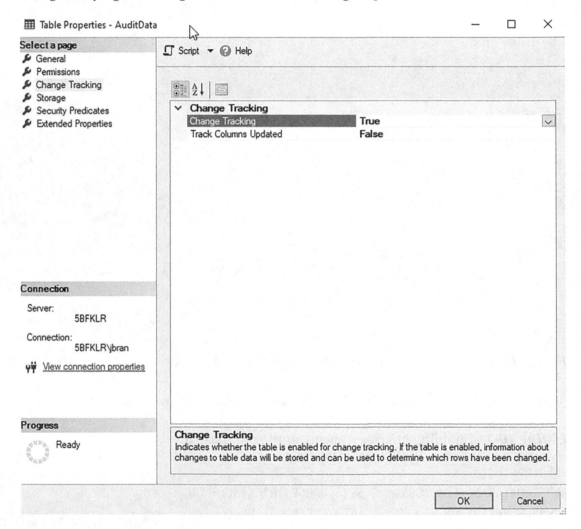

Figure 10-5. Enabling change tracking at the table level

Note   You need a primary key on any table you want to use change tracking on.

You can also enable change tracking with a SQL script as shown in Listing 10-2, making sure to change the database and table name to match what you want to use.

Listing 10-2. Enabling change tracking at the table level via script

```
USE [YourDBName];
ALTER TABLE [dbo].[YourTableName] ENABLE CHANGE_TRACKING
WITH (TRACK_COLUMNS_UPDATED = OFF);
```

Note   Track Columns Updated uses additional storage. It's disabled by default for this reason.

To view the change tracking data, execute the query in Listing 10-3.

Listing 10-3. Querying change tracking data

```
USE YourDBName;
SELECT CT.SYS_CHANGE_VERSION,
  CT.SYS_CHANGE_OPERATION, EM.*
  FROM CHANGETABLE
(CHANGES [AuditData],0) as CT
LEFT JOIN [dbo].[AuditData] EM
ON CT.ID = EM.ID
ORDER BY SYS_CHANGE_VERSION;
```

Listing 10-3 returns results of the changes to the table with change tracking enabled. Those results are shown in Figure 10-6. Your results will vary.

	SYS_CHANGE_VERSION	SYS_CHANGE_OPERATION	id	eventtime	sql
1	2	I	1	2022-04-29 00:00:00.000	select * from testing where col=1;
2	4	D	NULL	NULL	NULL

Figure 10-6. *Change tracking query results*

Figure 10-6 shows one row was inserted as noted by SYS_CHANGE_OPERATION = I. It also shows that one row was deleted as noted by SYS_CHANGE_OPERATION = D.

Tip   For more information on change tracking, visit `https://docs.microsoft.com/en-us/sql/relational-databases/track-changes/work-with-change-tracking-sql-server?view=sql-server-ver15`

Change tracking doesn't allow you to see how many times it's changed or the values of each change. If you need to know the exact changes made and how often they were made, then you need to use change data capture.

Tip   For a comparison of change tracking and change data capture, visit `https://docs.microsoft.com/en-us/sql/relational-databases/track-changes/track-data-changes-sql-server?view=sql-server-ver15#feature-differences-between-change-data-capture-and-change-tracking`

Change Data Capture

Change data capture (CDC) uses the SQL Server Agent to track DML changes made to a table. This allows you to see the changes made to data, the details of which are in a format that is easily consumed. This can be particularly useful to extract, transform, and load (ETL) applications or processes.

CDC has been optimized to minimize performance impacts, but there is overhead, so be careful implementing this, especially on tables with a lot of changes. In other words, think carefully before turning this on. It will also take up storage in the database, so you need to track storage usage carefully.

To determine if you have CDC enabled on a database, execute the query in Listing 10-4.

Listing 10-4. Determining if CDC is enabled

```
SELECT name, is_cdc_enabled
FROM sys.databases;
```

If it's enabled, you will see is_cdc_enabled = 1; if not, it will be 0.

Note   CDC requires exclusive use of the cdc schema and user because they are used as part of the CDC processes. CDC also requires use of the SQL Agent, so make sure that service is running and the agent is enabled and started.

To enable CDC, execute the query in Listing 10-5, making sure to use the database name you want to enable CDC on.

Listing 10-5. Enabling CDC at the database level

```
USE YourDBName;
EXEC sys.sp_cdc_enable_db;
```

After you enable CDC on the database, you can enable it on a table with the query in Listing 10-6.

Listing 10-6. Enabling CDC at the table level

```
USE [YourDBName];
EXEC sys.sp_cdc_enable_table
@source_schema = N'dbo',
@source_name   = N'YourTableName',
@role_name     = NULL,
@filegroup_name = NULL,
@supports_net_changes = 0;
```

To determine if you have CDC enabled on a table, execute the query in Listing 10-7.

Listing 10-7. Determining if CDC is enabled on any tables

```
USE YourDBName;
SELECT name, is_tracked_by_cdc
FROM sys.tables
WHERE is_tracked_by_cdc = 1;
```

If it's enabled, you will see is_cdc_enabled = 1; if not, it will be 0.

Tip   To understand the options in Listing 10-6, visit `https://docs.`
`microsoft.com/en-us/sql/relational-databases/track-changes/`
`enable-and-disable-change-data-capture-sql-server?view=sql-`
`server-ver15#enable-for-a-table`

Once you enable CDC on a table, you see a few things associated with it:

- **System tables in YourDBName**

    - **cdc.captured_columns** – Returns one row for each column
      tracked in a capture instance

    - **cdc.change_tables** – Returns one row for each change table in
      the database

    - **cdc.dbo_YourTableName_CT** – Returns one row for each change
      made to a captured column in the associated source table

    - **cdc.ddl_history** – Returns one row for each data definition
      language (DDL) change made to tables that are enabled for
      change data capture

    - **cdc.index_columns** – Returns one row for each index column
      associated with a change table

    - **cdc.lsn_time_mapping** – Returns one row for each transaction
      having rows in a change table. This table is used to map between
      log sequence number (LSN) commit values and the time the
      transaction was committed

- **System table stored in MSDB**

    - **dbo.cdc_jobs** – Returns the configuration parameters for change
      data capture agent jobs

- **Two agent jobs to capture and clean up CDC data**

  - **cdc.YourDBName_capture** – Executes the stored procedure sp_MScdc_capture_job, which captures the CDC data

  - **cdc.YourDBName_cleanup** – Executes the stored procedure sp_MScdc_cleanup_job, which starts by extracting the configured retention and threshold values for the cleanup job from msdb. dbo.cdc_jobs

---

Tip   To find out more about the CDC agent jobs, visit `https://docs.microsoft.com/en-us/sql/relational-databases/track-changes/administer-and-monitor-change-data-capture-sql-server?view=sql-server-ver15`

To find out more about the CDC system tables, visit `https://docs.microsoft.com/en-us/sql/relational-databases/system-tables/change-data-capture-tables-transact-sql?view=sql-server-ver15`

To see the changes CDC tracks, Microsoft recommends you query the cdc.fn_cdc_get_all_changes function instead of the system tables as shown in Listing 10-8.

Listing 10-8. Querying CDC data

```
USE YourDBName;
DECLARE @from_lsn binary(10), @to_lsn binary(10);
SET @from_lsn = sys.fn_cdc_get_min_lsn('dbo_YourTableName');
SET @to_lsn   = sys.fn_cdc_get_max_lsn();
SELECT *
FROM cdc.fn_cdc_get_all_changes_dbo_AuditData
     (@from_lsn, @to_lsn, N'all');
```

Note   SQL Agent needs to be enabled and started for CDC to capture data.

Your results will vary based on what changes happened on your table. Figure 10-7 shows you what the results could look like.

	__$start_lsn	__$seqval	__$operation	__$update_mask	id	eventtime	sql
1	0x00000026000005E30003	0x00000026000005E30002	4	0x04	2	2022-04-29 00:00:00.000	exec sp_code1;
2	0x00000026000005E50003	0x00000026000005E50002	4	0x04	2	2022-04-29 00:00:00.000	exec sp_code2;
3	0x00000026000006200003	0x00000026000006200002	4	0x04	2	2022-04-29 00:00:00.000	exec sp_code1;
4	0x000000260000062B0005	0x000000260000062B0002	1	0x07	2	2022-04-29 00:00:00.000	exec sp_code1;
5	0x00000026000006D60003	0x00000026000006D60002	2	0x07	3	2022-04-29 00:00:00.000	select col1 from auditdata;

Figure 10-7. *CDC query results*

The __$operation column values are

- **1** – Delete.

- **2** – Insert.

- **3** – Update. This will return the old value. It only works when the row filter option 'all update old' is specified. To set this, you need to specify N'all update old' instead of N'all' in Listing 10-8.

- **4** – Update, but only includes the column values after the update.

Tip   To get more information on cdc.fn_cdc_get_all_changes, visit `https://docs.microsoft.com/en-us/sql/relational-databases/system-functions/cdc-fn-cdc-get-all-changes-capture-instance-transact-sql?view=sql-server-ver15`

Temporal Tables

This built-in database feature allows you to see data stored in the table at any point in time. It's a system-versioned table that keeps a full history of data changes. The validity of each row is managed by the system, which is the database engine. The versioning is implemented as a pair of tables, current and history. Each of these tables has two datetime2 type columns to define the period of validity for each row. They are called the PERIOD columns. The current table contains the current value for each row. The history table contains each previous value for each row and the start time and end time for which it was valid.

Creating a Temporal Table

To create a temporal table with a default history table, use the script in Listing 10-9.

Listing 10-9. Creating a temporal table with a default history table

```
CREATE TABLE dbo.AuditChangesTemporal
(
    AuditID INT NOT NULL PRIMARY KEY CLUSTERED IDENTITY(1,1),
    [event_time] [datetime2](7) NOT NULL,
    [statement] [nvarchar](4000) NULL,
    ValidFrom DATETIME2 GENERATED ALWAYS AS ROW START NOT NULL,
    ValidTo DATETIME2 GENERATED ALWAYS AS ROW END NOT NULL,
    PERIOD FOR SYSTEM_TIME (ValidFrom, ValidTo)
)
WITH (SYSTEM_VERSIONING = ON (HISTORY_TABLE = dbo.
AuditChangesTemporalHistory));
```

The script in Listing 10-9 will create a temporal table, and the history table is accessible from under the table, as shown in Figure 10-8.

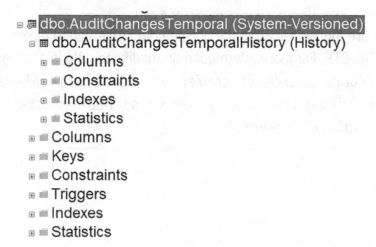

Figure 10-8. *Temporal table with its history table*

Modifying Data in a Temporal Table

If you don't hide the PERIOD columns, ValidTo and ValidFrom, you will need to account for them when modifying data. You can do this by specifying only the columns you want to INSERT into as shown in Listing 10-10. This will set default values for ValidTo and ValidFrom for you.

Listing 10-10. Inserting into a temporal table

```
INSERT INTO Auditing.dbo.AuditChangesTemporal
(event_time, statement)
SELECT DATEADD(mi, DATEPART(TZ, SYSDATETIMEOFFSET()), event_time) as event_
time, statement
FROM sys.fn_get_audit_file ('e:\sqlaudit\*.sqlaudit',default,default) af
WHERE DATEADD(mi, DATEPART(TZ, SYSDATETIMEOFFSET()), event_time) >
DATEADD(HOUR, -4, GETDATE());
```

If you do hide the PERIOD columns, ValidTo and ValidFrom, you won't need to account for them when modifying data. In other words, you can INSERT without having to specify columns.

Note   There are more rules around modifying data in temporal tables, such as for UPDATE and DELETE. For more information on modifying data in a temporal table, visit https://docs.microsoft.com/en-us/sql/relational-databases/tables/modifying-data-in-a-system-versioned-temporal-table?view=sql-server-ver16

Querying a Temporal Table

When you want the current data in a temporal table, you can query it the same way as any other table as shown in Figure 10-9.

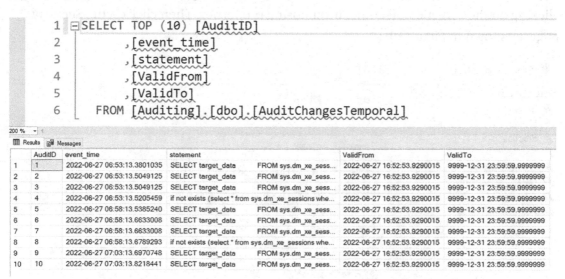

```
1  ⊟SELECT TOP (10) [AuditID]
2          ,[event_time]
3          ,[statement]
4          ,[ValidFrom]
5          ,[ValidTo]
6      FROM [Auditing].[dbo].[AuditChangesTemporal]
```

	AuditID	event_time	statement		ValidFrom	ValidTo
1	1	2022-06-27 06:53:13.3801035	SELECT target_data	FROM sys.dm_xe_sess...	2022-06-27 16:52:53.9290015	9999-12-31 23:59:59.9999999
2	2	2022-06-27 06:53:13.5049125	SELECT target_data	FROM sys.dm_xe_sess...	2022-06-27 16:52:53.9290015	9999-12-31 23:59:59.9999999
3	3	2022-06-27 06:53:13.5049125	SELECT target_data	FROM sys.dm_xe_sess...	2022-06-27 16:52:53.9290015	9999-12-31 23:59:59.9999999
4	4	2022-06-27 06:53:13.5205459	if not exists (select * from sys.dm_xe_sessions whe...		2022-06-27 16:52:53.9290015	9999-12-31 23:59:59.9999999
5	5	2022-06-27 06:58:13.5385240	SELECT target_data	FROM sys.dm_xe_sess...	2022-06-27 16:52:53.9290015	9999-12-31 23:59:59.9999999
6	6	2022-06-27 06:58:13.6633008	SELECT target_data	FROM sys.dm_xe_sess...	2022-06-27 16:52:53.9290015	9999-12-31 23:59:59.9999999
7	7	2022-06-27 06:58:13.6633008	SELECT target_data	FROM sys.dm_xe_sess...	2022-06-27 16:52:53.9290015	9999-12-31 23:59:59.9999999
8	8	2022-06-27 06:58:13.6789293	if not exists (select * from sys.dm_xe_sessions whe...		2022-06-27 16:52:53.9290015	9999-12-31 23:59:59.9999999
9	9	2022-06-27 07:03:13.6970748	SELECT target_data	FROM sys.dm_xe_sess...	2022-06-27 16:52:53.9290015	9999-12-31 23:59:59.9999999
10	10	2022-06-27 07:03:13.8218441	SELECT target_data	FROM sys.dm_xe_sess...	2022-06-27 16:52:53.9290015	9999-12-31 23:59:59.9999999

Figure 10-9. *Querying current data in temporal table*

If you want to query historical data, you will need to specify FOR SYSTEM_TIME AS OF, as shown in Listing 10-11.

Listing 10-11. Inserting into a temporal table

```
SELECT TOP (10) *
FROM [Auditing].[dbo].[AuditChangesTemporal]
FOR SYSTEM_TIME AS OF '2022-06-01 T10:00:00.7230011';
```

Nothing may return from that table based on whether there is actually something in the historical data for that SYSTEM_TIME.

Note   For more information about temporal tables, visit https://docs.
microsoft.com/en-us/sql/relational-databases/tables/getting-
started-with-system-versioned-temporal-tables?view=sql-
server-ver16

Successful and Failed Logins

One way to audit successful and/or failed logins is by enabling the login auditing in
SSMS, which will write to the SQL Server Log. You can enable this in SSMS by right-
clicking on the server connection and choosing properties. Then click on the Security
page, as shown in Figure 10-10.

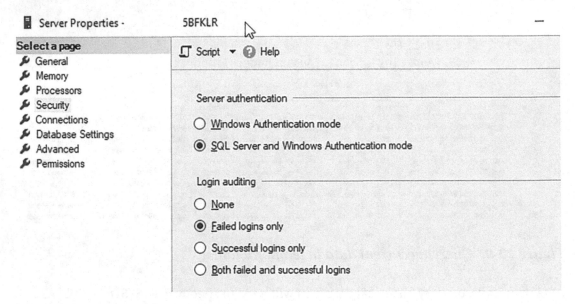

Figure 10-10. *Login auditing configuration*

Only failed logins are being captured on this server. If you change this setting, you
will need to restart SQL Server. Figure 10-11 shows you what a failed login message will
look like in the log.

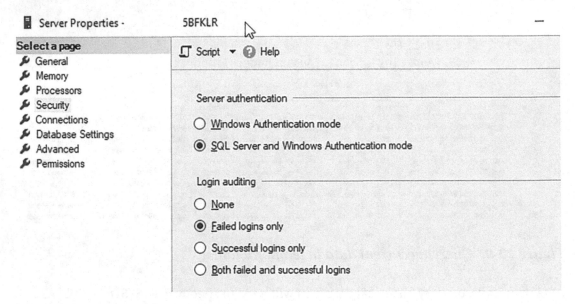

Figure 10-11. *Failed login in the SQL Server Log*

You can also query the log if you want to extract records from it, which was covered
in Chapter 9, "Tracking SQL Server Configuration Changes." The log isn't the best way to
track logins, though. A better way to track successful and failed logins is with either SQL
Server Audit or extended events.

SQL Server Audit for Successful and Failed Login Auditing

SQL Server Audit, covered in more detail in Chapter 3, "What Is SQL Server Audit?",
through Chapter 5, "Implementing SQL Server Audit via SQL Scripts," allows you to audit
successful and failed logins. You will need an audit to store the audit data and a server
audit specification to collect the login information. The server audit specification is
shown in Listing 10-12.

Listing 10-12. Server audit specification to capture successful and failed logins

```
USE [master];
CREATE SERVER AUDIT SPECIFICATION [ServerAuditSpecification]
FOR SERVER AUDIT [AuditSpecification]
ADD (FAILED_LOGIN_GROUP),
ADD (SUCCESSFUL_LOGIN_GROUP)
WITH (STATE = ON);
```

You can query your audit with the query in Listing 10-13.

Listing 10-13. Query to see audit results

```
USE master;
SELECT
        event_time,
        aa.name as audit_action,
        server_instance_name,
        server_principal_name,
        client_ip,
        application_name,
        host_name
FROM sys.fn_get_audit_file ('E:\audits\*.sqlaudit',default,default) af
INNER JOIN sys.dm_audit_actions aa
ON aa.action_id = af.action_id
WHERE event_time > DATEADD(HOUR, -4, GETDATE())
ORDER BY event_time DESC;
```

After having some logins fail and succeed, your audit results will look something like
Figure 10-12.

	event_time	audit_action	server_instance_name	server_principal_name	client_ip	application_name
1	2022-04-30 20:27:20.2082677	LOGIN FAILED	5BFKLR	sa	local machine	Microsoft SQL Serv
2	2022-04-30 20:25:09.9578812	LOGIN SUCCEEDED	5BFKLR	5BFKLR\jbran	local machine	Microsoft SQL Serv
3	2022-04-30 20:25:09.8797507	LOGIN SUCCEEDED	5BFKLR	5BFKLR\jbran	local machine	Microsoft SQL Serv
4	2022-04-30 20:25:09.8328778	LOGIN SUCCEEDED	5BFKLR	5BFKLR\jbran	local machine	Microsoft SQL Serv
5	2022-04-30 20:25:09.7859974	LOGIN SUCCEEDED	5BFKLR	5BFKLR\jbran	local machine	Microsoft SQL Serv
6	2022-04-30 20:25:09.6298013	LOGIN SUCCEEDED	5BFKLR	5BFKLR\jbran	local machine	Microsoft SQL Serv
7	2022-04-30 20:25:09.5985548	LOGIN SUCCEEDED	5BFKLR	5BFKLR\jbran	local machine	Microsoft SQL Serv
8	2022-04-30 20:25:09.5673040	LOGIN SUCCEEDED	5BFKLR	5BFKLR\jbran	local machine	Microsoft SQL Serv
9	2022-04-30 20:25:09.5204294	LOGIN SUCCEEDED	5BFKLR	5BFKLR\jbran	local machine	Microsoft SQL Serv
10	2022-04-30 20:25:07.9580501	LOGIN SUCCEEDED	5BFKLR	5BFKLR\jbran	local machine	Microsoft SQL Serv
11	2022-04-30 20:25:07.6141504	LOGIN SUCCEEDED	5BFKLR	5BFKLR\jbran	local machine	Microsoft SQL Serv
12	2022-04-30 20:25:00.8175054	LOGIN SUCCEEDED	5BFKLR	NT SERVICE\SQLSERVERAGENT	local machine	SQLAgent - Job Ma
13	2022-04-30 20:25:00.7554300	LOGIN SUCCEEDED	5BFKLR	NT SERVICE\SQLSERVERAGENT	local machine	SQLAgent - TSQL
14	2022-04-30 20:25:00.7397843	LOGIN SUCCEEDED	5BFKLR	NT SERVICE\SQLSERVERAGENT	local machine	SQLAgent - Job Ma
15	2022-04-30 20:24:25.1141366	LOGIN SUCCEEDED	5BFKLR	NT SERVICE\SQLTELEMETRY	local machine	SQLServerCEIP

Figure 10-12. *SQL Server Audit successful and failed login results*

You will see information about where the login came from such as client_ip and hostname only in more recent versions of SQL Server. Determining where a login came from is an important part of auditing, though. If you are on a SQL Server version older than 2016 SP1, you may want to consider using extended events instead.

Extended Events for Successful and Failed Login Auditing

Extended events, covered in more detail in Chapter 6, "What Is Extended Events?", through Chapter 8, "Implementing Extended Events via SQL Scripts," allows you to audit successful and failed logins, as well. The good thing about extended events is that no matter what version of SQL Server you are on, you can get the client hostname.

You will need to create a session that uses the login event and the error_reported event as shown in Listing 10-14.

Listing 10-14. Create an extended event to capture successful and failed logins

```
CREATE EVENT SESSION [AuditLogins] ON SERVER
ADD EVENT sqlserver.error_reported(
    ACTION(sqlserver.client_app_name,
           sqlserver.client_hostname,
           sqlserver.server_principal_name)
    WHERE (((([severity]=(14))
            AND ([error_number]=(18456)))
            AND ([state]>(1)))),
```

```
ADD EVENT sqlserver.login(
    ACTION(sqlserver.client_app_name,
           sqlserver.client_hostname,
           sqlserver.server_principal_name))
ADD TARGET package0.event_file(
            SET filename=N'E:\audits\AuditLogins.xel',
            max_file_size=(10),
            max_rollover_files=(10))
WITH (STARTUP_STATE=ON);
ALTER EVENT SESSION [AuditLogins] ON SERVER
STATE=START;
```

After having some logins fail and succeed, you can execute the query in Listing 10-15 to query your extended event.

Listing 10-15. Query your extended event

```
SELECT n.value('(@timestamp)[1]', 'datetime') as timestamp,
       n.value('(@name)[1]', 'nvarchar(15)') as name,
       n.value('(action[@name="client_hostname"]/value)[1]',
       'nvarchar(50)') as [client_hostname],
       n.value('(action[@name="server_principal_name"]/value)[1]',
       'nvarchar(50)') as [user],
       n.value('(action[@name="client_app_name"]/value)[1]',
       'nvarchar(50)') as [client_app_name],
       n.value('(data[@name="message"]/value)[1]', 'nvarchar(50)') as
       [message]
FROM (SELECT CAST(event_data as XML) as event_data
FROM sys.fn_xe_file_target_read_file('e:\audits\AuditLogins*.xel', NULL,
NULL, NULL)) ed
CROSS APPLY ed.event_data.nodes('event') as q(n)
WHERE n.value('(@timestamp)[1]', 'datetime') >= DATEADD(HOUR, -1,
GETDATE())
ORDER BY timestamp DESC;
```

The query in Listing 10-15 will produce results like the results in Figure 10-13. Note that the error_reported events, which are failed logins, don't have a user, but do have a message. The login events do have a user, but no message because there is no error message with successful logins.

	timestamp	name	client_hostname	user	client_app_name	message
7	2022-04-30 22:30:34.817	login	DESKTOP-15BFKLR	sa	Microsoft SQL Server Management Studio	NULL
8	2022-04-30 22:30:34.813	login	DESKTOP-15BFKLR	sa	Microsoft SQL Server Management Studio	NULL
9	2022-04-30 22:30:34.810	login	DESKTOP-15BFKLR	sa	Microsoft SQL Server Management Studio	NULL
10	2022-04-30 22:30:34.807	login	DESKTOP-15BFKLR	sa	Microsoft SQL Server Management Studio	NULL
11	2022-04-30 22:30:34.790	login	DESKTOP-15BFKLR	sa	Microsoft SQL Server Management Studio	NULL
12	2022-04-30 22:30:34.740	login	DESKTOP-15BFKLR	sa	Microsoft SQL Server Management Studio	NULL
13	2022-04-30 22:30:30.090	error_reported	DESKTOP-15BFKLR	NULL	Microsoft SQL Server Management Studio	Login failed for user 'sa'. Re.
14	2022-04-30 22:30:00.960	login	DESKTOP-15BFKLR	NT SERVICE\S...	SQLAgent - Job Manager	NULL
15	2022-04-30 22:30:00.933	login	DESKTOP-15BFKLR	NT SERVICE\S...	SQLAgent - TSQL JobStep (Job 0xC8C...	NULL
16	2022-04-30 22:30:00.923	login	DESKTOP-15BFKLR	NT SERVICE\S...	SQLAgent - Job Manager	NULL

Figure 10-13. *Audit results*

DDL Triggers

DDL triggers can be used to prevent changes, have something occur in response to a change, and record changes. You can do this at the server level or the database level. Triggers are much more useful for preventing changes or having something occur in response to a change. They are less useful for recording changes. I recommend using SQL Server Audit or extended events for those changes.

Tip   To learn more about DDL triggers, visit `https://docs.microsoft.com/ en-us/sql/relational-databases/triggers/ddl-triggers? view=sql-server-ver15`

In the next chapter, I will show you how to centralize your SQL Server audits and extended events data. This will make it much easier to query and report on because it's in one central location.

PART III

Centralizing and Reporting on Auditing Data

CHAPTER 11

Centralizing Audit Data

An important part of auditing is being able to easily query and report on multiple servers' audit data. In this chapter, you will learn how to centralize audit data with SQL Server Agent and linked servers. You will also learn how to set up audits on multiple servers with a registered servers list.

To centralize audit data, you will need these items:

- **Centralized audit database** – This is used to store the auditing data from all the audited servers.

- **Auditing user on the central server** – This user will be used on the linked server to connect back to the central server.

- **Linked server on audited servers** – This links to the centralized server that has the audit database.

- **SQL Server Agent audit collection job on audited servers** – This will send the audit data via the linked server to the centralized audit database.

- **SQL Server Agent job to clean up audit data on the centralized audit database** – This ensures you set a retention policy and enforce it.

Setting Up Audits on Multiple Servers

Setting up audits on multiple servers is easy with a registered servers list. Figure 11-1 shows you an example of a registered servers list.

© Josephine Bush 2022
J. Bush, *Practical Database Auditing for Microsoft SQL Server and Azure SQL*,
https://doi.org/10.1007/978-1-4842-8634-0_11

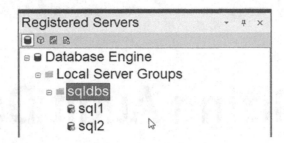

Figure 11-1. *Registered servers list*

Once you have the list set up, you can right-click on the folder that has all the servers you want to audit, and choose New Query as shown in Figure 11-2.

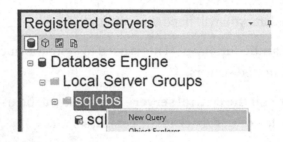

Figure 11-2. *Registered servers list New Query*

I like to keep all my audit data on the same drive letter across all the servers I'm auditing. Make sure you don't put audit files on the C drive. I don't recommend putting audit files on data drives or log drives either. We have an E drive for applications where I work. That's a great place for audit files to go.

Once the registered servers list query window is open, you will need to check the drives you have available on your servers as shown in Listing 11-1.

Listing 11-1. Check disk

```
DECLARE @drives TABLE
(driveletter VARCHAR(1), size INT);

INSERT INTO @drives
EXEC MASTER..xp_fixeddrives;

SELECT * FROM @drives
WHERE driveletter = 'E';
```

You will see something like the results in Figure 11-3. You may not have an E drive. In that case, you might want to consider adding a small drive for your audit files.

Results | Messages

	Server Name	driveletter	size
1	sql2	E	12546
2	sql1	E	10195

***Figure 11-3.** Drive space on registered servers*

The query results from Listing 11-1 does not show you how much disk space is free. You won't be using a lot of space, up to 200 MB, if you follow the instructions in Chapter 5, "Implementing SQL Server Audit via SQL Scripts." I recommended creating a folder on your drive for your audit files to live in. You will need to create this folder manually. If you want to automate this, you may be able to use PowerShell for this.

Once you have the drive folders in place, you can add the audit components with your registered server list query, as shown in Listing 11-2. This script will dynamically name your audit with the string _servername where server name will be the actual name of the server.

Listing 11-2. Setting up an audit on all your servers

```
USE [master];

DECLARE @statement NVARCHAR(max);
DECLARE @servername VARCHAR(50);
SET @servername = @@servername;

SELECT @statement = '
CREATE SERVER AUDIT [Audit_'+@servername+']
TO FILE
(       FILEPATH = N''E:\sqlaudit\''
        ,MAXSIZE = 50 MB
        ,MAX_ROLLOVER_FILES = 4
        ,RESERVE_DISK_SPACE = OFF
)
```

```
WITH
(       QUEUE_DELAY = 1000
        ,ON_FAILURE = CONTINUE
)
ALTER SERVER AUDIT [Audit_'+@servername+'] WITH (STATE = ON);';

EXEC sp_executesql @statement;
```

Figure 11-4 shows what the audit name may look like. It depends on what your server is named.

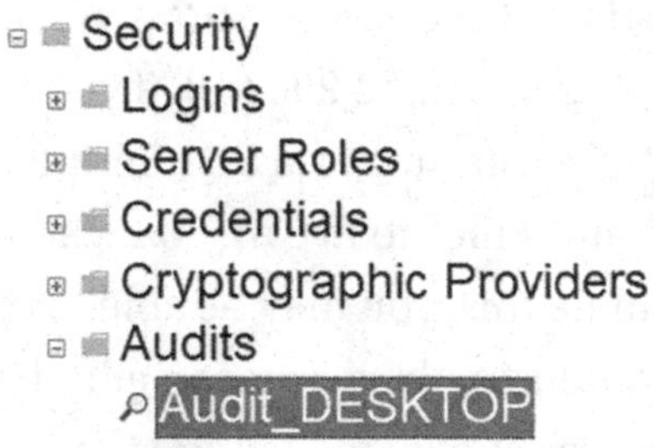

Figure 11-4. *Audit setup on server with script*

Next, you will need to set up the server audit specification on all your servers using the script in Listing 11-3. This script will dynamically name your server audit specification with the string _servername.

Listing 11-3. Set up server audit specification on all your servers

```
USE [master];

DECLARE @statement NVARCHAR(max)
DECLARE @servername VARCHAR(50)

SET @servername = @@servername

SELECT @statement = 'CREATE SERVER AUDIT SPECIFICATION
[ServerAuditSpecification_'+@servername+']
FOR SERVER AUDIT [Audit_'+@servername+']
ADD (DATABASE_CHANGE_GROUP),
ADD (AUDIT_CHANGE_GROUP),
ADD (APPLICATION_ROLE_CHANGE_PASSWORD_GROUP),
ADD (DATABASE_OBJECT_CHANGE_GROUP),
```

```
ADD (DATABASE_OWNERSHIP_CHANGE_GROUP),
ADD (DATABASE_PERMISSION_CHANGE_GROUP),
ADD (DATABASE_PRINCIPAL_CHANGE_GROUP),
ADD (DATABASE_ROLE_MEMBER_CHANGE_GROUP),
ADD (LOGIN_CHANGE_PASSWORD_GROUP),
ADD (SCHEMA_OBJECT_CHANGE_GROUP),
ADD (SCHEMA_OBJECT_OWNERSHIP_CHANGE_GROUP),
ADD (SCHEMA_OBJECT_PERMISSION_CHANGE_GROUP),
ADD (SERVER_OBJECT_CHANGE_GROUP),
ADD (SERVER_OBJECT_OWNERSHIP_CHANGE_GROUP),
ADD (SERVER_OBJECT_PERMISSION_CHANGE_GROUP),
ADD (SERVER_OPERATION_GROUP),
ADD (SERVER_PERMISSION_CHANGE_GROUP),
ADD (SERVER_PRINCIPAL_CHANGE_GROUP),
ADD (SERVER_ROLE_MEMBER_CHANGE_GROUP),
ADD (SERVER_STATE_CHANGE_GROUP),
ADD (USER_CHANGE_PASSWORD_GROUP)
WITH (STATE = ON);'

exec sp_executesql @statement;
```

Figure 11-5 shows what the server audit specification name may look like. It depends on what your server is named.

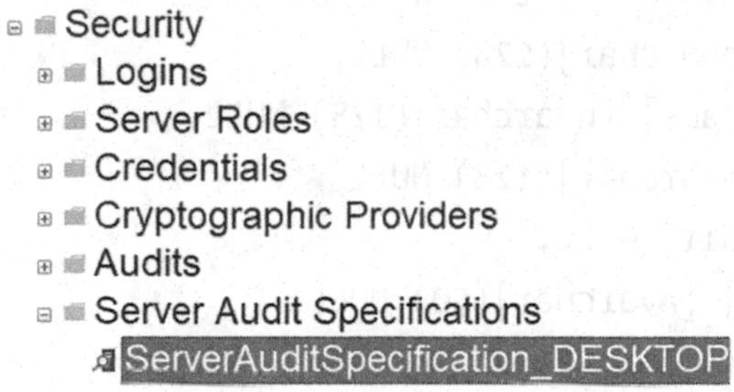

Figure 11-5. *Server audit specification setup on server with script*

You don't have to name the audit with _servername. This is how I've chosen to do it. You can name them differently, if you want, but I like to name them this way to tell them apart when querying system tables across multiple servers.

Creating a Centralized Audit Database and User

On the server you choose as your centralized audit database server, you need to set up an auditing database as shown in Listing 11-4.

Listing 11-4. Setting up auditing database

```
CREATE DATABASE [Auditing];
```

Next, you will need to set up a table to hold your auditing data as shown in Listing 11-5.

Listing 11-5. Setting up the auditing table

```
USE [Auditing];
CREATE TABLE [dbo].[AuditChanges](
      [event_time] [datetime2](7) NOT NULL,
      [statement] [nvarchar](4000) NULL,
      [server_instance_name] [nvarchar](128) NULL,
      [database_name] [nvarchar](128) NULL,
      [schema_name] [nvarchar](128) NULL,
      [session_server_principal_name] [nvarchar](128) NULL,
      [server_principal_name] [nvarchar](128) NULL,
      [object_Name] [nvarchar](128) NULL,
      [file_name] [nvarchar](260) NOT NULL,
      [client_ip] [nvarchar](128) NULL,
      [application_name] [nvarchar](128) NULL,
      [host_name] [nvarchar](128) NULL,
      [succeeded] [bit] NULL,
      [audit_action] [nvarchar](50) NULL
) ON [PRIMARY];
CREATE CLUSTERED INDEX [CIX_EventTime_User_Server_DB] ON [dbo].
[AuditChanges]
(
      [event_time] ASC
)WITH (PAD_INDEX = OFF, STATISTICS_NORECOMPUTE = OFF, SORT_IN_TEMPDB = OFF,
DROP_EXISTING = OFF, ONLINE = OFF, ALLOW_ROW_LOCKS = ON, ALLOW_PAGE_LOCKS =
ON) ON [PRIMARY];
```

Next, you will need an auditing user that has rights to the auditing database as shown in Listing 11-6. This way, the linked server on your audited servers can access the auditing database.

Listing 11-6. Setting up auditing user

```
USE [master];
CREATE LOGIN [sqlauditing] WITH PASSWORD=N'testing1234!',
DEFAULT_DATABASE=[master], CHECK_EXPIRATION=OFF, CHECK_POLICY=ON;
USE [Auditing];
CREATE USER [sqlauditing] FOR LOGIN [sqlauditing];
ALTER ROLE [db_datareader] ADD MEMBER [sqlauditing];
ALTER ROLE [db_datawriter] ADD MEMBER [sqlauditing];
```

Note   You will need the server authentication set as SQL Server and Windows Authentication mode to set up the sqlauditing user in Listing 11-6. For more information about authentication methods, visit `https://docs.microsoft.com/en-us/sql/relational-databases/security/choose-an-authentication-mode?view=sql-server-ver16`

Make sure to update the password in the script from its default value of 'testing1234!'.

Creating a Linked Server

You will need one linked server on each audited server to send the audit data to the centralized server. Listing 11-7 gives you the script to create this.

Listing 11-7. Setting up a linked server

```
USE [master];
EXEC master.dbo.sp_addlinkedserver @server = N'YourCentralizedAuditServer
Name', @srvproduct=N'SQL Server';

EXEC master.dbo.sp_addlinkedsrvlogin @rmtsrvname = N'
YourCentralizedAuditServerName ', @locallogin = NULL , @useself = N'False',
@rmtuser = N'sqlauditing', @rmtpassword = N'CreateStrongPasswordHere';
```

Make sure to update the @server variable to your central server's name. Also, make sure to update the @rmtpassword to the password you chose for you sqlauditing user.

SQL Agent Jobs to Collect and Clean Up Audit Data

You will need one SQL Server Agent job on each of the audited servers to send the audit data via the linked server to the centralized audit database. Listing 11-8 gives you the script to create this on a SQL Server that is version 2019 or later.

Listing 11-8. SQL Agent job to collect audit data

```
DECLARE @CentralServerName varchar(100);
DECLARE @AuditFilePath varchar(250);

/* CHANGE ONLY THESE TWO VARIABLES */
SET @CentralServerName = 'yourcentralservername';
SET @AuditFilePath = 'e:\sqlaudit\*.sqlaudit';

/*
DON'T CHANGE ANYTHING BELOW HERE UNLESS YOU ARE ON A SQL SERVER OLDER
THAN 2019
*/
DROP TABLE IF EXISTS ##tempvariables;
DECLARE @sql varchar(max);
SET @sql = N'INSERT INTO ' + @CentralServerName + '.Auditing.dbo.
AuditChanges
    SELECT DATEADD(mi, DATEPART(TZ, SYSDATETIMEOFFSET()), event_time) as
    event_time, statement,
    server_instance_name, database_name, schema_name, session_server_
    principal_name,
    server_principal_name, object_Name, file_name, client_ip,
    application_name,
    host_name, succeeded, aa.name AS audit_action
    FROM sys.fn_get_audit_file ('''+@AuditFilePath+''',default,
    default) af
    INNER JOIN sys.dm_audit_actions aa
    ON aa.action_id = af.action_id
```

```
        WHERE DATEADD(mi, DATEPART(TZ, SYSDATETIMEOFFSET()), event_time) >
        DATEADD(HOUR, -4, GETDATE());';

SELECT @CentralServerName AS servername,
@AuditFilePath as auditfilepath, @sql as stepsql
into ##tempvariables;

USE [msdb]
GO
BEGIN TRANSACTION
DECLARE @ReturnCode INT
SELECT @ReturnCode = 0
IF NOT EXISTS (SELECT name FROM msdb.dbo.syscategories WHERE
name=N'[Uncategorized (Local)]' AND category_class=1)
BEGIN
EXEC @ReturnCode = msdb.dbo.sp_add_category @class=N'JOB', @type=N'LOCAL',
@name=N'[Uncategorized (Local)]'
IF (@@ERROR <> 0 OR @ReturnCode <> 0) GOTO QuitWithRollback
END
DECLARE @jobId BINARY(16)
EXEC @ReturnCode =  msdb.dbo.sp_add_job @job_name=N'Audit Changes
Collection',
                @enabled=1,
                @notify_level_eventlog=0,
                @notify_level_email=0,
                @notify_level_netsend=0,
                @notify_level_page=0,
                @delete_level=0,
                @description=N'No description available.',
                @category_name=N'[Uncategorized (Local)]',
                @owner_login_name=N'sa', @job_id = @jobId OUTPUT
IF (@@ERROR <> 0 OR @ReturnCode <> 0) GOTO QuitWithRollback
DECLARE @stepsql varchar(max);
SET @stepsql = (SELECT stepsql from ##tempvariables);
EXEC @ReturnCode = msdb.dbo.sp_add_jobstep @job_id=@jobId,
@step_name=N'audit sql server changes',
```

```
                @step_id=1,
                @cmdexec_success_code=0,
                @on_success_action=1,
                @on_success_step_id=0,
                @on_fail_action=2,
                @on_fail_step_id=0,
                @retry_attempts=3,
                @retry_interval=3,
                @os_run_priority=0, @subsystem=N'TSQL',
                @command=@stepsql,
                @database_name=N'master',
                @flags=0
IF (@@ERROR <> 0 OR @ReturnCode <> 0) GOTO QuitWithRollback
EXEC @ReturnCode = msdb.dbo.sp_update_job @job_id = @jobId,
@start_step_id = 1
IF (@@ERROR <> 0 OR @ReturnCode <> 0) GOTO QuitWithRollback
EXEC @ReturnCode = msdb.dbo.sp_add_jobschedule @job_id=@jobId,
@name=N'every 4 hours get audit into from sqlaudit files on disk',
                @enabled=1,
                @freq_type=4,
                @freq_interval=1,
                @freq_subday_type=8,
                @freq_subday_interval=4,
                @freq_relative_interval=0,
                @freq_recurrence_factor=0,
                @active_start_date=20190812,
                @active_end_date=99991231,
                @active_start_time=0,
                @active_end_time=235959,
                @schedule_uid=N'c68b91ed-4f7f-4fe4-874a-670982cb20cb'
IF (@@ERROR <> 0 OR @ReturnCode <> 0) GOTO QuitWithRollback
EXEC @ReturnCode = msdb.dbo.sp_add_jobserver @job_id = @jobId, @server_name =
N'(local)'
IF (@@ERROR <> 0 OR @ReturnCode <> 0) GOTO QuitWithRollback
COMMIT TRANSACTION
```

```
GOTO EndSave
QuitWithRollback:
    IF (@@TRANCOUNT > 0) ROLLBACK TRANSACTION
EndSave:
GO
```

Make sure to set your @CentralServerName and @AuditFilePath variables at the top of the script in Listing 11-8. Don't change the @sql variable at this point for SQL Server 2019. This job will collect the audit data from one server and send it to the central server every four hours.

To query the audit data in SQL Server 2017, change the @sql variable and remove the column host_name because it isn't available in 2017. To query the audit data in a SQL Server version before 2017, change the @sql variable and remove the columns host_name, application_name, and client_ip because they aren't available in versions before 2017.

You will also need one SQL Server Agent job to clean up audit data on the centralized audit database to ensure you only retain as much auditing data as you need, not forever. I keep it 30 days. You can choose a time frame that suits your needs best. Listing 11-9 gives you the script to create this cleanup agent job.

Listing 11-9. SQL Agent job to clean up audit data

```
USE [msdb]
GO
BEGIN TRANSACTION
DECLARE @ReturnCode INT
SELECT @ReturnCode = 0
/****** Object:  JobCategory [[Uncategorized (Local)]]    Script Date:
5/8/2022 1:53:20 PM ******/
IF NOT EXISTS (SELECT name FROM msdb.dbo.syscategories WHERE
name=N'[Uncategorized (Local)]' AND category_class=1)
BEGIN
EXEC @ReturnCode = msdb.dbo.sp_add_category @class=N'JOB', @type=N'LOCAL',
@name=N'[Uncategorized (Local)]'
IF (@@ERROR <> 0 OR @ReturnCode <> 0) GOTO QuitWithRollback
END
DECLARE @jobId BINARY(16)
```

```
EXEC @ReturnCode =  msdb.dbo.sp_add_job @job_name=N'Audit Retention
Cleanup',
                @enabled=1,
                @notify_level_eventlog=0,
                @notify_level_email=0,
                @notify_level_netsend=0,
                @notify_level_page=0,
                @delete_level=0,
                @description=N'No description available.',
                @category_name=N'[Uncategorized (Local)]',
                @owner_login_name=N'sa', @job_id = @jobId OUTPUT
IF (@@ERROR <> 0 OR @ReturnCode <> 0) GOTO QuitWithRollback
/****** Object:  Step [only retain 30 days of audit data]    Script Date:
5/8/2022 1:53:20 PM ******/
EXEC @ReturnCode = msdb.dbo.sp_add_jobstep @job_id=@jobId, @step_
name=N'only retain 30 days of audit data',
                @step_id=1,
                @cmdexec_success_code=0,
                @on_success_action=1,
                @on_success_step_id=0,
                @on_fail_action=2,
                @on_fail_step_id=0,
                @retry_attempts=0,
                @retry_interval=0,
                @os_run_priority=0, @subsystem=N'TSQL',
                @command=N'USE [Auditing];
                DELETE FROM [dbo].[AuditChanges]
        WHERE event_time <= getdate()-30;',
                @database_name=N'master',
                @flags=0
IF (@@ERROR <> 0 OR @ReturnCode <> 0) GOTO QuitWithRollback
EXEC @ReturnCode = msdb.dbo.sp_update_job @job_id = @jobId, @start_
step_id = 1
IF (@@ERROR <> 0 OR @ReturnCode <> 0) GOTO QuitWithRollback
```

```
EXEC @ReturnCode = msdb.dbo.sp_add_jobschedule @job_id=@jobId,
@name=N'nightly audit tables retention cleanup',
            @enabled=1,
            @freq_type=4,
            @freq_interval=1,
            @freq_subday_type=1,
            @freq_subday_interval=0,
            @freq_relative_interval=0,
            @freq_recurrence_factor=0,
            @active_start_date=20190903,
            @active_end_date=99991231,
            @active_start_time=230000,
            @active_end_time=235959,
            @schedule_uid=N'39b449aa-2c4d-4d05-8a5f-c79598ef52bb'
IF (@@ERROR <> 0 OR @ReturnCode <> 0) GOTO QuitWithRollback
EXEC @ReturnCode = msdb.dbo.sp_add_jobserver @job_id = @jobId, @server_name =
N'(local)'
IF (@@ERROR <> 0 OR @ReturnCode <> 0) GOTO QuitWithRollback
COMMIT TRANSACTION
GOTO EndSave
QuitWithRollback:
    IF (@@TRANCOUNT > 0) ROLLBACK TRANSACTION
EndSave:
GO
```

Once you have your audit data centralized, it makes it a lot easier to query and report on it. In the next chapter, I will show you how you can report on your audit data with SQL Server Agent jobs and PowerShell.

## CHAPTER 12

Create Reports from Audit Data

After centralizing your audit data, you may want to query and report on it. This chapter will show you how you can create and send HTML reports with either SQL Server Agent or PowerShell.

HTML Reports with SQL Server Agent

Since the goal is to email the HTML report with SQL Server Agent, you will need to configure database mail first.

Tip For more information on setting up database mail, visit `https://docs.microsoft.com/en-us/sql/relational-databases/database-mail/configure-database-mail?view=sql-server-ver15`

You can check to see if you have database mail already set up by executing the script in Listing 12-1.

Listing 12-1. Verify any current database mail setup

```
EXEC msdb.dbo.sysmail_help_account_sp;
```

If you already have database mail set up, note the name returned by the query in Listing 12-1. You will need this to set up the agent job later in this chapter.

If you don't already have database mail set up, you will need to enable Database Mail XPs using the script in Listing 12-2. Note that you will need to set show advanced options to 1 before enabling database mail.

© Josephine Bush 2022
J. Bush, *Practical Database Auditing for Microsoft SQL Server and Azure SQL*,
https://doi.org/10.1007/978-1-4842-8634-0_12

Listing 12-2. Enabling database mail

```
USE master
GO
sp_configure 'show advanced options',1
reconfigure
GO
sp_configure 'Database Mail XPs',1
reconfigure
GO
```

Now that you've enabled database mail, you need to configure it. Listing 12-3 gives you a script to configure it.

Listing 12-3. Configuring database mail

```
DECLARE @profilename varchar(30);
DECLARE @emailaddress varchar(100);
DECLARE @displayname varchar(50);
DECLARE @mailserver varchar(50);

/* CHANGE ONLY THESE FOUR VARIABLES */
SET @profilename = 'yourdbmailprofilename';
SET @emailaddress = 'youremail@domain.com';
SET @displayname = 'yourservername SQL Server Alerting';
SET @mailserver = 'smtp.domain.com';

IF NOT EXISTS(SELECT * FROM msdb.dbo.sysmail_profile WHERE  name =
'yourdbmailprofilename')
  BEGIN
    EXECUTE msdb.dbo.sysmail_add_profile_sp
      @profile_name = @profilename,
      @description  = '';
  END

IF NOT EXISTS(SELECT * FROM msdb.dbo.sysmail_account
WHERE  name = @profilename)
  BEGIN
    EXECUTE msdb.dbo.sysmail_add_account_sp
```

```
    @account_name      = @profilename,
    @email_address     = @emailaddress,
    @display_name      = @displayname,
    @replyto_address   = @emailaddress,
    @description       = '',
    @mailserver_name   = @mailserver,
    @mailserver_type   = 'SMTP',
    @port              = '25',
    @username          = NULL ,
    @password          = NULL ,
    @use_default_credentials = 0 ,
    @enable_ssl              = 0 ;
END

IF NOT EXISTS(SELECT *
              FROM msdb.dbo.sysmail_profileaccount pa
                INNER JOIN msdb.dbo.sysmail_profile p
    ON pa.profile_id = p.profile_id
                INNER JOIN msdb.dbo.sysmail_account a
                ON pa.account_id = a.account_id
              WHERE p.name = @profilename
                AND a.name = @profilename)
  BEGIN
    EXECUTE msdb.dbo.sysmail_add_profileaccount_sp
      @profile_name = @profilename,
      @account_name = @profilename,
      @sequence_number = 1 ;
END
```

You only need to update the variables at the top of the script in Listing 12-3:

- **@profilename** – This is what you want your database mail profile to be named.

- **@emailaddress** – This will be the email address that is both the send to and send from email.

- **@displayname** – This will be the name that is displayed as the from
  in the emails you sent with your database mail profile. For example,
  instead of seeing user@domain.com as the from, you will see the
  @displayname as the from, such as yourservername SQL Server
  Alerting (youremail@domain.com).

- **@mailserver** – You will need to fill this out with your mail server
  usually something like stmp.domain.com.

You will use HTML formatting on the job step that will send the daily report. The
entire script for the job is in Listing 12-4.

Listing 12-4. SQL Server Agent job to send daily auditing report

```
DECLARE @profilename varchar(30);
DECLARE @mailrecipients varchar(100);

/* CHANGE ONLY THESE TWO VARIABLES */
SET @profilename = '''yourdbmailprofilename''';
SET @mailrecipients = '''youremail@domain.com''';

/* DON'T CHANGE ANYTHING BELOW HERE */

DROP TABLE IF EXISTS ##tempvariables;
DECLARE @sql varchar(max);
SET @sql = N'IF (select count(event_time)
     FROM [Auditing].[dbo].[AuditChanges]
     WHERE event_time > getdate()-1) > 0
     BEGIN
     DECLARE @tableHTML  NVARCHAR(MAX) ;
     SET @tableHTML =
     N''<style type="text/css">
     #box-table
     {
     font-family: "Lucida Sans Unicode", "Lucida Grande", Sans-Serif;
     font-size: 12px;
     text-align: left;
     border: #aaa;
     }
```

```
#box-table th
{
font-size: 13px;
font-weight: normal;
background: #f38630;;
border: 2px solid #aaa;
text-align: left;
color: #039;
cellpadding: 10px;
cellspacing: 10px;
}

#box-table td
{
border-right: 1px solid #aabcfe;
border-left: 1px solid #aabcfe;
border-bottom: 1px solid #aabcfe;
cellpadding: 10px;
cellspacing: 10px;
}

tr:nth-of-type(odd)
{ background-color:#aaa; color: #ccc }

tr:nth-of-type(even)
{ background-color:#ccc; color: #aaa }

</style>''+

N''<H2>SQL Server Auditing Findings</H2>'' +
N''<table border="1" id="box-table">'' +
N''<tr><th>Event Time</th><th>Partial Statement</th>'' +
N''<th>Server</th><th>Database</th><th>Schema</th>'' +
N''<th>User</th><th>Successful</th></tr>'' +
CAST ( (
        SELECT td = convert(varchar, [event_time], 22),          '''',
        td = [audit_action], '''',
        td = left([statement], 50), '''',
```

```
            td = [server_instance_name], '''',
            td = [database_name], '''',
            td = [schema_name], '''',
            td = [session_server_principal_name] '''',
            td = [succeeded]
            FROM [Auditing].[dbo].[AuditChanges]
            WHERE event_time > getdate()-1
            ORDER BY event_time ASC
            FOR XML PATH(''tr''), TYPE) AS NVARCHAR(MAX) ) +
            N''</table>'' ;

EXEC msdb.dbo.sp_send_dbmail
@recipients='+@mailrecipients+',
@subject = ''Audit Findings - Changes on Production Servers Last 24
Hours'',
@body = @tableHTML,
@profile_name = '+@profilename+',
@body_format = ''HTML'';
END';

SELECT @sql as stepsql
into ##tempvariables;

USE [msdb]
GO
BEGIN TRANSACTION
DECLARE @ReturnCode INT
SELECT @ReturnCode = 0
IF NOT EXISTS (SELECT name FROM msdb.dbo.syscategories WHERE
name=N'[Uncategorized (Local)]' AND category_class=1)
BEGIN
EXEC @ReturnCode = msdb.dbo.sp_add_category @class=N'JOB', @type=N'LOCAL',
@name=N'[Uncategorized (Local)]'
IF (@@ERROR <> 0 OR @ReturnCode <> 0) GOTO QuitWithRollback
END
```

```
DECLARE @jobId BINARY(16)
EXEC  @ReturnCode =  msdb.dbo.sp_add_job
@job_name=N'Audit Daily Email of Database Server Changes',
@enabled=1,
        @notify_level_eventlog=0,
        @notify_level_email=2,
        @notify_level_netsend=0,
        @notify_level_page=0,
        @delete_level=0,
        @description=N'No description available.',
        @category_name=N'[Uncategorized (Local)]',
        @owner_login_name=N'sa',
        @job_id = @jobId OUTPUT
IF (@@ERROR <> 0 OR @ReturnCode <> 0) GOTO QuitWithRollback
DECLARE @stepsql varchar(max);
SET @stepsql = (SELECT stepsql from ##tempvariables);
EXEC  @ReturnCode = msdb.dbo.sp_add_jobstep
@job_id=@jobId,
@step_name=N'audit findings of changed items on prod servers',
        @step_id=1,
        @cmdexec_success_code=0,
        @on_success_action=1,
        @on_success_step_id=0,
        @on_fail_action=2,
        @on_fail_step_id=0,
        @retry_attempts=0,
        @retry_interval=0,
        @os_run_priority=0,
        @subsystem=N'TSQL',
        @command=@stepsql,
@database_name=N'master',
@flags=0

IF (@@ERROR <> 0 OR @ReturnCode <> 0) GOTO QuitWithRollback
EXEC @ReturnCode = msdb.dbo.sp_update_job @job_id = @jobId, @start_
step_id = 1
```

```
IF (@@ERROR <> 0 OR @ReturnCode <> 0) GOTO QuitWithRollback
EXEC @ReturnCode = msdb.dbo.sp_add_jobschedule @job_id=@jobId,
@name=N'daily 11am auditing findings',
                @enabled=1,
                @freq_type=4,
                @freq_interval=1,
                @freq_subday_type=1,
                @freq_subday_interval=0,
                @freq_relative_interval=0,
                @freq_recurrence_factor=0,
                @active_start_date=20190812,
                @active_end_date=99991231,
                @active_start_time=110000,
                @active_end_time=235959,
                @schedule_uid=N'8ed67b50-2fa6-4683-a714-9c4518fc1453'
IF (@@ERROR <> 0 OR @ReturnCode <> 0) GOTO QuitWithRollback
EXEC @ReturnCode = msdb.dbo.sp_add_jobserver @job_id = @jobId, @server_name =
N'(local)'
IF (@@ERROR <> 0 OR @ReturnCode <> 0) GOTO QuitWithRollback
COMMIT TRANSACTION
GOTO EndSave
QuitWithRollback:
    IF (@@TRANCOUNT > 0) ROLLBACK TRANSACTION
EndSave:
GO
```

There are some things you need to be aware of or update in the script in Listing 12-4:

- The SQL statement that is sent in the email will only include the first 50 characters. Otherwise, the HTML formatting doesn't work right. The full statement is in the database for reference, if needed.

- Update the variables at the top of the script:

  - **@profilename** – This is what you named your database mail profile.

  - **@mailrecipients** – This will be who receives this auditing report email.

The email will look something like the table in Figure 12-1. Your results will vary depending on what happens on your database servers.

SQL Server Auditing Findings

Event Time	Audit Action	Partial Statement	Server	Database	Schema	Username	Successful
03/05/21 4:27:01 PM	ALTER	ALTER SERVER ROLE [sysadmin] ADD MEMBER [domain\group]	Sql1	master		josephine	1
03/05/21 4:08:58 PM	CREATE	CREATE LOGIN [domain\group] FROM	Sql1	master		josephine	1
03/05/21 2:06:43 PM	ALTER	TRUNCATE TABLE [dbo].[tablename]	Sql2	userdb	dbo	appuser	0
03/05/21 1:27:00 PM	DROP	DROP DATABASE db	Sql3	master		sa	1
03/05/21 12:27:00 PM	ALTER	ALTER VIEW [dbo].[tablename_view] AS SELECT	Sql4	userdb	dbo	anotherappuser	1

Figure 12-1. *SQL Server Agent job auditing report example*

HTML Reports with PowerShell

If you want to create an HTML file with your audit query results. Instead, you can use PowerShell. Listing 12-5 gives you an example PowerShell script. This script will capture all audit data from the last seven days.

Listing 12-5. Using PowerShell to create and send an HTML document via email

```
# UPDATE THESE VARIABLES TO YOUR VALUES

$OutputFile = "E:\powershell\sqlserverauditfindings.html"
$CentralServerName = "yourcentralserver"
$SendEmailFrom = "youremail@domain.com"
$SendEmailTo = "recipient@domain.com"
$SMTPServer = "smtp.domain.com"
$EmailSubject = "Audit Findings - Changes on SQL Server Production Servers
in Last 7 Days"
```

```
# DON'T CHANGE ANYTHING BELOW

$Header = @"
<style>
TABLE {border-width: 1px; border-style: solid; border-color: black;
border-collapse: collapse;}
TD {border-width: 1px; padding: 3px; border-style: solid; border-
color: black;}
TH {border-width: 1px; padding: 3px; border-style: solid; border-color:
black; text-align: left;}
BODY {width:800px;}
td:nth-child(2) {max-width: 400px;}
</style>
"@

#get rid of the file if it somehow still exists from a previous run
if (Test-Path $OutputFile){ Remove-Item -Path $OutputFile -Force}

# make sure query returns at least one row
$querycount = Invoke-Sqlcmd -Query "SELECT count(event_time) as count FROM
[Auditing].[dbo].[AuditChanges] a
WHERE event_time > getdate()-7" -ServerInstance $CentralServerName

# query audit data if there is at least one row and create an HTML file
if($querycount.count -gt 0) {
#query the last 7 days of audit events and convert to html file
Invoke-Sqlcmd -Query "SELECT convert(varchar, MAX([event_time]), 22) as
event_time, [audit_action], [succeeded], [statement], [server_instance_
name], [database_name],[schema_name],
[session_server_principal_name]
FROM [Auditing].[dbo].[AuditChanges] a
WHERE event_time > getdate()-7
GROUP BY [audit_action], [succeeded], [statement], [server_instance_name],
[database_name], [schema_name], [session_server_principal_name]
ORDER BY server_instance_name, database_name, schema_name, session_server_
principal_name DESC" `
-ServerInstance $CentralServerName | ConvertTo-HTML `
```

```
-Head $Header `
-Property event_time,audit_action,succeeded,statement,server_instance_
name,database_name,schema_name,session_server_principal_name,name_in_ad `
| Out-File $OutputFile -Encoding utf8

# email file
Send-MailMessage -From $SendEmailFrom `
                  -To $SendEmailTo `
                  -Subject $EmailSubject `
                  -Attachments $OutputFile `
                  -SmtpServer $SMTPServer

# remove html file
Remove-Item –path $OutputFile
}

# no file is created because there weren't any audit rows
else {
Write-Output "nothing happened bc there were zero rows"
}
```

The only things you need to update in the script in Listing 12-5 are the variables at the top:

- **$OutputFile** – Needs to be a path that you have on your server

- **$ServerInstance** – Needs to point to your central auditing database server, which is set up in Chapter 11, "Centralizing Audit Data"

- **$SendEmailFrom** – Set this to the email address you are sending from

- **$SendEmailTo** – Set this to the email address you are sending to

- **$SMTPServer** – Set this to the SMTP server you are using

- **$EmailSubject** – Whatever you want the subject to be and I've included the subject I like to use

The HTML file will look like the screenshot in Figure 12-2. Your results will vary depending on what happens on your database servers. The file will be named sqlserverauditfindings.html unless you change it in the $OutputFile variable.

event_time	audit_action	succeeded	statement	server_instance_name	database_name	schema_name	session_server_principal_name
04/13/22 12:06:32 PM	ALTER	True	RECONFIGURE WITH OVERRIDE	sql1	master		anotheruser
04/13/22 6:11:46 PM	ALTER CONNECTION	True	kill 174	sql1	master		sa
04/13/22 4:14:12 PM	ALTER	True	UPDATE STATISTICS dbo.sometable	sql2	userdb	dbo	jbush

Figure 12-2. *PowerShell HTML file example*

Sending your audit results via email makes it easy to stay on top of what changes are happening on your database servers. Here's the schedule I have for my audit reports:

- **SQL Server Agent job schedule** – Sends daily email with audit results and partial SQL statements for the last 24 hours in the body of the email

- **PowerShell schedule** – Sends weekly email weekly to our ticketing system with an HTML attachment that has the audit results and full SQL statements for the last seven days included

You can schedule the PowerShell script to execute using a SQL Server Agent job. Figure 12-3 shows you what the PowerShell Agent job step will look like. Make sure to select the Type of PowerShell.

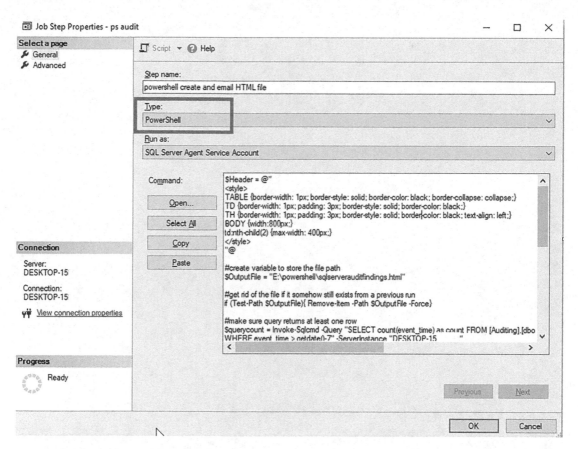

Figure 12-3. *PowerShell Agent job step*

Tip   To find out more information about creating a PowerShell job step, visit
https://docs.microsoft.com/en-us/sql/powershell/run-windows-
powershell-steps-in-sql-server-agent?view=sql-server-
ver15#PShellJob

In the next chapter, you will learn how to audit SQL Databases in Azure. You will also learn how to centralize and report on the audit data in Azure.

PART IV

Cloud Auditing Options

CHAPTER 13

Auditing Azure SQL Databases

This chapter will show you how to audit your Azure SQL Databases. In some ways, it's very much like SQL Server auditing, and in other ways, it's fairly different.

There is a high-level comparison of Azure auditing vs. SQL Server auditing in Table 13-1.

Table 13-1. *SQL Server and Azure SQL auditing comparisons*

Cloud solution	SQL Server Audit	Extended Events	Auditing differences
SQL Server VM	Yes	Yes	The same as if you are using SQL Server on premises
Azure SQL Database	No	Yes	SQL Audit equivalent available in the Azure portal

Read earlier chapters of this book for more guidance on SQL Server Audit and extended events on a VM.

Auditing Azure SQL Database via the Portal

To audit Azure SQL Database, you will need to navigate to the Azure portal, `https://portal.azure.com`. Auditing is built into the portal.

You have the option to audit your databases at the server level or at the database level. If you enable server-level auditing, it will audit all the databases. If you enable database-level auditing, it will only audit that one database. Don't enable it at the server

213

© Josephine Bush 2022
J. Bush, *Practical Database Auditing for Microsoft SQL Server and Azure SQL*,
https://doi.org/10.1007/978-1-4842-8634-0_13

level and the database level. This will cause duplicate audit data. I enable it at the server level because I want to see audit data for all my databases.

Note   Auditing is available in pricing tiers.

By default, Azure auditing will capture everything happening on your Azure SQL databases. This can create a lot of audit data. I will show you how to modify the default policy. This way, you can specify what you do and don't want to be audited. First, let's take a look at how you enable auditing.

Enabling and Configuring Auditing

Figure 13-1 shows you how to enable auditing at the server level. To access the auditing page, you will need to navigate to the SQL Server for your databases, and then click Auditing in the menu on the left side of the page.

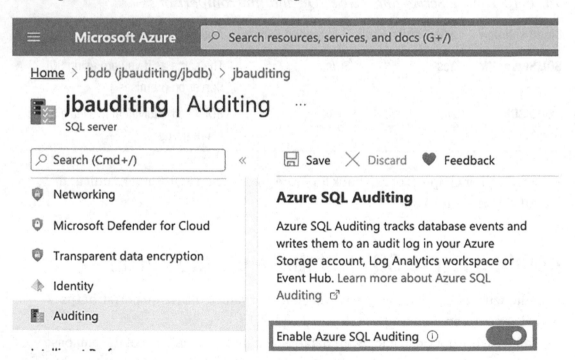

Figure 13-1. *Enabling server-level auditing in Azure SQL*

Once you are on the Auditing page, you will see a radio button. It will be set to off, and you need to turn it on to enable the auditing as shown in Figure 13-1.

You will see multiple choices for where you can store the audit data as shown in Figure 13-2.

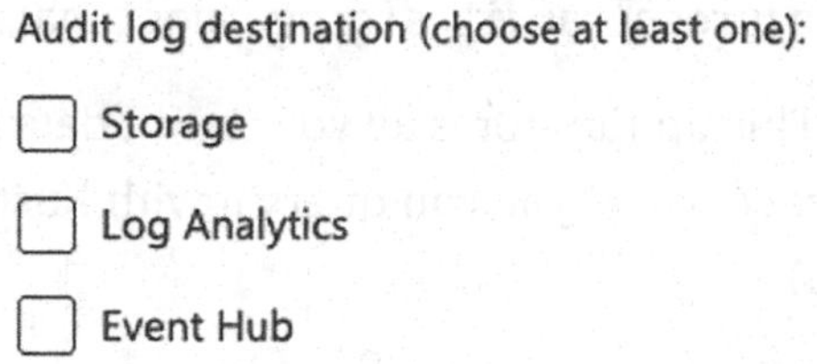

Audit log destination (choose at least one):

☐ Storage

☐ Log Analytics

☐ Event Hub

Figure 13-2. *Audit log destinations for Azure SQL auditing*

You can choose one or more of these options to store your audit data. If you store audit data in multiple locations, you will be charged for that data in multiple locations. I recommend you pick your favorite one.

You can also audit Microsoft support operations as shown in Figure 13-3.

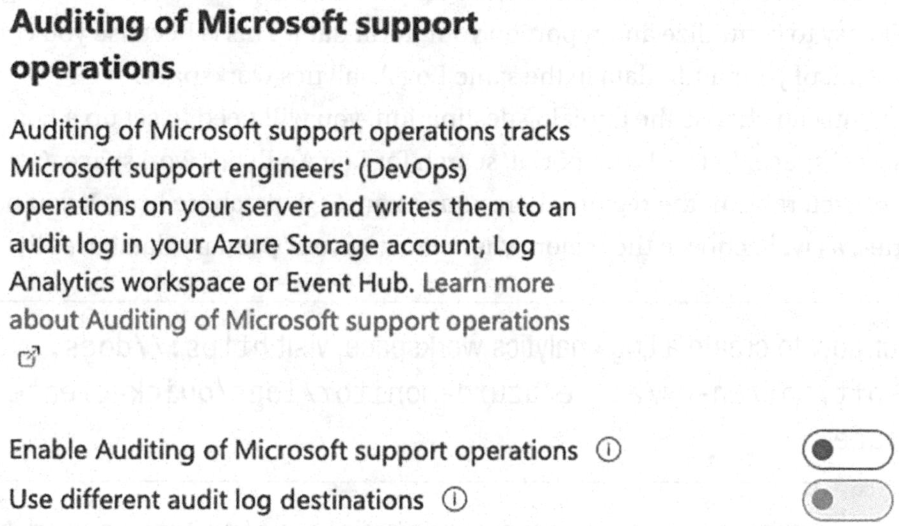

Auditing of Microsoft support operations

Auditing of Microsoft support operations tracks Microsoft support engineers' (DevOps) operations on your server and writes them to an audit log in your Azure Storage account, Log Analytics workspace or Event Hub. Learn more about Auditing of Microsoft support operations ☐

Enable Auditing of Microsoft support operations ⓘ

Use different audit log destinations ⓘ

Figure 13-3. *Auditing Microsoft support operations*

You can choose to enable this and store it in the same or a different location than your other audit data. I tend to enable this and store it in the same location as my audit data to make it easy to query everything in one place.

For audit log destination, you have three options:

- **Storage** – This means a storage account. Your files will be stored in .xel format in a folder structure. For more information, visit `https://docs.microsoft.com/en-us/azure/azure-sql/database/auditing-overview?view=azuresql#audit-storage-destination`

- **Log Analytics** – This option stores all your audit data in a Log Analytics workspace where you can query it with Kusto Query Language (Kusto).

- **Event Hub** – You need to set up a stream to consume events and write them to a target. They are stored using JSON formatting. For more information, visit `https://docs.microsoft.com/en-us/azure/azure-sql/database/auditing-overview?view=azuresql#audit-event-hub-destination`

My favorite is Log Analytics, and at first, it might not seem like the easiest choice because you have to learn Kusto, but Kusto is easy to learn if you already know SQL. Plus, it makes it easy to centralize and report on your audit data. This is because you can store most, if not all, of your audit data in the same Log Analytics workspace.

Before you can choose the audit log destination, you will need to set up a Log Analytics workspace. In the Azure portal, search for Log Analytics workspace. Create a workspace, preferably in the region where your Azure SQL database lives. If you have secondaries, as well, choose the region where most of your primary databases live.

Tip   For how to create a Log Analytics workspace, visit `https://docs.microsoft.com/en-us/azure/azure-monitor/logs/quick-create-workspace`

It's important to set the data retention after creating your Log Analytics workspace. You can do this by clicking Usage and estimated costs in your workspace and then clicking Data Retention as shown in Figure 13-4.

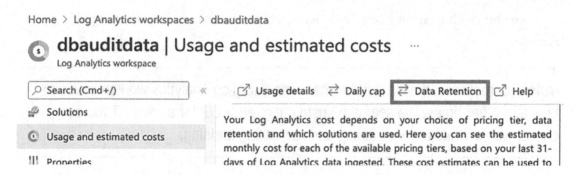

Figure 13-4. *Accessing data retention settings*

By default, 31 days of retention is included with your pricing plan as shown in Figure 13-5. You choose to retain your files for up to 730 days for an additional cost. I leave it on the default of 31 days. I don't need more audit data than that, and I will also report on it daily, so I will see it long before 31 days go by.

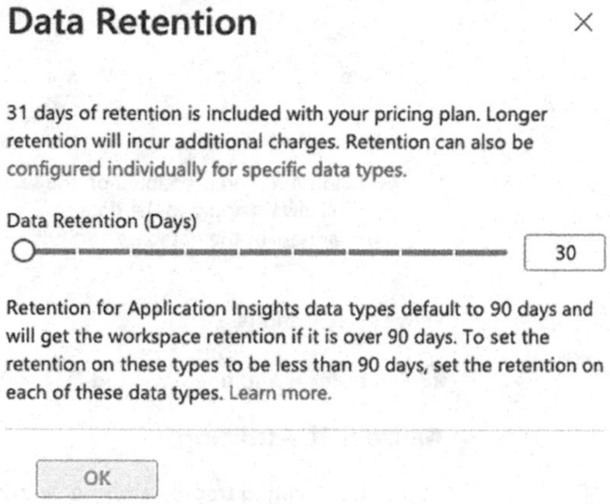

Data Retention   ✕

31 days of retention is included with your pricing plan. Longer retention will incur additional charges. Retention can also be configured individually for specific data types.

Data Retention (Days)

〇━━━━━━━━━━━━━━━━━━━━━   30

Retention for Application Insights data types default to 90 days and will get the workspace retention if it is over 90 days. To set the retention on these types to be less than 90 days, set the retention on each of these data types. Learn more.

    OK

Figure 13-5. *Data retention settings*

Go back to your server auditing options, choose Log Analytics, and then choose your subscription and workspace, as shown in Figure 13-6.

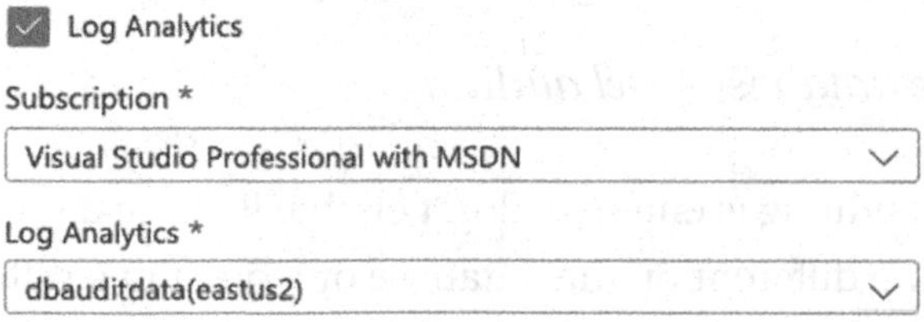

☑ Log Analytics

Subscription *

Visual Studio Professional with MSDN   ∨

Log Analytics *

dbauditdata(eastus2)   ∨

Figure 13-6. *Choosing a Log Analytics workspace for Azure SQL auditing*

Once you've chosen your Log Analytics workspace, click Save near the top of the page.

Note   Sometimes, the audit data writes into your Log Analytics workspace quite fast, and other times, I've seen the Kusto query error out for a while. If you see errors, wait a while or try disabling and reenabling auditing.

If you want to audit only one Azure SQL database, you can enable it at the database level. Navigate to the database, and choose the Auditing option. This will show you a page to enable auditing at the database level. It will also show you if the server audit is already enabled as shown in Figure 13-7.

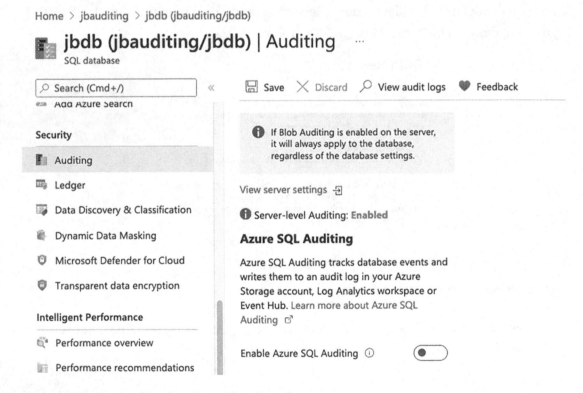

Figure 13-7. *Enable database-level auditing*

If the server-level auditing is enabled, don't enable it at the database level. If you want to audit something different on the database or store it in a different location, then you could turn it on at the database level. You may still wind up with duplicate audit data, though, so use caution with this option.

Viewing Audit Data

There are two ways to see your audit data in your Log Analytics workspace. You can go into each database and click the Auditing page following the steps in Figure 13-8.

Tip   You will need to trigger an event before it can be audited. Since you turned on the auditing in the last section, it will audit everything happening. You can log into the SQL database with SSMS or Azure Data Studio, and those events will be audited.

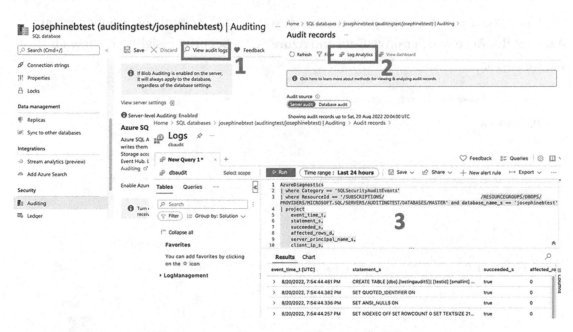

Figure 13-8. *Access auditing logs from an Azure SQL database*

Note   It can take a while for audit data to appear in your Log Analytics workspace. Keep this in mind if you aren't seeing audit data right away. It can take upward of an hour, and in that time frame, it may not be capturing any auditable events.

You can also go to your Log Analytics workspace to view the audit logs. This is a better option because there is a summary and an easy way to drill into the data.

Navigate to your Log Analytics workspace, and then click Workspace summary as shown in Figure 13-9.

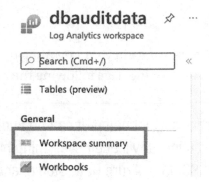

Figure 13-9. *Log Analytics navigating to Workspace summary*

Once you are in the Workspace summary, you will see a couple of options such as Azure SQL – Access to Sensitive Data and Azure SQL – Security Insights, as shown in Figure 13-10.

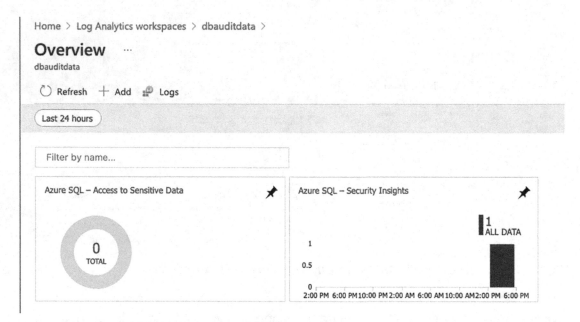

Figure 13-10. *Log Analytics Workspace summary options*

You may have other stuff in this workspace, as well, but I recommend storing only Azure SQL audit data here for simplicity. Click the Azure SQL – Security Insights box. This will give you a dashboard view of the audit data in your Log Analytics workspace as shown in Figure 13-11.

Figure 13-11. *Log Analytics SQLSecurityInsights*

You will see many categories of audit data:

- **Audit distribution** – Shows you which audited actions have been taken and what the count is on each action

- **Distribution by database** – Shows you which databases have audited actions and a count of the actions for each database

- **Distribution by IP** – Shows you which IP addresses have audited actions and a count of the actions for each IP

- **Distribution by principal** – Shows you which principals have audited actions and a count of the actions for each principal

- **Distribution by success** – Shows you a count of successful and failed audited actions

You can click on any of these boxes to drill down for more information. This will bring you to a screen with a Kusto query prepopulated for you. This gives you good information for each of those categories. To query the audit data as a whole, I recommend clicking the Logs button near the top of the page as shown in Figure 13-12.

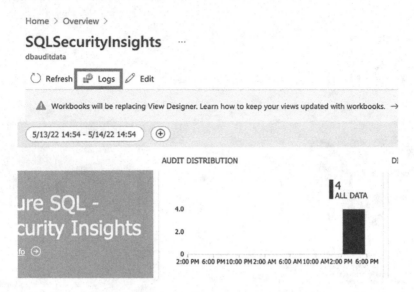

Figure 13-12. *Log Analytics SQLSecurityInsights Logs button*

After clicking Logs, you will see a page with suggested queries. You can close that because none of those will help you query the audit data.

Use the Kusto query in Listing 13-1 to get your audit data.

Listing 13-1. Log Analytics Kusto query

```
AzureDiagnostics
| where Category == 'SQLSecurityAuditEvents'
   and TimeGenerated > ago(1d)
| project
   event_time_t,
   database_name_s,
   statement_s,
   server_principal_name_s,
   succeeded_s,
   client_ip_s,
   application_name_s,
   additional_information_s,
   data_sensitivity_information_s
| order by event_time_t desc
```

Tip   For more information on Kusto, visit `https://docs.microsoft.com/en-us/azure/data-explorer/kusto/query/`

The Kusto query will return results like the results in Figure 13-13. The results will depend on what happened on your audited system.

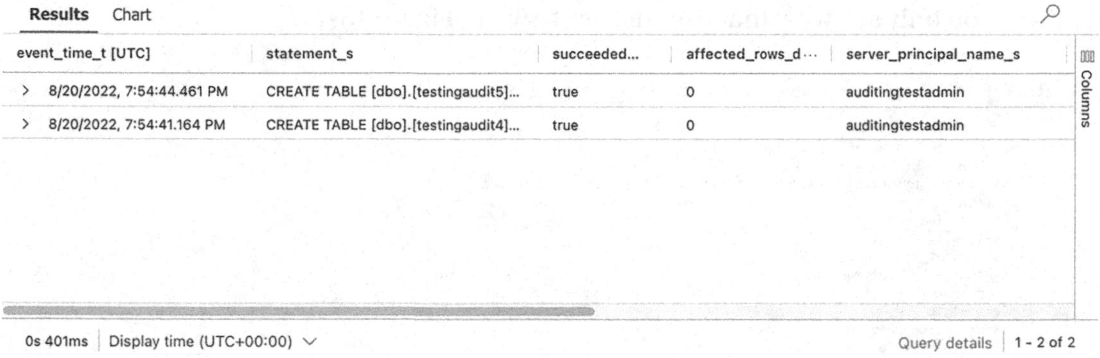

event_time_t [UTC]	statement_s	succeeded...	affected_rows_d···	server_principal_name_s
> 8/20/2022, 7:54:44.461 PM	CREATE TABLE [dbo].[testingaudit5]...	true	0	auditingtestadmin
> 8/20/2022, 7:54:41.164 PM	CREATE TABLE [dbo].[testingaudit4]...	true	0	auditingtestadmin

Results   Chart

0s 401ms | Display time (UTC+00:00) ⌄   Query details | 1 - 2 of 2

Figure 13-13. *Log Analytics Kusto query results*

Even though I do not recommend it for SQL Server Audit, I recommend filtering with a Kusto query after the audit data has been captured in your Log Analytics workspace. This is because the audit functionality in Azure doesn't let you filter before you collect the data. For example, you may only want to see what a specific user does in your audit. You can filter with Kusto by adding another where clause such as and `server_principal_name_s == 'josephine'`.

An example of a Kusto query with that filter is shown in Listing 13-2.

Listing 13-2. Kusto query with additional filter

```
AzureDiagnostics
| where Category == 'SQLSecurityAuditEvents'
    and TimeGenerated > ago(1d)
    and server_principal_name_s == 'josephine'
| project
    event_time_t,
    database_name_s,
    statement_s,
    server_principal_name_s,
```

```
    succeeded_s,
    client_ip_s,
    application_name_s,
    additional_information_s,
    data_sensitivity_information_s
| order by event_time_t desc
```

Now you only see what that user did as shown in Figure 13-14.

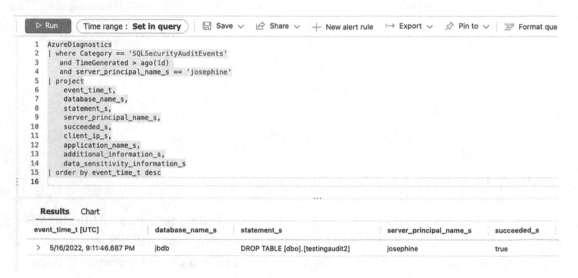

Figure 13-14. *Kusto query results with additional filter*

Modifying Azure SQL Database Auditing

The results you see in Figure 13-13 are that way because I modified the default auditing policy. Otherwise, you wind up with so much audit data that it's not easy to weed through it to see what you want or need to see. What you would see with the default audit settings is more like Figure 13-15.

	event_time_t [UTC]	database_na...	statement_s	server_principal_name_s	succeeded_s	client_ip_s	applica
>	5/14/2022, 9:39:59.615 PM	jbdb	SELECT ISNULL(SESSIONPR...	azureadmin	true	67.1ᵢ	azdata
>	5/14/2022, 9:39:59.615 PM	jbdb	exec sp_executesql N'SELEC...	azureadmin	true	67.1ᵢ	azdata
>	5/14/2022, 9:39:59.490 PM	jbdb	SELECT CONVERT(NVARCHA...	azureadmin	true	67.1ᵢ	azdata
>	5/14/2022, 9:39:59.443 PM	jbdb	SELECT CAST(ISNULL(SERVE...	azureadmin	true	67.1ᵢ	azdata
>	5/14/2022, 9:39:59.365 PM	jbdb	SELECT ISNULL(SESSIONPR...	azureadmin	true	67.1ᵢ	azdata
>	5/14/2022, 9:39:59.365 PM	jbdb	SELECT SERVERPROPERTY('I...	azureadmin	true	67.1ᵢ	azdata
>	5/14/2022, 9:39:59.255 PM	jbdb	SELECT CAST(case when 'a' ...	azureadmin	true	67.1ᵢ	azdata

Figure 13-15. *Audit results without filtering*

Notice how in Figure 13-15 there are a lot more statements audited. We will want to filter that out before it writes to the audit.

By default, all Azure SQL databases get these audit actions:

- BATCH_COMPLETED_GROUP

- SUCCESSFUL_DATABASE_AUTHENTICATION_GROUP

- FAILED_DATABASE_AUTHENTICATION_GROUP

These audit actions will audit all queries and stored procedures executed against the database, as well as all successful and failed logins. As you can imagine, this can be a lot of audit data. I'm mainly concerned with changes like schema or permissions. To get only these changes, you need to change the default auditing policy to use different audit action groups.

If you are familiar with SQL Server Audit, some of the audit action groups will be the same, but some are different. Figure 13-16 shows the accepted values for audit action groups in Azure.

Type:	AuditActionGroups[]
Accepted values:	BATCH_STARTED_GROUP, BATCH_COMPLETED_GROUP, APPLICATION_ROLE_CHANGE_PASSWORD_GROUP, BACKUP_RESTORE_GROUP, DATABASE_LOGOUT_GROUP, DATABASE_OBJECT_CHANGE_GROUP, DATABASE_OBJECT_OWNERSHIP_CHANGE_GROUP, DATABASE_OBJECT_PERMISSION_CHANGE_GROUP, DATABASE_OPERATION_GROUP, DATABASE_PERMISSION_CHANGE_GROUP, DATABASE_PRINCIPAL_CHANGE_GROUP, DATABASE_PRINCIPAL_IMPERSONATION_GROUP, DATABASE_ROLE_MEMBER_CHANGE_GROUP, FAILED_DATABASE_AUTHENTICATION_GROUP, SCHEMA_OBJECT_ACCESS_GROUP, SCHEMA_OBJECT_CHANGE_GROUP, SCHEMA_OBJECT_OWNERSHIP_CHANGE_GROUP, SCHEMA_OBJECT_PERMISSION_CHANGE_GROUP, SUCCESSFUL_DATABASE_AUTHENTICATION_GROUP, USER_CHANGE_PASSWORD_GROUP, LEDGER_OPERATION_GROUP, DBCC_GROUP, DATABASE_OWNERSHIP_CHANGE_GROUP, DATABASE_CHANGE_GROUP

Figure 13-16. *Audit action groups in Azure*

Getting and Setting Your Auditing Policy

Let's look at the PowerShell commands you can use to see and change your auditing policy:

- **Get-AZSqlServerAudit** – This allows you to see the current policy.

- **Set-AZSqlServerAudit** – This allows you to change the current policy.

To use these PowerShell commands, you need the Azure CLI. In the Azure portal, click the cloud shell button near the upper right of the page as shown in Figure 13-17.

Figure 13-17. *Accessing the cloud shell*

> **Tip**   To find out more about using PowerShell in the Azure CLI, visit `https://docs.microsoft.com/en-us/azure/cloud-shell/quickstart-powershell`

You will get a box like the one in Figure 13-18 at the bottom of the browser. Make sure you are using PowerShell, not Bash.

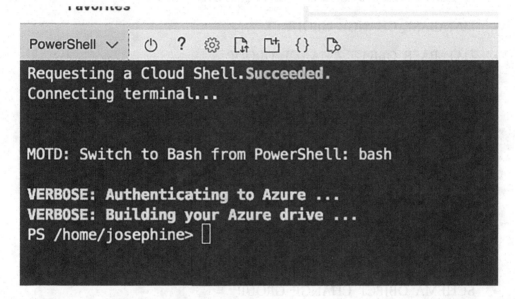

Figure 13-18.   Cloud shell using PowerShell

To get the auditing policy, you will need to specify the ResourceGroupName and the Servername, as shown in Listing 13-3.

Listing 13-3.   Get the current auditing policy

```
Get-AzSqlServerAudit -ResourceGroupName 'yourresourcegroup' -Servername 'yourservername'
```

Make sure to change the variables to the correct resource group and server name in your Azure account.

Figure 13-19 shows you the results of executing the Get-AzSqlServerAudit in my Azure portal.

```
PS /home/josephine> Get-AzSqlServerAudit -ResourceGroupName 'dbops' -Servername 'jbauditing'

ServerName                    : jbauditing
AuditActionGroup              : {BATCH_COMPLETED_GROUP, SUCCESSFUL_DATABASE_AUTHENTICATION_GROUP, FAILED_DATABASE_AUTHENTICATION_GROUP}
PredicateExpression           :
```

Figure 13-19. *Get the current auditing policy results*

The default auditing policy is still in place on this database server. I recommend changing the policy to capture these actions to minimize auditing data:

- APPLICATION_ROLE_CHANGE_PASSWORD_GROUP

- DATABASE_CHANGE_GROUP

- DATABASE_OBJECT_CHANGE_GROUP

- DATABASE_OBJECT_OWNERSHIP_CHANGE_GROUP

- DATABASE_OBJECT_PERMISSION_CHANGE_GROUP

- DATABASE_OWNERSHIP_CHANGE_GROUP

- DATABASE_PERMISSION_CHANGE_GROUP

- DATABASE_PRINCIPAL_CHANGE_GROUP

- DATABASE_PRINCIPAL_IMPERSONATION_GROUP

- DATABASE_ROLE_MEMBER_CHANGE_GROUP

- SCHEMA_OBJECT_CHANGE_GROUP

- SCHEMA_OBJECT_OWNERSHIP_CHANGE_GROUP

- SCHEMA_OBJECT_PERMISSION_CHANGE_GROUP

- USER_CHANGE_PASSWORD_GROUP

Tip   To find out more information about these audit action groups, visit https://
docs.microsoft.com/en-us/sql/relational-databases/security/
auditing/sql-server-audit-action-groups-and-actions?view=
sql-server-ver15#database-level-audit-action-groups

Those audit actions will get schema and security changes. To use these audit actions, you will need to execute the script in Listing 13-4.

Listing 13-4. Modify auditing policy

```
Set-AzSqlServerAudit -ResourceGroupName 'yourresourcegroup' -Servername
'yourservername' -AuditActionGroup APPLICATION_ROLE_CHANGE_PASSWORD_
GROUP, DATABASE_CHANGE_GROUP, DATABASE_OBJECT_CHANGE_GROUP, DATABASE_
OBJECT_OWNERSHIP_CHANGE_GROUP, DATABASE_OBJECT_PERMISSION_CHANGE_GROUP,
DATABASE_OWNERSHIP_CHANGE_GROUP, DATABASE_PERMISSION_CHANGE_GROUP,
DATABASE_PRINCIPAL_CHANGE_GROUP, DATABASE_PRINCIPAL_IMPERSONATION_GROUP,
DATABASE_ROLE_MEMBER_CHANGE_GROUP, SCHEMA_OBJECT_CHANGE_GROUP, SCHEMA_
OBJECT_OWNERSHIP_CHANGE_GROUP, SCHEMA_OBJECT_PERMISSION_CHANGE_GROUP, USER_
CHANGE_PASSWORD_GROUP
```

Make sure to change the variables to the correct resource group and server name in your Azure account.

Figure 13-20 shows you the results of executing the Set-AzSqlServerAudit after changing the auditing policy.

```
PS /home/josephine> Get-AzSqlServerAudit -ResourceGroupName 'dbops' -Servername 'jbauditing'

ServerName                        : jbauditing
AuditActionGroup                  : {APPLICATION_ROLE_CHANGE_PASSWORD_GROUP, DATABASE_CHANGE_GROUP, DATABASE_OBJECT_CHANGE_GROUP,
                                    DATABASE_OBJECT_OWNERSHIP_CHANGE_GROUP…}
```

Figure 13-20. *Get the current auditing policy results after you modify it*

You can choose to keep the default auditing policy. Depending on what you want to capture with auditing, this may be a good idea for you. I don't want to see everything happening and think this modified policy is a better way to audit.

Auditing Azure SQL Database with Extended Events

Another way to audit Azure SQL Databases is with extended events. You can set up an extended event via SSMS. The main difference between extended events on SQL Server and Azure SQL Database is the storage location.

Creating Storage Account and Container

With Azure SQL Database, you will need to store your .xel files in a storage account and then set up a credential to access the storage account. In the Azure portal, search for storage accounts. Click Create. At this point, you need to choose the following:

- **Subscription** – Select a subscription.

- **Resource group** – You may want to put it in the same resource group as the SQL database.

- **Storage account name** – Must be unique across Azure.

- **Region** – I recommend putting this storage account in the same region as the database.

- **Performance** – Standard is fine for performance.

- **Redundancy** – Choose based on how important the audit data is for you.

Click Review + Create. Then click Create. Figure 13-21 shows an example of the settings I chose.

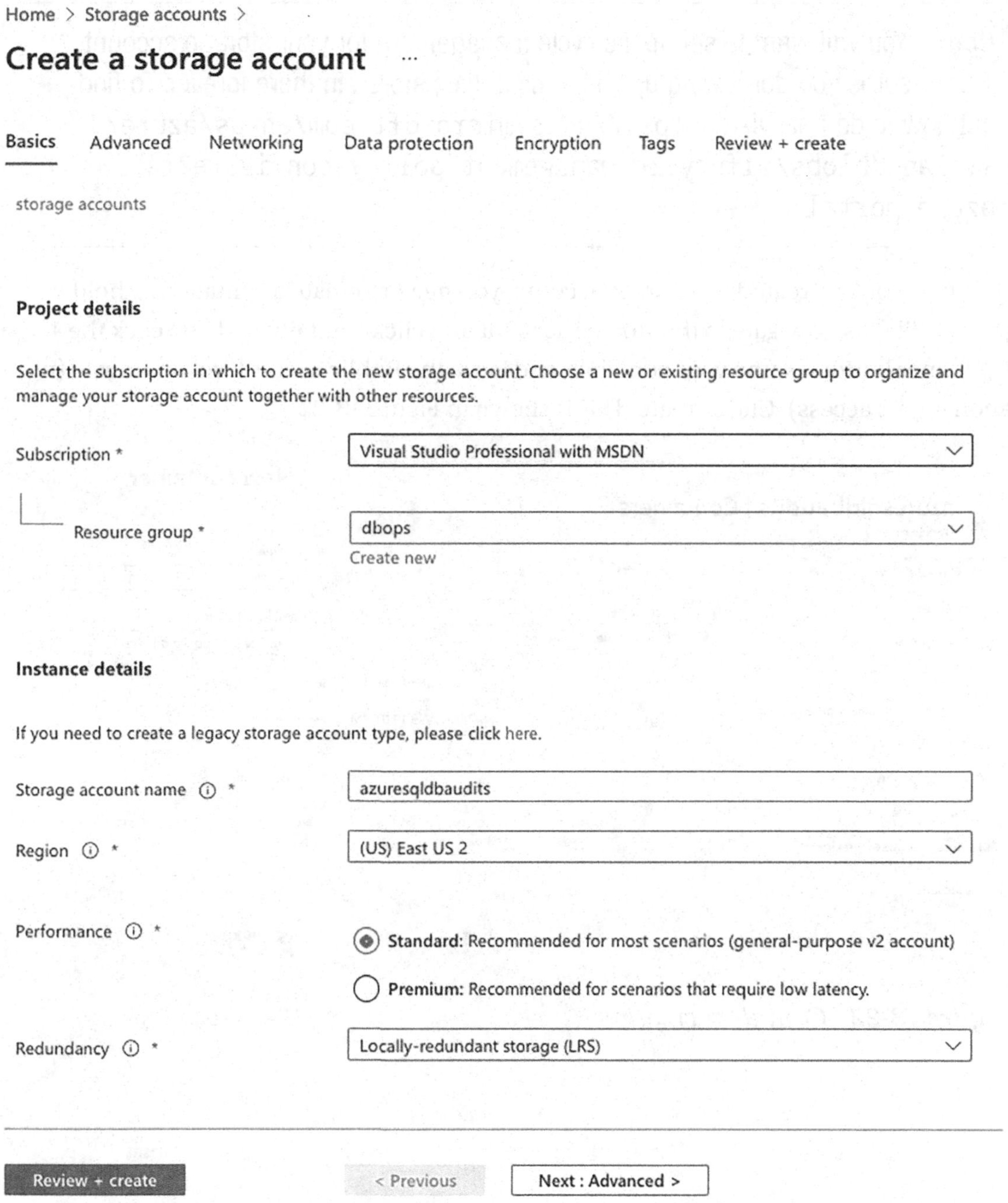

Home > Storage accounts >

Create a storage account ...

Basics   Advanced   Networking   Data protection   Encryption   Tags   Review + create

storage accounts

Project details

Select the subscription in which to create the new storage account. Choose a new or existing resource group to organize and manage your storage account together with other resources.

Subscription *	Visual Studio Professional with MSDN ⌄
Resource group *	dbops ⌄
	Create new

Instance details

If you need to create a legacy storage account type, please click here.

Storage account name ⓘ *	azuresqldbaudits
Region ⓘ *	(US) East US 2 ⌄
Performance ⓘ *	⦿ **Standard:** Recommended for most scenarios (general-purpose v2 account)
	◯ **Premium:** Recommended for scenarios that require low latency.
Redundancy ⓘ *	Locally-redundant storage (LRS) ⌄

Review + create   < Previous   Next : Advanced >

Figure 13-21. *Configure storage account*

Note   You will want to set up life cycle management for your storage account. This ensures you don't wind up with tons of files stored in there forever. To find out how to do this, visit `https://docs.microsoft.com/en-us/azure/storage/blobs/lifecycle-management-policy-configure?tabs=azure-portal`

Once you've created the storage account, you need to create a container to hold your audit files. Navigate to the storage account and click Containers. Then click the + Container button. Name your container and leave the Public access level on Private (no anonymous access). Click Create. This is shown in Figure 13-22.

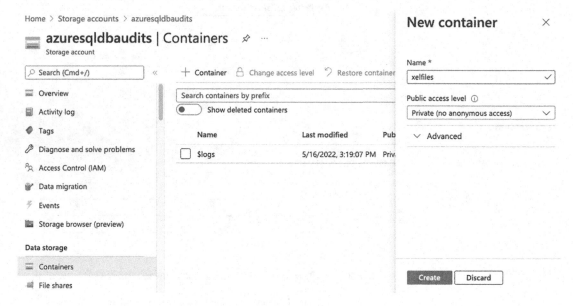

Figure 13-22. *Container creation*

After clicking Create, you will see your container listed. Click the container and choose Properties. Copy the URL for the next steps as shown in Figure 13-23.

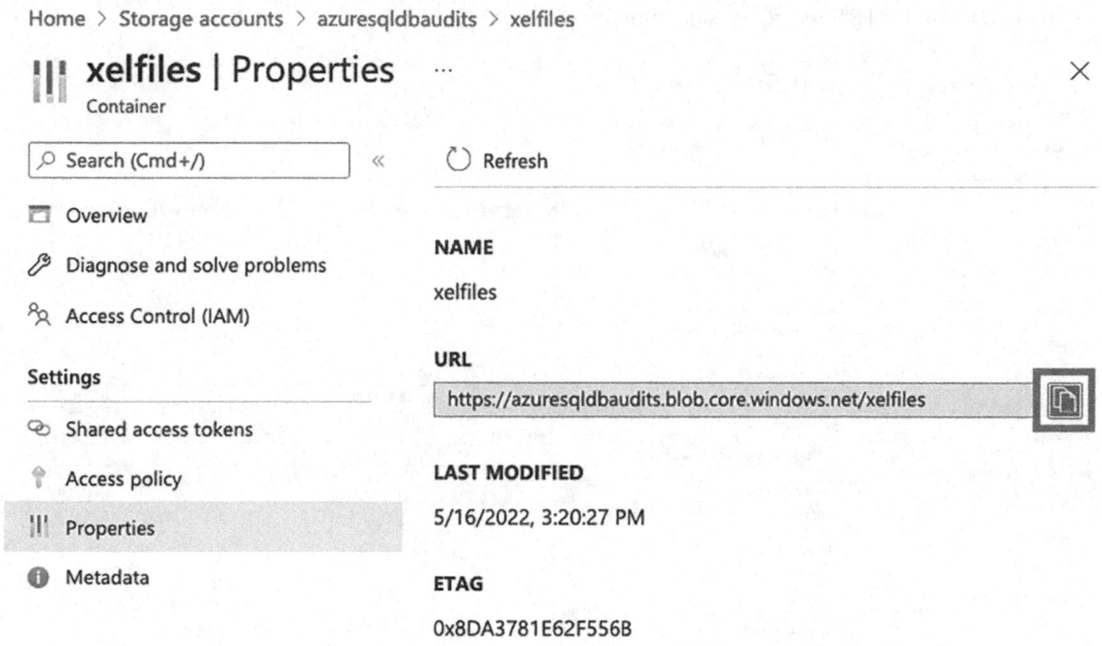

Home > Storage accounts > azuresqldbaudits > xelfiles

||| xelfiles | Properties   ...   ✕
Container

| 🔍 Search (Cmd+/)   ≪ | ◌ Refresh |

🗔 Overview

🔧 Diagnose and solve problems

🗝 Access Control (IAM)

Settings

🔗 Shared access tokens

🔑 Access policy

||| Properties

ⓘ Metadata

NAME

xelfiles

URL

https://azuresqldbaudits.blob.core.windows.net/xelfiles

LAST MODIFIED

5/16/2022, 3:20:27 PM

ETAG

0x8DA3781E62F556B

Figure 13-23. *Copy container URL*

Then navigate back up to the storage account and click Shared access signature. Make sure to create your settings for this key based on the screenshot in Figure 13-24.

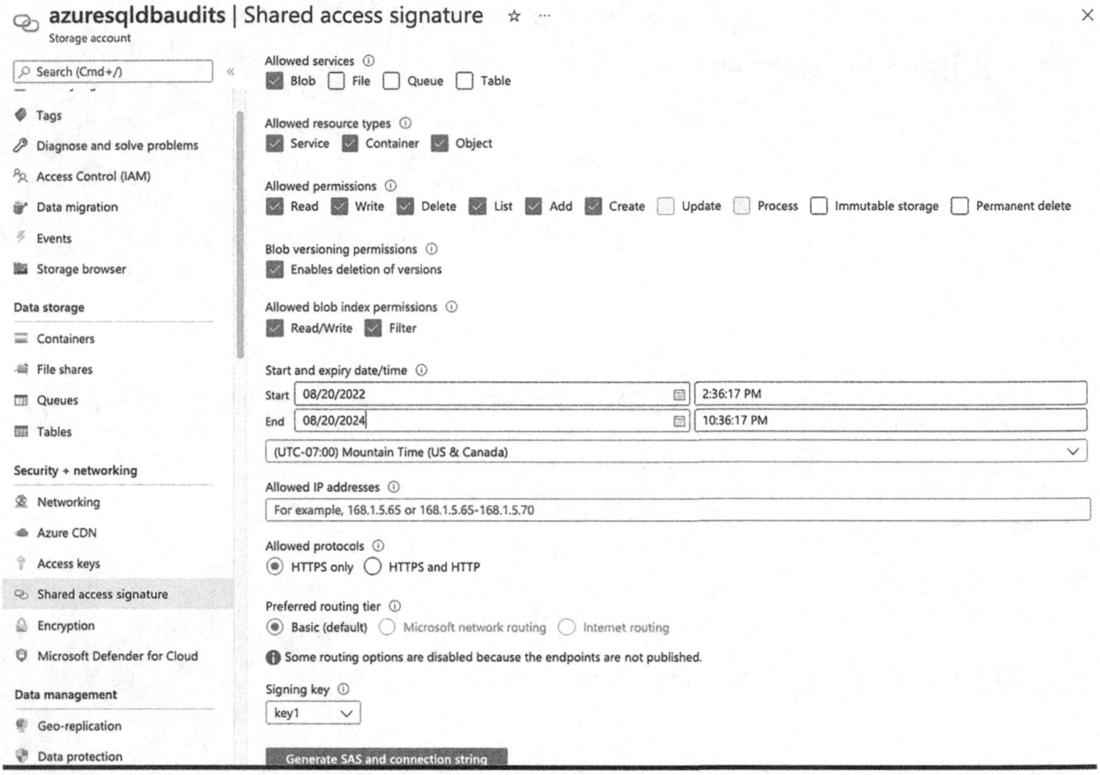

Figure 13-24. *Create shared access signature*

The settings I've chosen for my shared access signature are

- **Allowed services** – Blob.

- **Allowed resource types** – Service, Container, Object.

- **Allowed permissions** – Read, Write, Delete, List, Add, Create.

- **Blob versioning permissions** – Allows version deletion.

- **Allowed blob index permissions** – Read/Write, Filter.

- **Start and expiry date/time** – If it expires, your managed instance will not be able to access the container anymore. You will need to generate a new shared access signature. Then update your managed instance credential with the new token. I tend to set the expiry for years out to avoid issues with not being able to access the storage account.

- **Allowed protocols** – HTTPS only.

- **Preferred routing tier** – Basic (default).

- **Signing key** – Key 1.

Click Generate SAS and connection string. The SAS token will load on that page. Do not navigate off of this page. You can't get the SAS token ever again. If you need a new token, you have to generate a new SAS setup. Copy the SAS token for the next steps as shown in Figure 13-25.

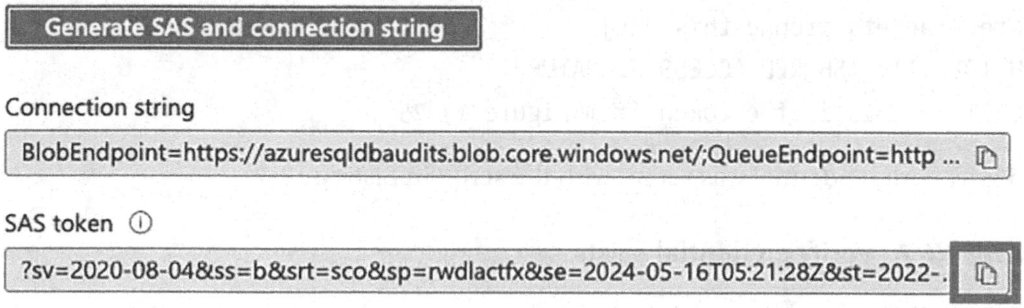

Figure 13-25. *Copy SAS token*

Note   You need to remove the question mark (?) from the beginning of the token when adding it to the SQL Server credential.

Creating Database Credential

Connect to your Azure SQL Database in SSMS. You will need a master key. Your database may already have one, so if you get an error saying the master key already exists, you can proceed to the script in Listing 13-6. The script in Listing 13-5 needs to be executed on the database you want to audit, not in the master database.

Listing 13-5. Create master key encryption

```
CREATE MASTER KEY ENCRYPTION
BY PASSWORD='Testing1234!';
```

You need to create a credential so your database can access your storage account as shown in Listing 13-6. This also needs to be executed on the database you want to audit, not in the master database. The square brackets are needed around the URL. For example, [https://whateveryourazurebloburlis] will the correct syntax for the name of the database scoped credential.

Listing 13-6. Create credential

```
CREATE DATABASE SCOPED CREDENTIAL [URL from Figure 13-23 and keep these
square brackets around this URL]
WITH IDENTITY='SHARED ACCESS SIGNATURE'
,SECRET = 'this is the token from Figure 13-25';
```

Verify your credential was set up with the script in Listing 13-7.

Listing 13-7. Verify credential exists

```
SELECT * FROM sys.database_credentials;
```

Creating Extended Event

You are ready to set up your extended event using the script in Listing 13-8. This also needs to be executed on the database you want to audit, not master. Make sure to update the filename to the storage account URL from Figure 13-23.

Listing 13-8. Create extended event

```
CREATE EVENT SESSION [auditxel] ON DATABASE
ADD EVENT sqlserver.rpc_completed(   ACTION(sqlserver.client_app_
name,sqlserver.client_hostname,sqlserver.database_name,sqlserver.sql_
text,sqlserver.username)
    WHERE ([sqlserver].[username]=N'josephine')),
ADD EVENT sqlserver.sql_batch_completed(   ACTION(sqlserver.client_app_
name,sqlserver.client_hostname,sqlserver.database_name,sqlserver.sql_
text,sqlserver.username)
    WHERE ([sqlserver].[username]=N'josephine'))
ADD TARGET package0.event_file(SET filename=N'https://azuresqldbaudits.
blob.core.windows.net/xelfiles/xelauditdata.xel',max_file_size=(10),max_
rollover_files=(5))
WITH (MAX_MEMORY=4096 KB,EVENT_RETENTION_MODE=ALLOW_SINGLE_EVENT_LOSS,MAX_
DISPATCH_LATENCY=30 SECONDS,MAX_EVENT_SIZE=0 KB,MEMORY_PARTITION_
MODE=NONE,TRACK_CAUSALITY=OFF,STARTUP_STATE=ON);
ALTER EVENT SESSION [auditxel] ON DATABASE
STATE=START;
```

Once the extended event is started, it will place a file in the Azure storage account as shown in Figure 13-26. Five files up to 10 MB each will be placed there because that's what's specified in the script in Listing 13-6.

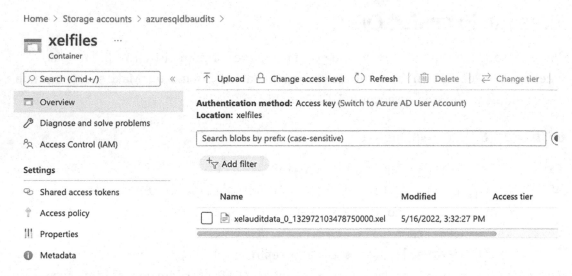

Figure 13-26. *.xel files in Azure storage account*

Querying Extended Event

To query the .xel files, you will need to know the exact file names. You can use the Azure Storage connection in SSMS to find out the names as shown in Figure 13-27.

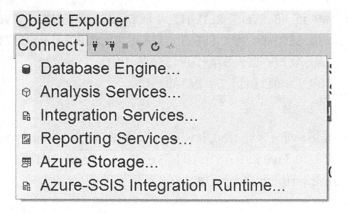

Figure 13-27. *Azure Storage connection*

Sign in to Azure and pick the right storage account and container from the drop-down as shown in Figure 13-28.

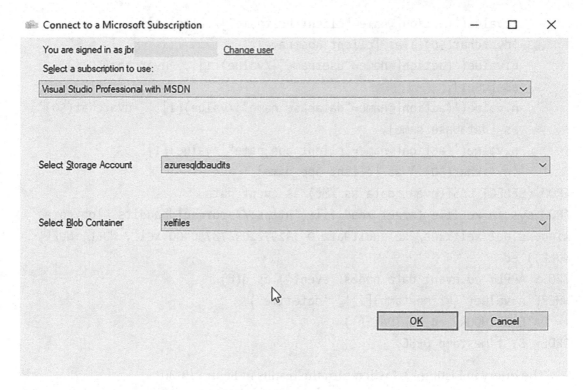

Figure 13-28. *Log in to Azure and select storage account and container*

Click OK. This connects you to this storage account and lists the files in the container as shown in Figure 13-29.

☐ ▧ azuresqldbaudits (Azure Storage Account - Encrypted)
☐ ■ Containers
☐ ■ xelfiles
☐ xelauditdata_0_132972103478750000.xel

Figure 13-29. *Container list of files*

Once you know the names of the files, you can query them with the script in Listing 13-9.

Listing 13-9. Query .xel files

```
SELECT n.value('(@timestamp)[1]', 'datetime') as timestamp,
      n.value('(action[@name="sql_text"]/value)[1]', 'nvarchar(max)')
      as [sql],
```

```
        n.value('(action[@name="client_hostname"]/value)[1]',
        'nvarchar(50)') as [client_hostname],
        n.value('(action[@name="username"]/value)[1]', 'nvarchar(50)')
        as [user],
        n.value('(action[@name="database_name"]/value)[1]', 'nvarchar(50)')
        as [database_name],
        n.value('(action[@name="client_app_name"]/value)[1]',
        'nvarchar(50)') as [client_app_name]
FROM (SELECT CAST(event_data as XML) as event_data
FROM sys.fn_xe_file_target_read_file('https://azuresqldbaudits.blob.core.
windows.net/xelfiles/ xelauditdata_0_132972103478750000.xel', NULL, NULL,
NULL)) ed
CROSS APPLY ed.event_data.nodes('event') as q(n)
WHERE n.value('(@timestamp)[1]', 'datetime')
>= DATEADD(HOUR, -4, GETDATE())
ORDER BY timestamp DESC;
```

The query in Listing 13-7 will return the results in Figure 13-30.

	timestamp	sql	client_hostname	user	database_n...	client_app_name
1	2022-05-16 22:03:57.890	(@_msparam_0 nvarchar(4000))SEL...	DESKTOP-15	josephine	jbdb	Microsoft SQL Server Manage
2	2022-05-16 22:03:57.640	SELECT sqllog.name AS [Name], sqll...	DESKTOP-15	josephine	jbdb	Microsoft SQL Server Manage
3	2022-05-16 22:03:57.570	SELECT sqllog.name AS [Name], sqll...	DESKTOP-15	josephine	jbdb	Microsoft SQL Server Manage
4	2022-05-16 22:03:57.497	DECLARE @edition sysname; SET @...	DESKTOP-15	josephine	jbdb	Microsoft SQL Server Manage
5	2022-05-16 22:03:57.007	(@_msparam_0 nvarchar(4000))SEL...	DESKTOP-15	josephine	jbdb	Microsoft SQL Server Manage
6	2022-05-16 22:03:56.833	SELECT CAST(serverproperty(...	DESKTOP-15	josephine	jbdb	Microsoft SQL Server Manage
7	2022-05-16 22:03:56.753	select SERVERPROPERTY(N'server...	DESKTOP-15	josephine	jbdb	Microsoft SQL Server Manage
8	2022-05-16 22:03:56.683	DECLARE @edition sysname; SET @...	DESKTOP-15	josephine	jbdb	Microsoft SQL Server Manage
9	2022-05-16 22:03:55.257	/****** Script for SelectTopNRows com...	DESKTOP-15	josephine	jbdb	Microsoft SQL Server Manage
10	2022-05-16 22:03:55.157	SELECT @@SPID;	DESKTOP-15	josephine	jbdb	Microsoft SQL Server Manage

Figure 13-30. *.xel files results*

I don't recommend using extended events in Azure SQL Database to audit anything you want to easily query and report on. I recommend using Azure SQL auditing, which is built into the portal. It's a better way to audit changes on your database because it's easier to query from Log Analytics. It's also easier to centralize and report on.

Centralizing and Reporting on Azure SQL Audit Data

Centralizing is as easy as putting all your audit data in the same Log Analytics workspace. This makes for easy querying and reporting on audit data.

To report on data, I use a Logic App. This way, I can send an email attachment daily with any changes captured by the audit. Figure 13-31 shows you the high-level setup of the Logic App.

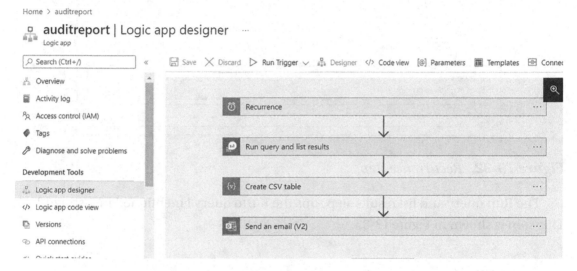

Figure 13-31. *Logic app to report on audit data*

Tip   To learn how to create a logic app, visit `https://docs.microsoft.com/en-us/azure/logic-apps/quickstart-create-first-logic-app-workflow`

The logic app consists of four steps. Let's walk through them one by one. The Recurrence step determines how often this app will run as shown in Figure 13-32. This logic app will run once a day at 10. This is in UTC, so make sure to account for that if you want it to run at 10 in another time zone instead.

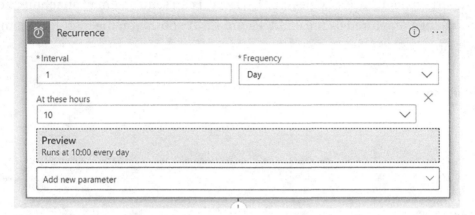

Figure 13-32. *Recurrence step*

The Run query and list results step runs the Kusto query I mentioned in Listing 13-1. This step is shown in Figure 13-33.

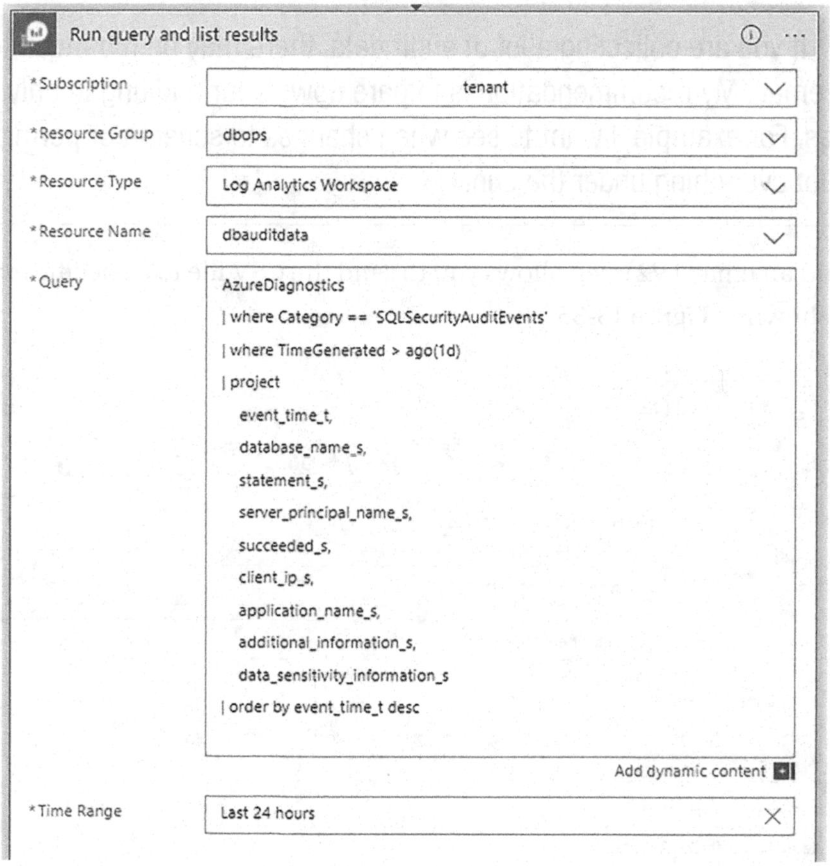

Figure 13-33. *Run query and list results step*

The Create CSV table step creates a CSV file of the results as shown in Figure 13-34. The contents of the CSV come from the previous step. I create a CSV file because the Kusto query results are not easily formatted into the body of an email.

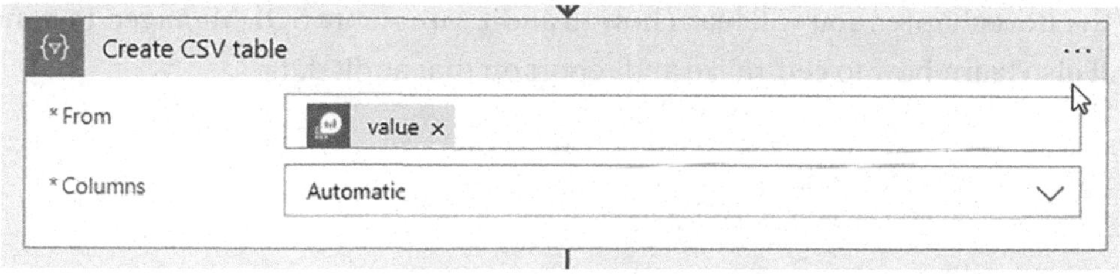

Figure 13-34. *Create CSV table step*

> **Caution**   If you are collecting a lot of audit data, there may be too much to send in a daily email. My recommendation is to pare down your auditing to only the necessities. For example, I want to see when changes to schema or permissions happen, not everything under the sun.

The Send an email (V2) step allows you to send the CSV file to a specific email address as shown in Figure 13-35.

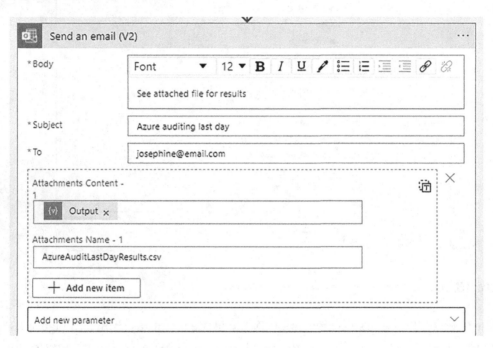

Figure 13-35. *Send an email (V2)*

In the next chapter, you will learn how to audit with Azure SQL Managed Instance. You will also learn how to centralize and report on that audit data.

CHAPTER 14

Auditing Azure SQL Managed Instance

This chapter will show you how to audit your Azure SQL Managed Instance. In some cases, it's similar to SQL Server auditing, and in other cases, it's different.

Let's start with a high-level comparison of Azure auditing vs. SQL Server auditing.

Table 14-1. *SQL Server and Azure SQL auditing comparisons*

Cloud solution	SQL Server Audit	Extended Events	Auditing differences
SQL Server VM	Yes	Yes	The same as if you are using SQL Server on premises
Azure SQL Managed Instance	Yes	Yes	Need to use a storage account to hold your audit files

Read earlier chapters of this book for more guidance on SQL Server Audit and extended events on a VM.

Auditing Azure SQL Managed Instance with Diagnostic Settings

Turning on diagnostic settings is the easiest way to audit an Azure SQL Managed Instance. If you haven't used diagnostic settings before, you will have to turn them on for each server you want to audit.

© Josephine Bush 2022
J. Bush, *Practical Database Auditing for Microsoft SQL Server and Azure SQL*,
https://doi.org/10.1007/978-1-4842-8634-0_14

Enabling and Configuring Diagnostic Setting

Navigate to your managed instance in the Azure portal, and then Navigate to Diagnostic settings. You will need to add a diagnostic setting by clicking + Add diagnostic setting as shown in Figure 14-1.

Figure 14-1. *Add diagnostic setting*

Name your diagnostic setting, and then choose SQLSecurityAuditEvents. If you also want to audit the actions Microsoft is taking on your managed instance, you can choose DevOpsOperationsAudit. Select your destination details. In this case, I'm putting the data in a Log Analytics workspace as shown in Figure 14-2.

Diagnostic setting ⋯

🖫 Save   ✕ Discard   🗑 Delete   ⭐ Feedback

A diagnostic setting specifies a list of categories of platform logs and/or metrics that you want to collect from a resource, and one or more destinations that you would stream them to. Normal usage charges for the destination will occur. Learn more about the different log categories and contents of those logs

Diagnostic setting name *   [miauditing   ✓]

Logs   **Destination details**

Category groups ⓘ   ☑ Send to Log Analytics workspace

  ☐ allLogs   ☐ audit   Subscription
                                                 [Dev   ⌄]
Categories
  ☐ ResourceUsageStats   Log Analytics workspace
                                                 [dbopsaudit (eastus2)   ⌄]
  ☐ DevOpsOperationsAudit
                                                 ☐ Archive to a storage account
  ☑ SQLSecurityAuditEvents

Figure 14-2. *Configure the diagnostic setting*

Click Save and you will see your diagnostic setting listed as shown in Figure 14-3.

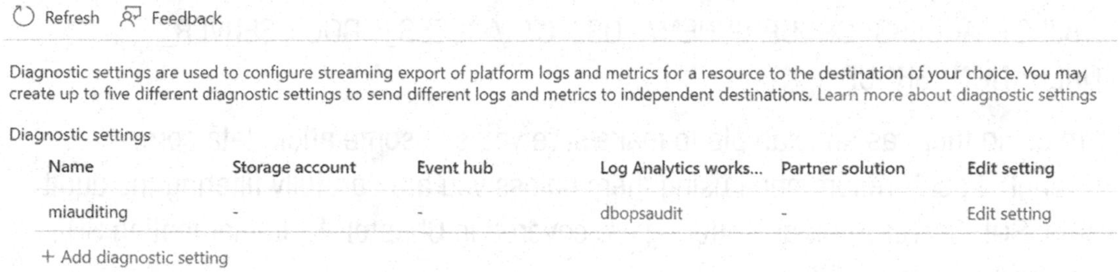

○ Refresh   ⌕ Feedback

Diagnostic settings are used to configure streaming export of platform logs and metrics for a resource to the destination of your choice. You may create up to five different diagnostic settings to send different logs and metrics to independent destinations. Learn more about diagnostic settings

Diagnostic settings

Name	Storage account	Event hub	Log Analytics works...	Partner solution	Edit setting
miauditing	-	-	dbopsaudit	-	Edit setting

+ Add diagnostic setting

Figure 14-3. *Diagnostic setting saved*

Creating and Configuring SQL Server Audit

Once you've configured your diagnostic settings, you will need to set up a SQL Server Audit on your managed instance. First, you will need to set up an audit using the script in Listing 14-1.

Listing 14-1. Setting up an audit

```
USE [master];
CREATE SERVER AUDIT [miaudit] TO EXTERNAL_MONITOR;
ALTER SERVER AUDIT [miaudit] WITH (STATE = ON);
```

Then you need to create a server audit associated with your audit using the script in Listing 14-2.

Listing 14-2. Setting up a server audit

```
USE [master];
CREATE SERVER AUDIT SPECIFICATION [miserveraudit]
FOR SERVER AUDIT [miaudit]
ADD (DATABASE_OBJECT_ACCESS_GROUP),
ADD (SCHEMA_OBJECT_ACCESS_GROUP),
ADD (AUDIT_CHANGE_GROUP),
ADD (SERVER_OPERATION_GROUP)
WITH (STATE = ON);
```

> **Caution**   These audit action groups can create a lot of audit data: DATABASE_
> OBJECT_ACCESS_GROUP, SCHEMA_OBJECT_ACCESS_GROUP, SERVER_
> OPERATION_GROUP.
>
> I'm using them as an example to make sure you see some audit data come
> through. I don't recommend using them unless you are carefully filtering the audit
> data. SQL Server Audit and filtering are covered in Chapter 4, "Implementing SQL
> Server Audit via the GUI."

Querying Audit Data

To access the audit data, you will need to go to the Log Analytics workspace you chose in
your diagnostic setting and then click Workspace summary. This summary is shown in
Figure 14-4.

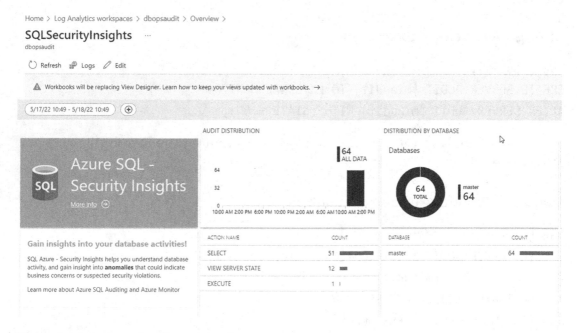

Figure 14-4. Log Analytics Workspace summary

> **Note**   For more information about how to access and use the Log Analytics workspace, please review Chapter 13, "Auditing Azure SQL Databases."

You can click on any of these boxes to drill down for more information. This will bring you to a screen with a Kusto query prepopulated for you. It provides you with detailed information for each of those categories. To query the audit data as a whole, I recommend clicking the Logs button near the top of the page, as shown in Figure 14-5.

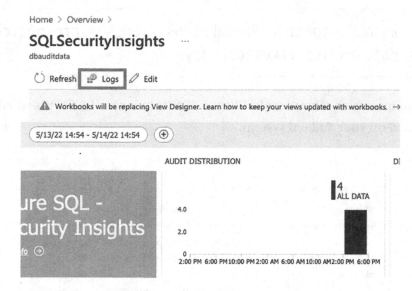

Figure 14-5.   *Log Analytics SQLSecurityInsights Logs button*

After clicking Logs, you will see a page with suggested queries. You can close that because none of those will help you query the audit data. Use the Kusto query in Listing 14-3 to see your audit data.

Listing 14-3.   Log Analytics Kusto query

```
AzureDiagnostics
| where Category == 'SQLSecurityAuditEvents'
   and TimeGenerated > ago(1d)
| project
    event_time_t,
    database_name_s,
```

```
    statement_s,
    server_principal_name_s,
    succeeded_s,
    client_ip_s,
    application_name_s,
    additional_information_s,
    data_sensitivity_information_s
| order by event_time_t desc
```

Tip   For more information on Kusto, visit `https://docs.microsoft.com/en-us/azure/data-explorer/kusto/query/`

The Kusto query will return results like the results in Figure 14-6. This will depend on what happened on your audited system.

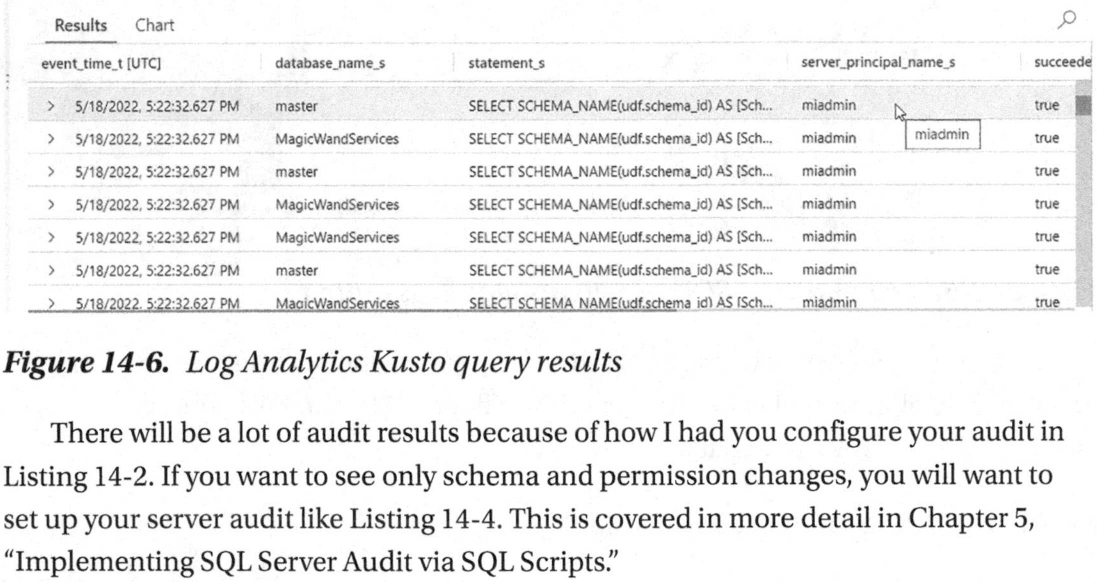

Figure 14-6. *Log Analytics Kusto query results*

There will be a lot of audit results because of how I had you configure your audit in Listing 14-2. If you want to see only schema and permission changes, you will want to set up your server audit like Listing 14-4. This is covered in more detail in Chapter 5, "Implementing SQL Server Audit via SQL Scripts."

Listing 14-4. SQL Server Audit

```
USE [master];
CREATE SERVER AUDIT SPECIFICATION [miserveraudit]
FOR SERVER AUDIT [miaudit]
ADD (DATABASE_OBJECT_ACCESS_GROUP),
```

```
ADD (SCHEMA_OBJECT_ACCESS_GROUP),
ADD (DATABASE_ROLE_MEMBER_CHANGE_GROUP),
ADD (SERVER_ROLE_MEMBER_CHANGE_GROUP),
ADD (AUDIT_CHANGE_GROUP),
ADD (DBCC_GROUP),
ADD (DATABASE_PERMISSION_CHANGE_GROUP),
ADD (SCHEMA_OBJECT_PERMISSION_CHANGE_GROUP),
ADD (SERVER_OBJECT_PERMISSION_CHANGE_GROUP),
ADD (SERVER_PERMISSION_CHANGE_GROUP),
ADD (DATABASE_CHANGE_GROUP),
ADD (DATABASE_OBJECT_CHANGE_GROUP),
ADD (DATABASE_PRINCIPAL_CHANGE_GROUP),
ADD (SCHEMA_OBJECT_CHANGE_GROUP),
ADD (SERVER_OBJECT_CHANGE_GROUP),
ADD (SERVER_PRINCIPAL_CHANGE_GROUP),
ADD (SERVER_OPERATION_GROUP),
ADD (APPLICATION_ROLE_CHANGE_PASSWORD_GROUP),
ADD (LOGIN_CHANGE_PASSWORD_GROUP),
ADD (SERVER_STATE_CHANGE_GROUP),
ADD (DATABASE_OWNERSHIP_CHANGE_GROUP),
ADD (SCHEMA_OBJECT_OWNERSHIP_CHANGE_GROUP),
ADD (SERVER_OBJECT_OWNERSHIP_CHANGE_GROUP),
ADD (USER_CHANGE_PASSWORD_GROUP)
WITH (STATE = ON);
```

Auditing Azure SQL Managed Instance with SQL Server Audit

SQL Server Audit on Azure SQL Managed Instance is very similar to SQL Server running on a VM. The main difference is the storage location. You will need to use a storage account to write audit files. The setup is the same as SQL Server otherwise. See earlier chapters in this book on how to set up SQL Server Audit.

Creating Storage Account and Container

In the Azure portal, search for storage accounts. Click Create. At this point, you need to choose:

- **Subscription** – Select a subscription.

- **Resource group** – You may want to put it in the same resource group as the managed instance.

- **Storage account name** – Must be unique across Azure.

- **Region** – I recommend putting this storage account in the same region as the database.

- **Performance** – Standard is fine for performance.

- **Redundancy** – Choose based on how important the audit data is for you.

Click Review + Create. Then click Create. Figure 14-7 shows an example of the settings I chose.

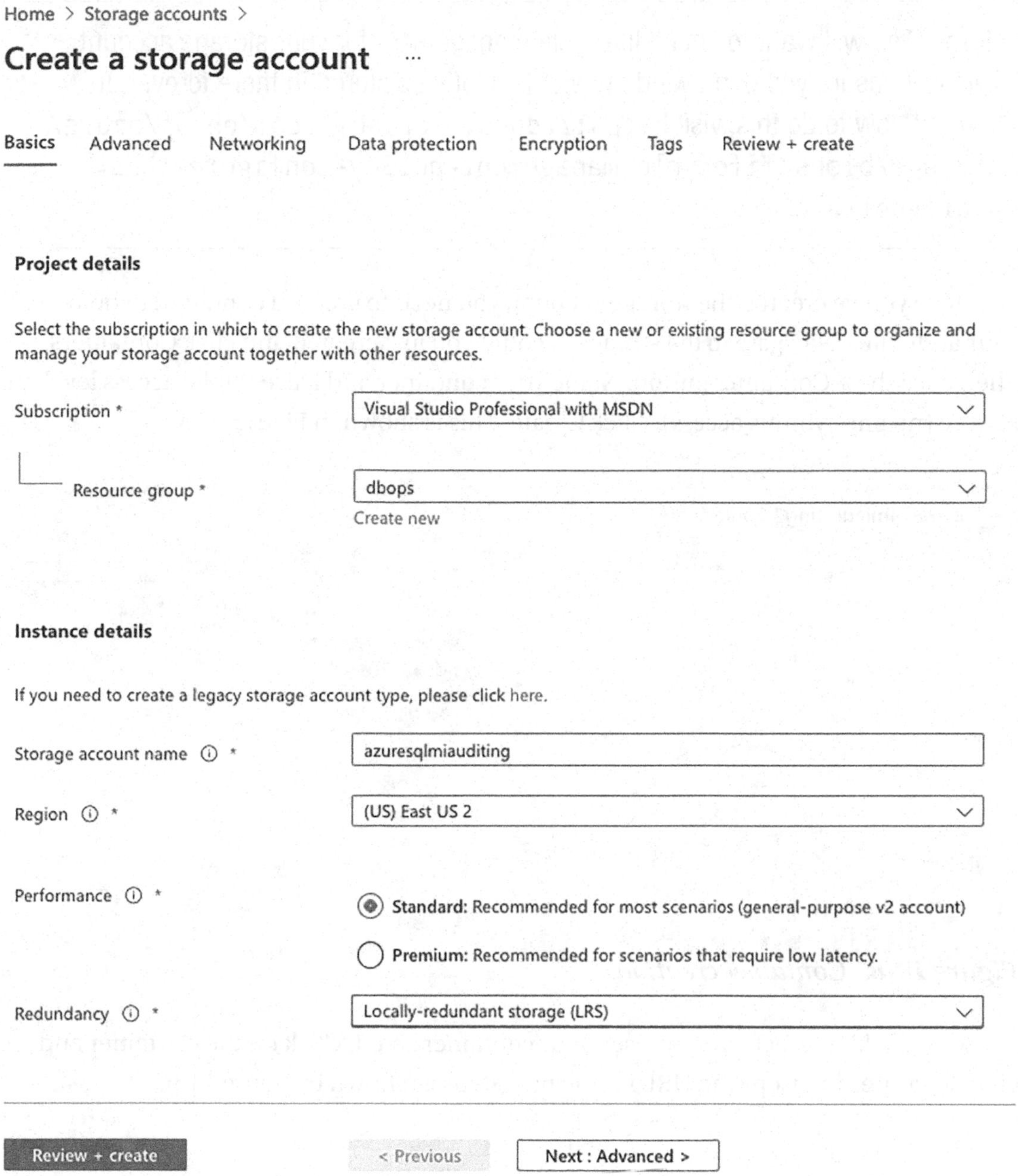

Home > Storage accounts >

Create a storage account   ...

Basics   Advanced   Networking   Data protection   Encryption   Tags   Review + create

Project details

Select the subscription in which to create the new storage account. Choose a new or existing resource group to organize and manage your storage account together with other resources.

Subscription *   Visual Studio Professional with MSDN   ∨

└── Resource group *   dbops   ∨
                                  Create new

Instance details

If you need to create a legacy storage account type, please click here.

Storage account name ⓘ *   azuresqlmiauditing

Region ⓘ *   (US) East US 2   ∨

Performance ⓘ *   ⦿ **Standard:** Recommended for most scenarios (general-purpose v2 account)

                                   ◯ **Premium:** Recommended for scenarios that require low latency.

Redundancy ⓘ *   Locally-redundant storage (LRS)   ∨

[Review + create]   < Previous   [Next : Advanced >]

Figure 14-7. *Creating storage account*

> **Note**   You will want to set up life cycle management for your storage account.
> This will ensure you don't wind up with tons of files stored in there forever. To
> find out how to do this, visit `https://docs.microsoft.com/en-us/azure/`
> `storage/blobs/lifecycle-management-policy-configure?tabs=`
> `azure-portal`

Once you've created the storage account, you need to create a container to hold
your audit files. Navigate to the storage account you just created and click Containers.
Then click the + Container button. Name your container and leave Public access level on
Private (no anonymous access). Click Create. This is shown in Figure 14-8.

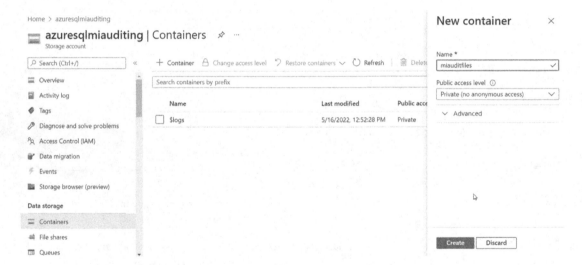

Figure 14-8. *Container creation*

After clicking Create, you will see your container listed. Click on the container and
choose Properties. Copy the URL for the next steps as shown in Figure 14-9.

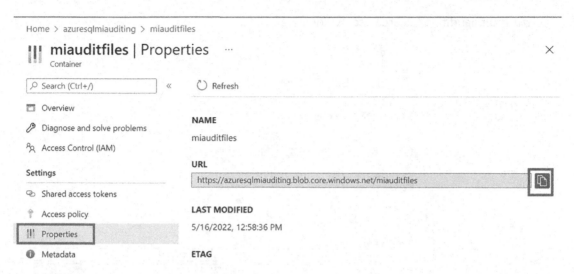

Figure 14-9. *Copy container URL*

Navigate back up to the storage account and click Shared access signature. Make sure to create your settings for this key based on the screenshot in Figure 14-10. You will need to set the expiry date for longer than the default if you want to continue using this storage account for your audit files for longer than just eight hours.

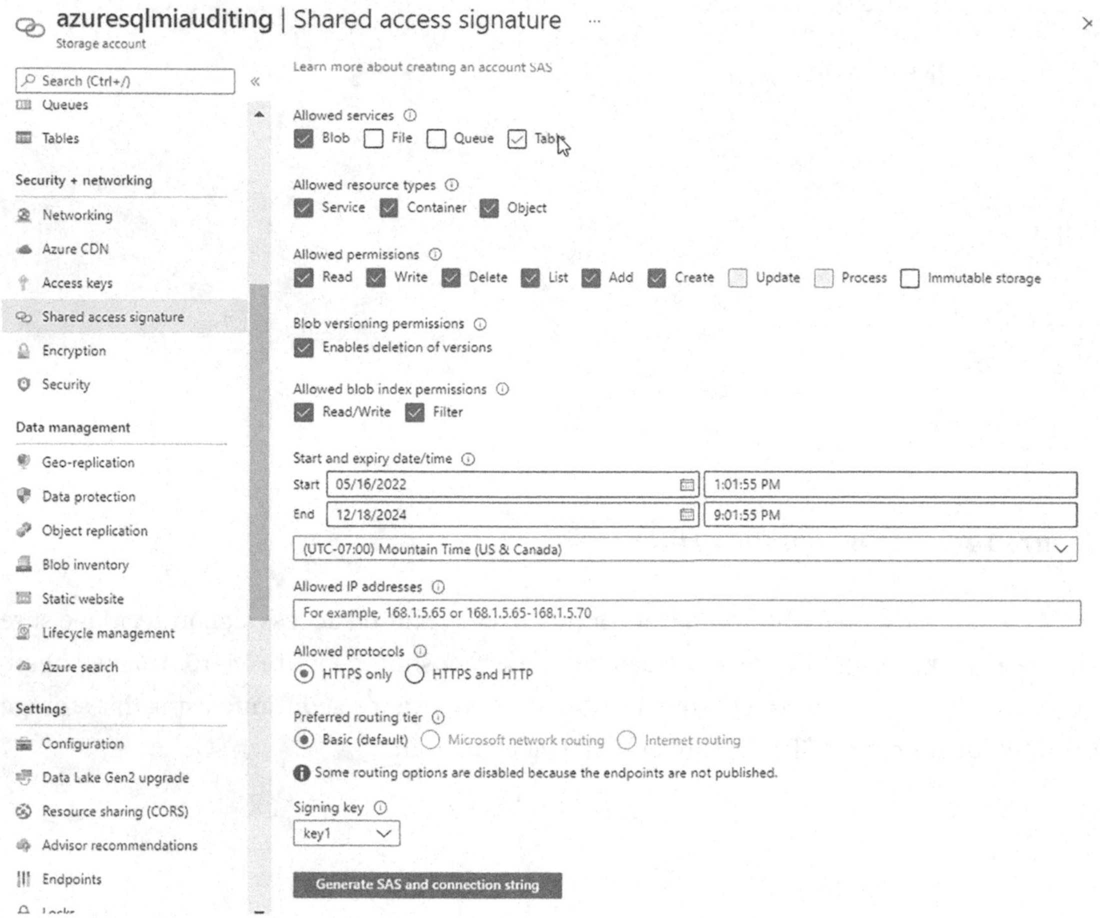

Figure 14-10. *Create a shared access signature*

The settings I've chosen for my shared access signature are

- **Allowed services** – Blob.

- **Allowed resource types** – Service, Container, Object.

- **Allowed permissions** – Read, Write, Delete, List, Add, Create.

- **Blob versioning permissions** – Allows version deletion.

- **Allowed blob index permissions** – Read/Write, Filter.

- **Start and expiry date/time** – If it expires, your managed instance will not be able to access the container anymore. You will need to generate a new shared access signature. Then update your managed instance credential with the new token. I tend to set the expiry out for years out to avoid issues with not being able to access the storage account.

- **Allowed protocols** – HTTPS only.

- **Preferred routing tier** – Basic (default).

- **Signing key** – Key 1.

Click Generate SAS and connection string. The SAS token will load on that page. Do not navigate off of this page. You can't get the SAS token ever again. If you need a new token, you have to generate a new SAS setup. Copy the SAS token for the next steps as shown in Figure 14-11.

Note   You need to remove the question mark (?) from the beginning of the token when adding it to the SQL Server credential.

```
Generate SAS and connection string
```

Connection string

```
BlobEndpoint=https://azuresqlmiauditing.blob.core.windows.net/;QueueEndpoint=https://azuresqlmiauditing.queue...
```

SAS token ⓘ

```
?sv=2020-08-04&ss=b&srt=sco&sp=rwdlactfx&se=2024-12-19T04:01:55Z&st=2022-05-16T19:01:55Z&spr=https&s..
```

Figure 14-11. *Copy the SAS token*

Creating Database Credential

Connect to your managed instance in SSMS. You need to create a credential so your managed instance can access your storage account as shown in Listing 14-5.

Listing 14-5. Create credential in SSMS

```
CREATE CREDENTIAL [URL from Figure 14-9]
WITH IDENTITY='SHARED ACCESS SIGNATURE',
SECRET = 'token from Figure 14-11';
```

Creating SQL Server Audit

You can create your SQL Server Audit using the script in Listing 14-6.

Listing 14-6. Create audit in SSMS

```
CREATE SERVER AUDIT miauditstorage
TO URL
(
PATH = 'URL from Figure 14-9',
RETENTION_DAYS = 30
);
ALTER SERVER AUDIT [miauditstorage] WITH (STATE = ON);
```

RETENTION_DAYS = 30 means that the storage account will only store 30 days' worth of audit files before they are deleted. 0 means forever. I like 30 because it's enough time for me to analyze audit data before it goes away.

No audit data will be collected until you set up either a server or database audit. You can set up a server audit with the script in Listing 14-7.

Listing 14-7. Create server audit in SSMS

```
USE [master];
CREATE SERVER AUDIT SPECIFICATION [miserverauditstorage]
FOR SERVER AUDIT [miauditstorage]
ADD (DATABASE_OBJECT_ACCESS_GROUP),
ADD (SCHEMA_OBJECT_ACCESS_GROUP),
ADD (AUDIT_CHANGE_GROUP),
ADD (SERVER_OPERATION_GROUP)
WITH (STATE = ON);
```

Querying SQL Server Audit Files

This starts writing .xel files to your Azure storage account as shown in Figure 14-12.

Figure 14-12. *SQL Audit files in Azure storage account*

You will see they are saved as .xel files, even though on SQL Server on a VM, they will be saved as .sqlaudit files. Also, note there is a folder structure for the files by server, database, container, and date. It's hard to query multiple files because you have to loop through them.

As with SQL Server on a VM, you can right-click the audit to View Audit Logs, as shown in Figure 14-13.

Figure 14-13. *View audit logs*

There is a way to merge audit files by clicking File ➤ Open ➤ Merge Audit Files as shown in Figure 14-14.

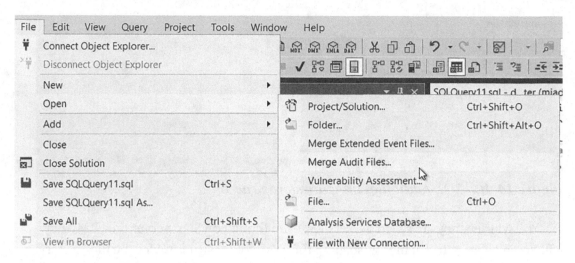

Figure 14-14. *Merge Audit Files menu item*

Merge Audit Files will bring up a dialog box. Click Add. This will bring up another dialog box where you can add your audit files as shown in Figure 14-15.

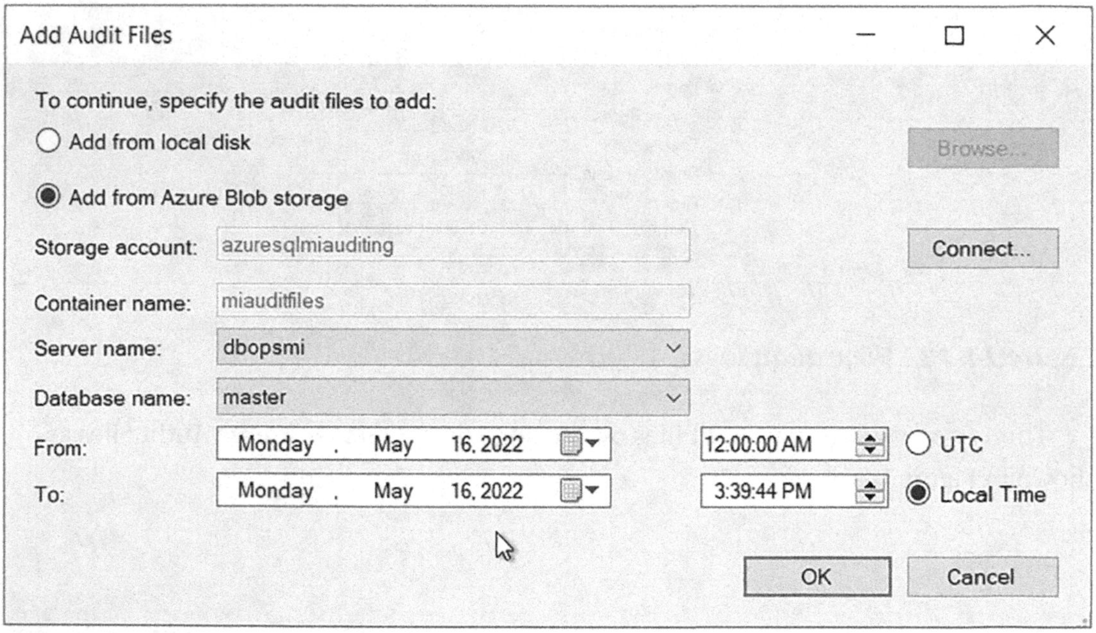

Figure 14-15. *Merge Audit Files*

You are limited to merging only one database's audit files. This may not prove very useful if you have multiple databases you are auditing. This is why I like the diagnostic setting that allows you to store your audit data in a Log Analytics workspace. This makes for easy querying across multiple databases or servers.

Auditing Azure SQL Managed Instance with Extended Events

Extended events on Azure SQL Managed Instance is very similar to SQL Server on a VM. The main difference is the storage location. You will need to use a storage account to write audit files. The setup is the same as SQL Server otherwise. See earlier chapters in this book on how to set up extended events.

You will need to create a storage account and container to hold your audit files. The storage account, container, container URL, SAS token, and credential can be used in the last section. This setup will be the same as for SQL Server Audit in the last section.

You need to specify the URL in the filename when creating the extended event as shown in Listing 14-8.

Listing 14-8. Create server audit in SSMS

```
CREATE EVENT SESSION [auditxel] ON SERVER
ADD EVENT sqlserver.rpc_completed(   ACTION(sqlserver.client_app_name,
sqlserver.client_hostname,sqlserver.database_name,sqlserver.sql_text,
sqlserver.username)
    WHERE ([sqlserver].[username]=N'josephine')),
ADD EVENT sqlserver.sql_batch_completed(   ACTION(sqlserver.client_app_
name,sqlserver.client_hostname,sqlserver.database_name,sqlserver.sql_
text,sqlserver.username)
    WHERE ([sqlserver].[username]=N'josephine'))
ADD TARGET package0.event_file(SET filename=N'https://azuremiauditing.blob.
core.windows.net/miauditfiles/xelauditdata.xel',max_file_size=(10),max_
rollover_files=(5))
```

```
WITH (MAX_MEMORY=4096 KB,EVENT_RETENTION_MODE=ALLOW_SINGLE_EVENT_LOSS,MAX_
DISPATCH_LATENCY=30 SECONDS,MAX_EVENT_SIZE=0 KB,MEMORY_PARTITION_
MODE=NONE,TRACK_CAUSALITY=OFF,STARTUP_STATE=ON);
ALTER EVENT SESSION [auditxel] ON SERVER
STATE=START;
```

Make sure to update the filename to the path to your storage account and container. This will be the one you set up a credential for. Refer to the SQL Server Audit section in this chapter for more details.

Once the extended event is started, it will place a file in the Azure storage account as shown in Figure 14-16. Five files up to 10 MB each will be placed there because that's what's specified in the script in Listing 14-8.

Figure 14-16. *.xel files in Azure storage account*

To query the .xel files, you will need to know the exact file names. You can use the Azure Storage connection in SSMS to find out the names as shown in Figure 14-17.

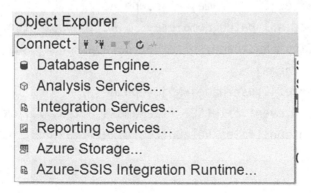

Figure 14-17. *Azure Storage connection*

Sign in to Azure and pick the right storage account and container from the drop-down as shown in Figure 14-18.

Connect to a Microsoft Subscription	—	□	×

You are signed in as jbr   Change user

Select a subscription to use:

Visual Studio Professional with MSDN	∨

Select Storage Account | azuresqldbaudits | ∨ |
| --- | --- |

Select Blob Container | xelfiles | ∨ |
| --- | --- |

OK	Cancel

Figure 14-18. *Log in to Azure and select a storage account and container*

Click OK. This connects you to this storage account and it lists the files in the container as shown in Figure 14-19.

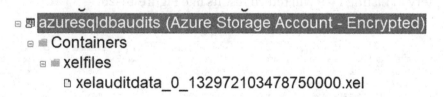

```
azuresqldbaudits (Azure Storage Account - Encrypted)
  Containers
    xelfiles
      xelauditdata_0_132972103478750000.xel
```

Figure 14-19. *Container list of files*

Once you know the names of the files, you can query them with the script in Listing 14-9.

Listing 14-9. Query .xel files

```
SELECT n.value('(@timestamp)[1]', 'datetime') as timestamp,
       n.value('(action[@name="sql_text"]/value)[1]', 'nvarchar(max)')
       as [sql],
       n.value('(action[@name="client_hostname"]/value)[1]',
       'nvarchar(50)') as [client_hostname],
       n.value('(action[@name="username"]/value)[1]', 'nvarchar(50)')
       as [user],
       n.value('(action[@name="database_name"]/value)[1]', 'nvarchar(50)')
       as [database_name],
       n.value('(action[@name="client_app_name"]/value)[1]',
       'nvarchar(50)') as [client_app_name]
FROM (SELECT CAST(event_data as XML) as event_data
FROM sys.fn_xe_file_target_read_file(N'https://azuremiauditing.blob.core.
windows.net/miauditfiles/xelauditdata_0_132972103478750000.xel', NULL,
NULL, NULL)) ed
CROSS APPLY ed.event_data.nodes('event') as q(n)
WHERE n.value('(@timestamp)[1]', 'datetime')
>= DATEADD(HOUR, -4, GETDATE())
ORDER BY timestamp DESC;
```

The query in Listing 14-9 will return results like Figure 14-20.

	timestamp	sql	client_hostname	user	database_n...	client_app_name
1	2022-05-16 22:03:57.890	(@_msparam_0 nvarchar(4000))SEL...	DESKTOP-15	josephine	jbdb	Microsoft SQL Server Manage
2	2022-05-16 22:03:57.640	SELECT sqllog.name AS [Name], sqll...	DESKTOP-15	josephine	jbdb	Microsoft SQL Server Manage
3	2022-05-16 22:03:57.570	SELECT sqllog.name AS [Name], sqll...	DESKTOP-15	josephine	jbdb	Microsoft SQL Server Manage
4	2022-05-16 22:03:57.497	DECLARE @edition sysname; SET @...	DESKTOP-15	josephine	jbdb	Microsoft SQL Server Manage
5	2022-05-16 22:03:57.007	(@_msparam_0 nvarchar(4000))SEL...	DESKTOP-15	josephine	jbdb	Microsoft SQL Server Manage
6	2022-05-16 22:03:56.833	SELECT CAST(serverproperty(...	DESKTOP-15	josephine	jbdb	Microsoft SQL Server Manage
7	2022-05-16 22:03:56.753	select SERVERPROPERTY(N'server...	DESKTOP-15	josephine	jbdb	Microsoft SQL Server Manage
8	2022-05-16 22:03:56.683	DECLARE @edition sysname; SET @...	DESKTOP-15	josephine	jbdb	Microsoft SQL Server Manage
9	2022-05-16 22:03:55.257	/****** Script for SelectTopNRows com...	DESKTOP-15	josephine	jbdb	Microsoft SQL Server Manage
10	2022-05-16 22:03:55.157	SELECT @@SPID;	DESKTOP-15	josephine	jbdb	Microsoft SQL Server Manage

Figure 14-20. *.xel files results*

Querying the .xel files is difficult because you need to know the exact file name. You can't easily query multiple .xel files at the same time. This is why I like the diagnostic settings that allow you to store your audit data in a Log Analytics workspace. This makes for easy querying across multiple databases or servers.

Centralizing and Reporting on Azure SQL Managed Instance Audit Data

Centralizing is as easy as putting all your audit data in the same Log Analytics workspace. This makes for easy querying and reporting on audit data.

To report on data, I use a Logic App. This way, I can send an email attachment with any changes captured by the audit daily. Figure 14-21 shows you the high-level setup of the Logic App.

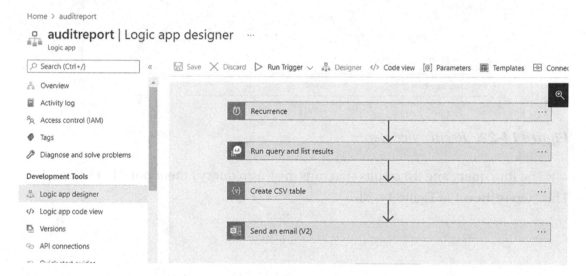

Figure 14-21. *Logic app to report on audit data*

> **Tip**   To learn how to create a logic app, visit `https://docs.microsoft.`
> `com/en-us/azure/logic-apps/quickstart-create-first-logic-`
> `app-workflow`

The logic app consists of four steps. Let's walk through them one by one. The Recurrence step determines how often this app will run as shown in Figure 14-22. This logic app will run once a day at 10. This is in UTC, so make sure to account for that if you want it to run at 10 in another time zone instead.

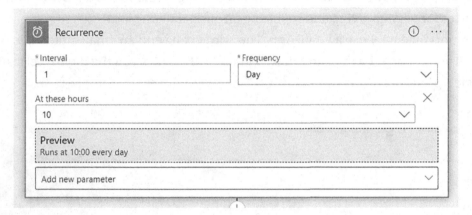

Figure 14-22.   *Recurrence step*

The Run query and list results step runs the Kusto query I mentioned in Listing 14-3. This step is shown in Figure 14-23.

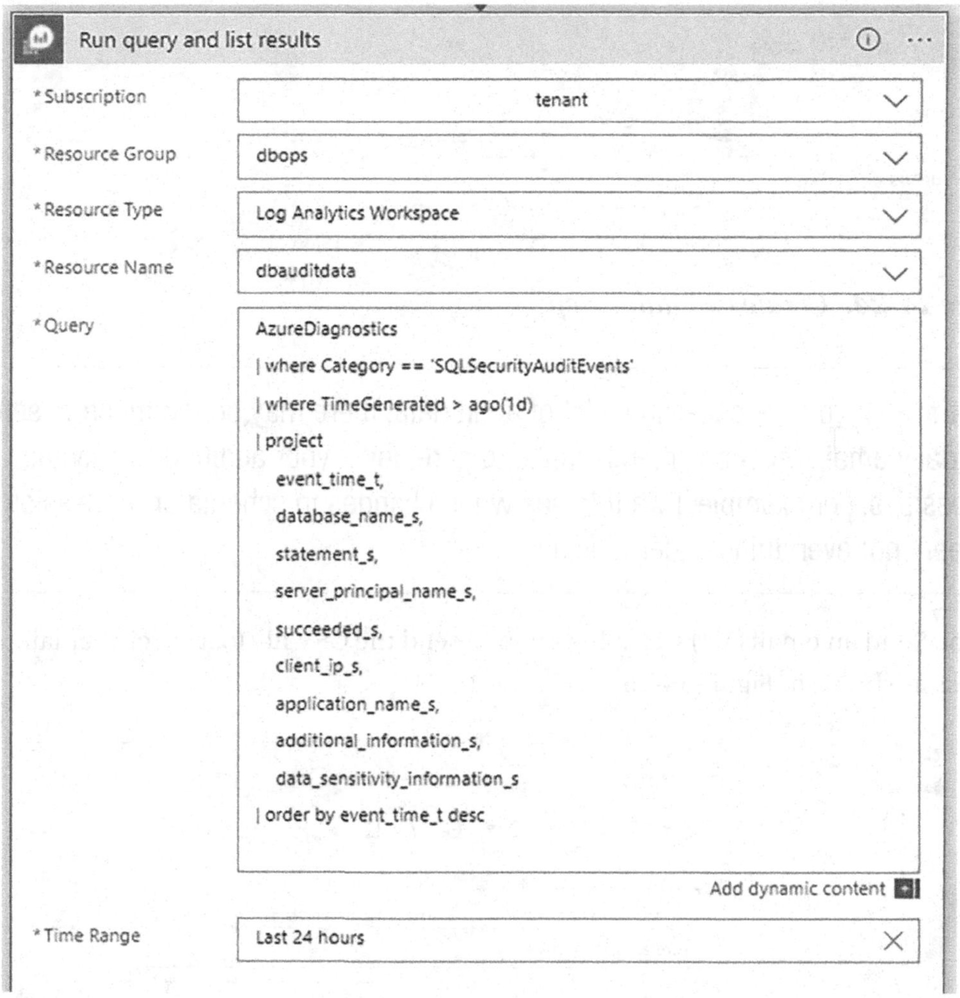

Figure 14-23. *Run query and list results step*

The Create CSV table step creates a CSV file of the results as shown in Figure 14-24. The contents of the CSV come from the previous step. I create a CSV file because the Kusto query results are not easily formatted into the body of an email.

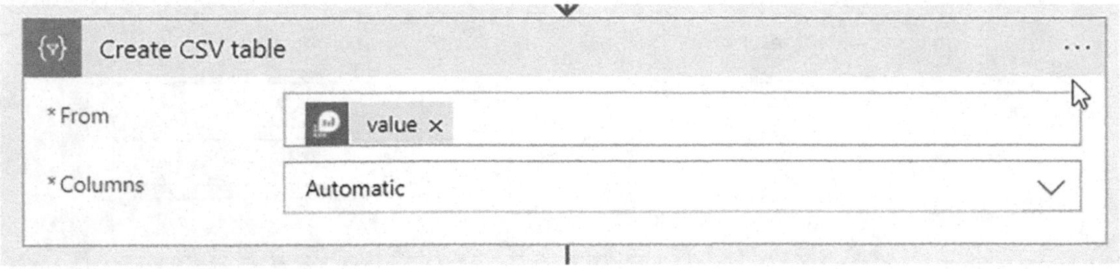

Figure 14-24. *Create CSV table step*

Caution   If you are collecting a lot of audit data, there may be too much to send in a daily email. My recommendation is to pare down your auditing to only the necessities. For example, I want to see when changes to schema or permissions happen, not everything under the sun.

The Send an email (V2) step allows you to send the CSV file to a specific email address as shown in Figure 14-25.

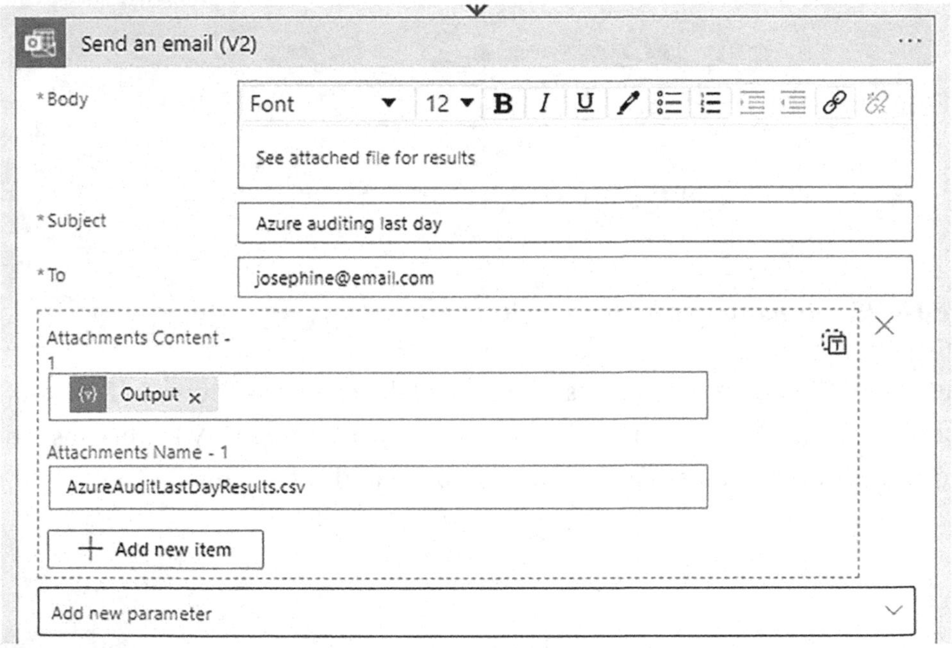

Figure 14-25. *Send an email (V2)*

In the next chapter, you will learn about auditing SQL databases with Amazon Web Services and Google Cloud.

CHAPTER 15

Other Cloud Provider Auditing Options

Since not everyone uses Azure for their cloud databases, this chapter will cover auditing options for Amazon Web Services (AWS) Relational Database Service (RDS) and Google Cloud.

AWS RDS SQL Server Audit

There are a few components required to make SQL Server Audit work on AWS RDS SQL Server instances:

- **S3 bucket** – To store audit files.

- **Option group** – To allow RDS SQL Server to use audit functionality. This also determines which S3 bucket and IAM role to use.

- **IAM role** – This will allow your RDS instance to access your S3 bucket.

- **SQL Server Audit and Server or Database Audit** – To audit actions on SQL Server.

Creating an S3 Bucket

If you don't already have an S3 bucket, you will need to create one to store the audit files. Search for and click on S3 as shown in Figure 15-1.

© Josephine Bush 2022
J. Bush, *Practical Database Auditing for Microsoft SQL Server and Azure SQL*,
https://doi.org/10.1007/978-1-4842-8634-0_15

Figure 15-1. *Search for and click on S3 in search results*

Click the Create bucket button as shown in Figure 15-2.

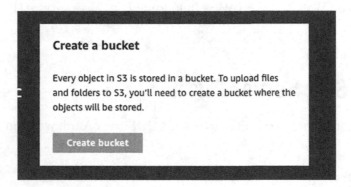

Figure 15-2. *Create an S3 bucket*

Note   For more information about creating an S3 bucket, visit `https://docs.` `aws.amazon.com/AmazonRDS/latest/UserGuide/Appendix.SQLServer.` `Options.Audit.html#Appendix.SQLServer.Options.Audit.S3bucket`

This will bring up a Create bucket page as shown in Figure 15-3. You will need to name it something unique across all of AWS. This bucket must be in the same region as the database.

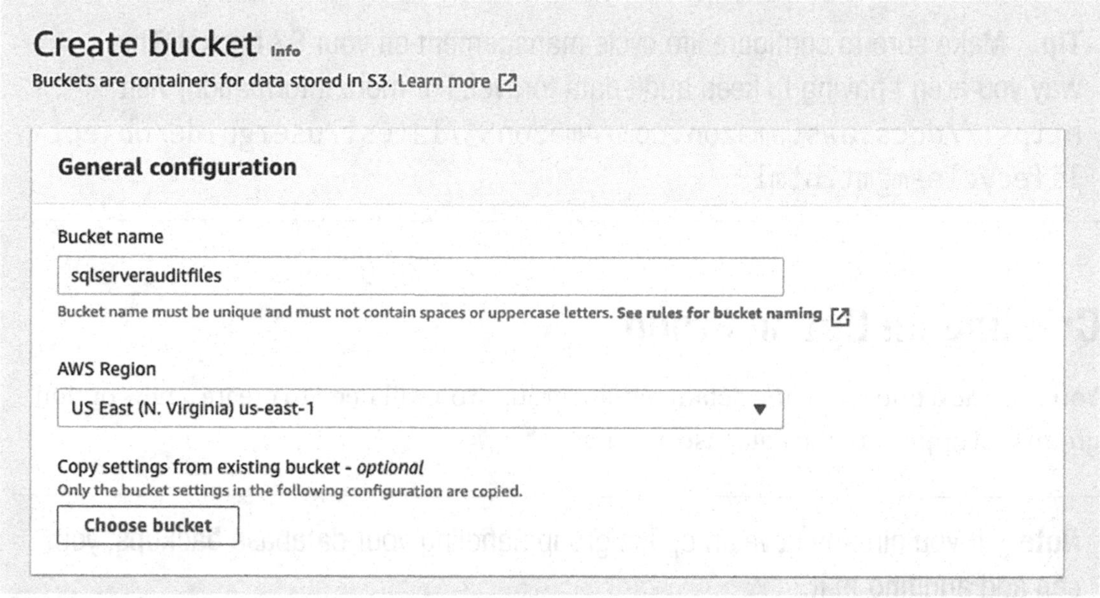

Figure 15-3. *Create bucket settings*

You can leave all the defaults in place on the rest of the Create bucket page and then click Create bucket.

Note   Your S3 bucket can't be open to the public, and it can't use S3 object lock for audit files.

You will see the new bucket listed in your portal as shown in Figure 15-4.

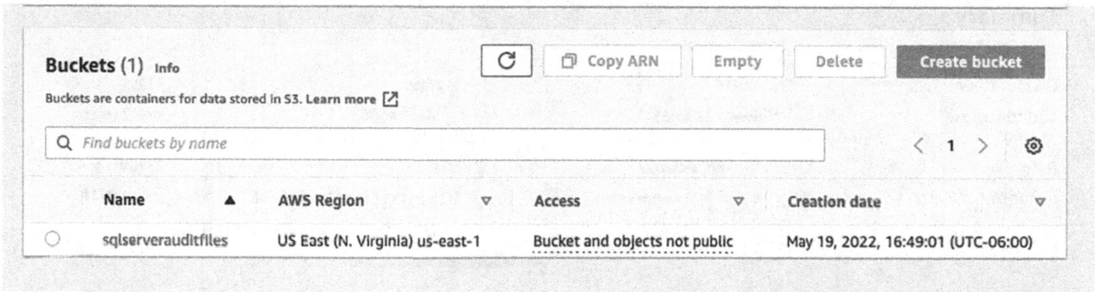

Figure 15-4. *S3 bucket listing*

> **Tip**   Make sure to configure life cycle management on your S3 bucket. This way you aren't paying to keep audit data forever. For more information, visit https://docs.aws.amazon.com/AmazonS3/latest/userguide/object-lifecycle-mgmt.html

Creating an Option Group

You can't add options to the default option group. You will need to create a new option group and apply it to the database instance.

> **Note**   If you already have an option group handling your database backups, you can add auditing to it.

To create a new option group, search for and click on RDS. You will need the engine and its version to create the new option group. First, let's check the engine of your RDS Instance. Click on your RDS instance. In the Summary section, you will see the Engine as shown in Figure 15-5. Make note of that engine. Then click Configuration as shown in Figure 15-5.

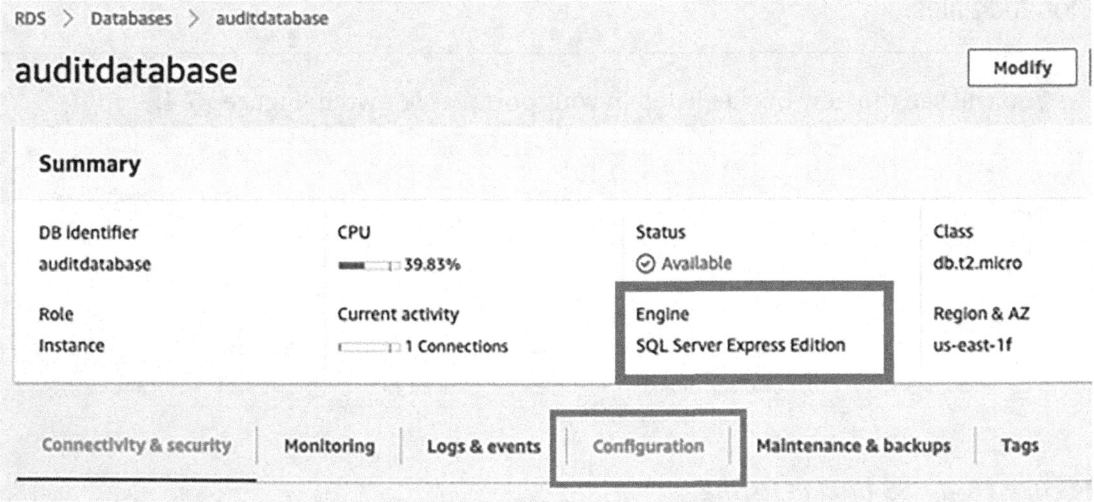

Figure 15-5.   *RDS Configuration*

Make a note of your Engine version as shown in Figure 15-6.

Instance

Configuration

DB Instance ID
auditdatabase

Engine version
14.00.3421.10.v1

Figure 15-6. *The engine version*

To set up a new option group, click Option groups as shown in Figure 15-7.

Amazon RDS

Dashboard
Databases
Query Editor
Performance Insights
Snapshots
Automated backups
Reserved Instances
Proxies

Subnet groups
Parameter groups
Option groups
Custom engine versions

Figure 15-7. *Option groups menu item*

Since I only have the default option group right now, I will create a new option group. Click the Create group button as shown in Figure 15-8.

Figure 15-8. *Create group button*

Once you are on the Create group page, you will have four fields to fill out as shown in Figure 15-9.

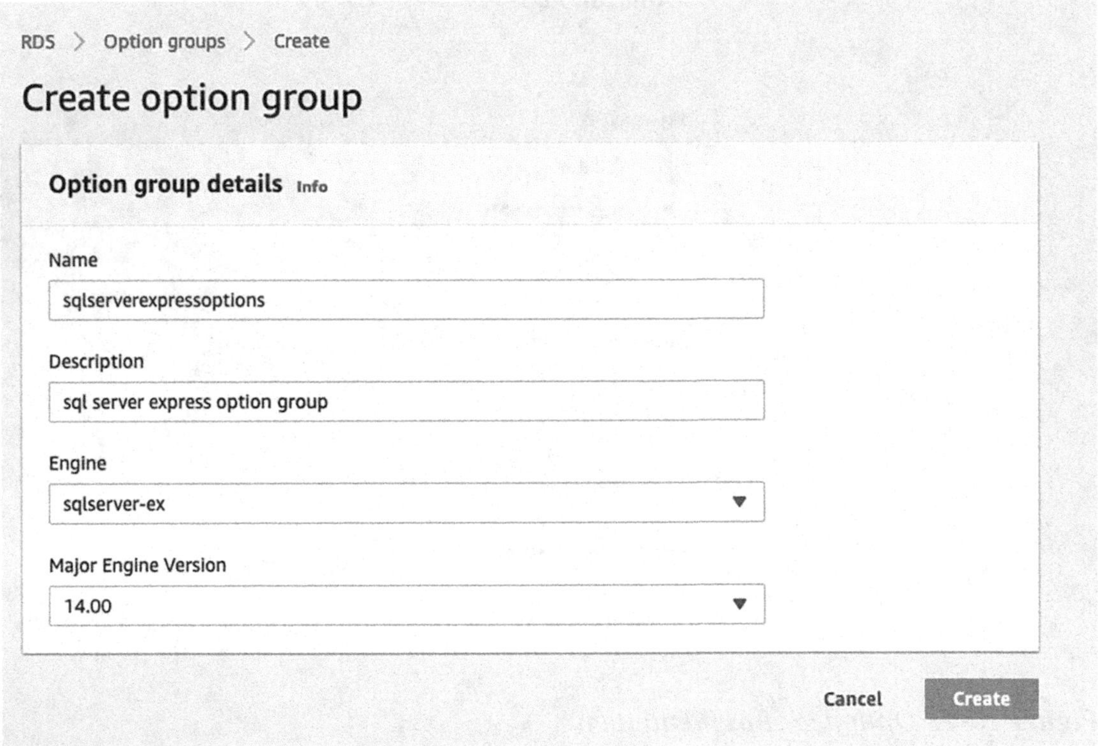

RDS > Option groups > Create

Create option group

Option group details Info

Name

sqlserverexpressoptions

Description

sql server express option group

Engine

sqlserver-ex ▼

Major Engine Version

14.00 ▼

Cancel   Create

Figure 15-9. *Create option group settings*

For the settings on the Create option group page:

- **Name** – You can name it whatever you want. It's best to name it something descriptive enough that you can tell what it's for. You can have multiple options in the group, though, so you don't have to put auditing in the name.

- **Description** – To help you determine what is in the option group.

- **Engine** – Choose the engine you got from your RDS summary in Figure 15-5.

- **Major Engine Version** – Choose the major engine version you got from your engine version configuration setting in Figure 15-6.

Click Create. Now your option group is ready for options to be added to it.

Adding Auditing Option to New Option Group

Once it's created, click on it in the list as shown in Figure 15-10.

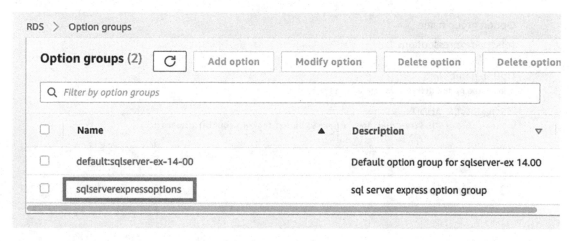

Figure 15-10. *Click on the new option group*

Scroll down to the Options box and click Add Option as shown in Figure 15-11.

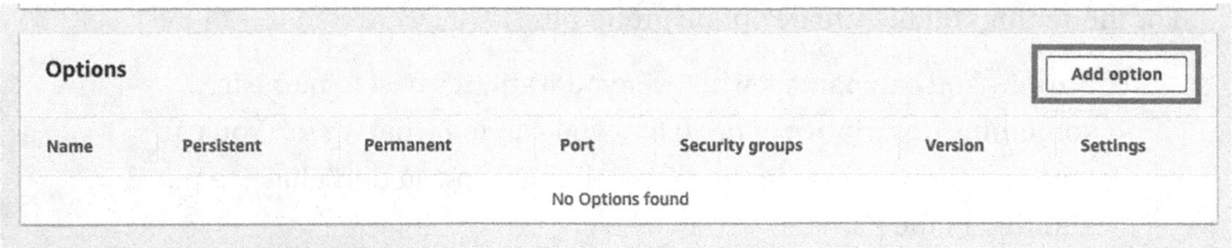

Options						Add option
Name	Persistent	Permanent	Port	Security groups	Version	Settings
			No Options found			

Figure 15-11. *Add option button*

On the Add Option page, you need to choose SQLSERVER_AUDIT and your S3 bucket as shown in Figure 15-12. You can choose a prefix on your S3 bucket. If you don't put in a prefix, the audit files will be placed in the root folder of the bucket.

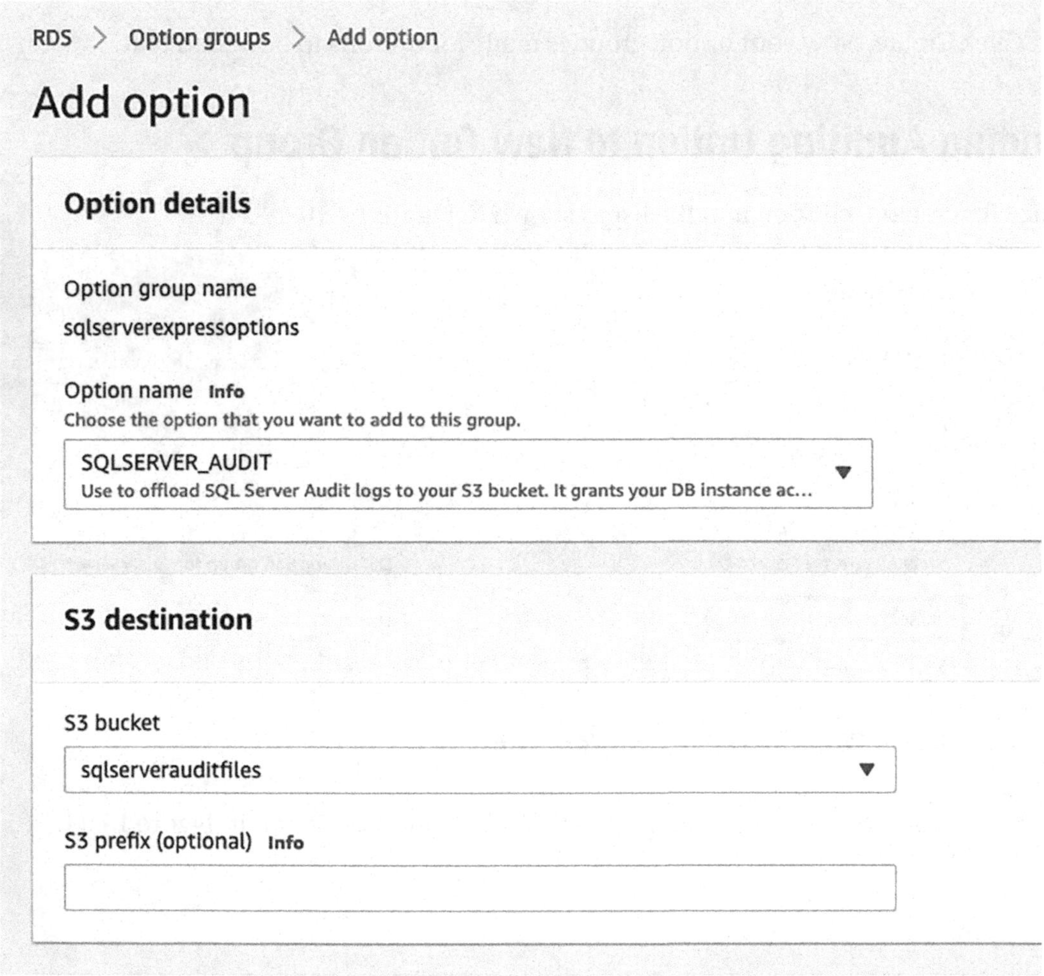

RDS > Option groups > Add option

Add option

Option details

Option group name
sqlserverexpressoptions

Option name **Info**
Choose the option that you want to add to this group.

SQLSERVER_AUDIT
Use to offload SQL Server Audit logs to your S3 bucket. It grants your DB instance ac... ▼

S3 destination

S3 bucket

sqlserverauditfiles ▼

S3 prefix (optional) **Info**

Figure 15-12. *Add option settings*

You will need an IAM role. If you don't already have an S3 role, create one now. This role will allow your RDS instance to talk to the bucket. Choose Create new role in the IAM role drop-down as shown in Figure 15-13.

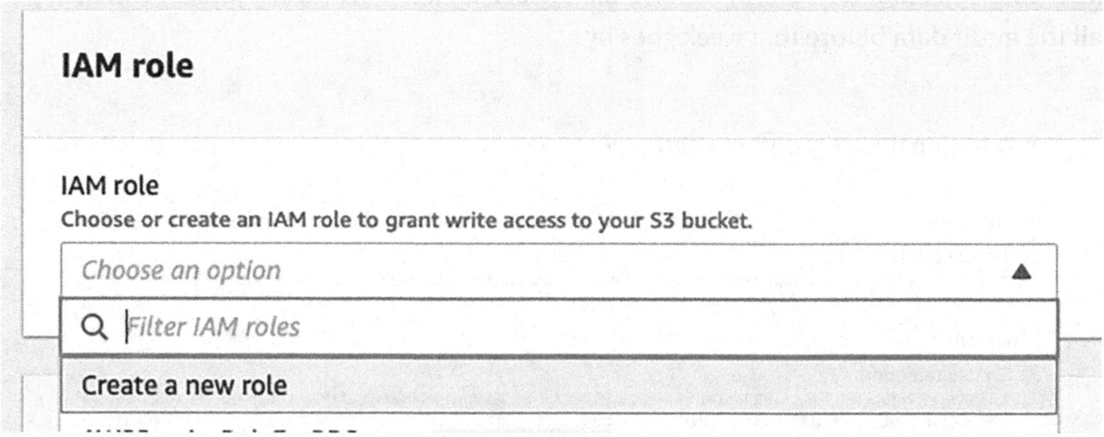

IAM role

IAM role
Choose or create an IAM role to grant write access to your S3 bucket.

Choose an option ▲

Q Filter IAM roles

Create a new role

Figure 15-13. *Create a new IAM role*

You can name the new role something like AWSServiceS3forRDS as shown in Figure 15-14.

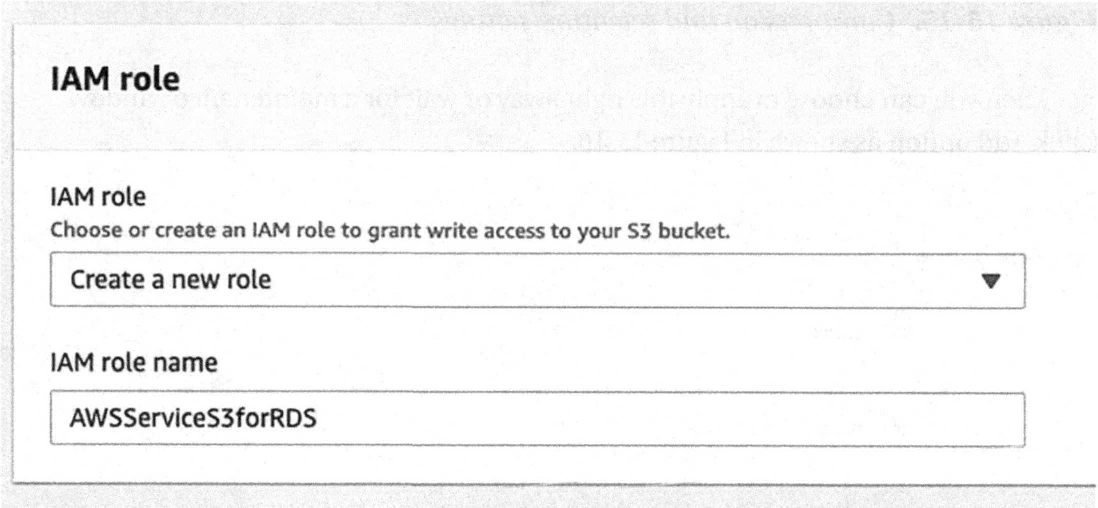

IAM role

IAM role
Choose or create an IAM role to grant write access to your S3 bucket.

Create a new role ▼

IAM role name

AWSServiceS3forRDS

Figure 15-14. *Creating IAM role name*

Expand the Additional configuration section. Leave the compression enabled and enable the retention as shown in Figure 15-15. You can retain between 1 and 840 hours of audit logs. If you leave retention disabled, the audit logs will be removed immediately after they are offloaded from your RDS instance. I set it to a week, so I know I can query all the audit data before that week goes by.

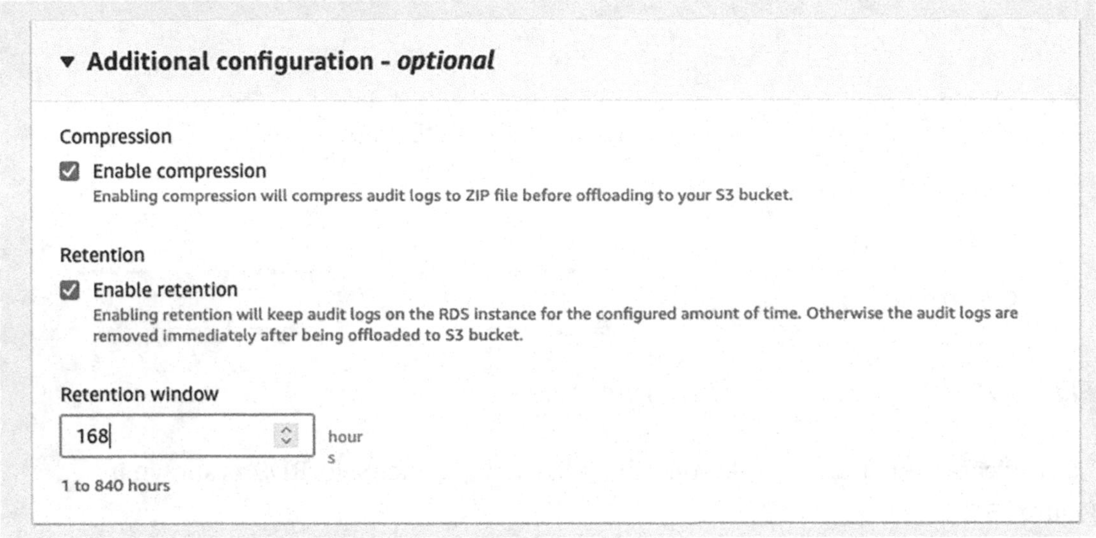

Figure 15-15. *Compression and retention settings*

Then you can choose to apply this right away or wait for a maintenance window. Click Add option as shown in Figure 15-16.

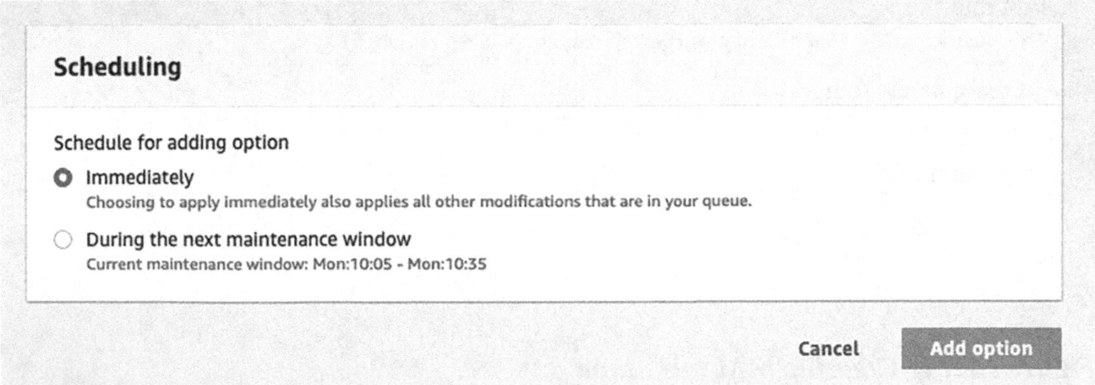

Figure 15-16. *Schedule and add option*

After clicking Add option, you are taken back to your option group listing page. Click on the option group you just created and verify the settings you implemented as shown in Figure 15-17.

Options							Add option
Name	Persistent	Permanent	Port	Security groups	Version	Settings	
SQLSERVER_AUDIT	No	No	-	-	-	ENABLE_COMPRESSION true S3_BUCKET_ARN arn:aws:s3:::sqlserverauditfiles IAM_ROLE_ARN arn:aws:iam::656251904757:role/service-role/AWSServiceS3forRDS RETENTION_TIME 168	

Figure 15-17. *Verify new option group settings*

Adding the New Option Group to RDS Instance

Navigate to your RDS instance. You will need to modify it to use this new option group. Click Modify on your database instance as shown in Figure 15-18.

RDS > Databases > auditdatabase

auditdatabase   [Modify] [Actions ▼]

Summary

Figure 15-18. *Modify RDS instance*

Scroll down to the database options settings. Change the option group to the new group you just created as shown in Figure 15-19.

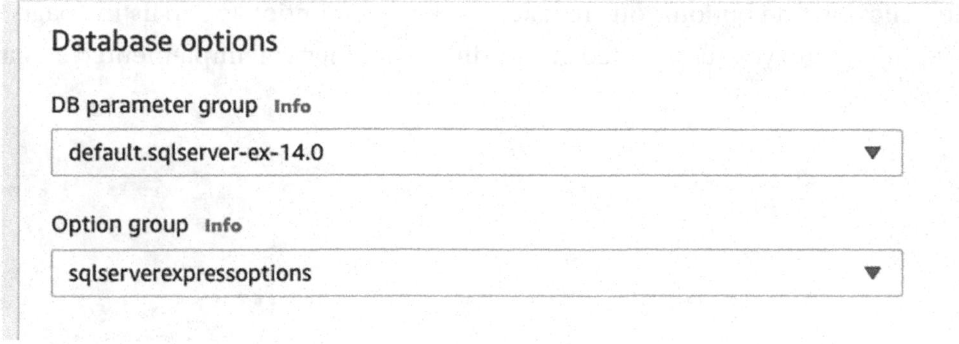

Database options

DB parameter group Info

default.sqlserver-ex-14.0   ▼

Option group Info

sqlserverexpressoptions   ▼

Figure 15-19. Choose the new option group

Scroll down and click Continue. Choose whether to apply this during the next maintenance window or immediately. Then click Modify DB Instance as shown in Figure 15-20.

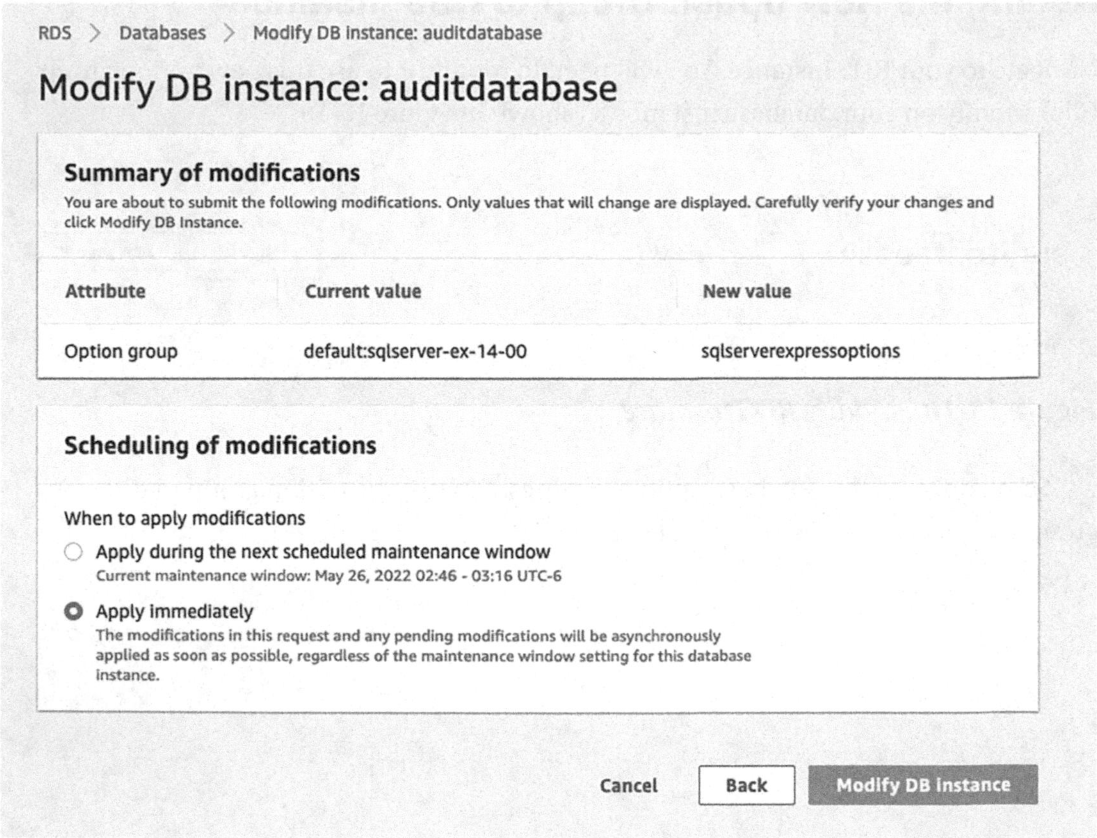

RDS > Databases > Modify DB instance: auditdatabase

Modify DB instance: auditdatabase

Summary of modifications

You are about to submit the following modifications. Only values that will change are displayed. Carefully verify your changes and click Modify DB Instance.

Attribute	Current value	New value
Option group	default:sqlserver-ex-14-00	sqlserverexpressoptions

Scheduling of modifications

When to apply modifications

○ Apply during the next scheduled maintenance window
Current maintenance window: May 26, 2022 02:46 - 03:16 UTC-6

● Apply immediately
The modifications in this request and any pending modifications will be asynchronously applied as soon as possible, regardless of the maintenance window setting for this database instance.

Cancel   **Back**   **Modify DB instance**

Figure 15-20. Modify RDS instance with new option group immediately

---

Caution   Apply immediately can cause your database to be unavailable for some time while the change is applied.

Click back to the Configuration page of the RDS instance. You will see the new option group is in a status of Pending apply as shown in Figure 15-21.

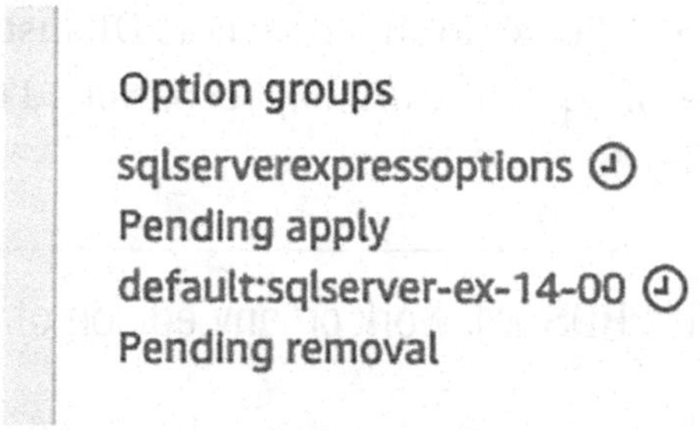

Option groups

sqlserverexpressoptions ⊙
Pending apply
default:sqlserver-ex-14-00 ⊙
Pending removal

Figure 15-21.   Option group pending apply

On the database listing page, you will see the database is in a status of Modifying as shown in Figure 15-22.

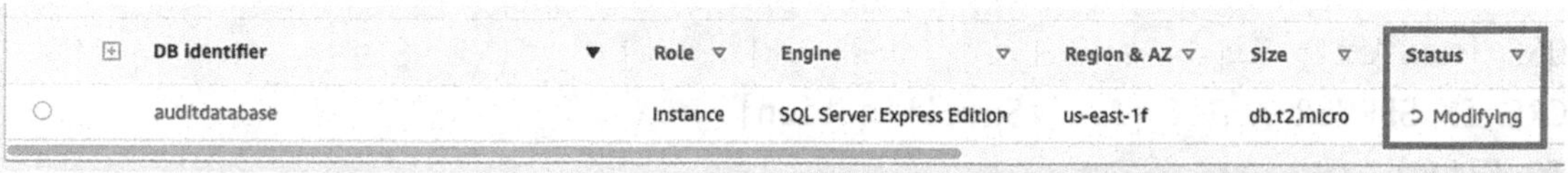

	DB identifier	▼	Role ▽	Engine	▽	Region & AZ ▽	Size ▽	Status ▽
○	auditdatabase		Instance	SQL Server Express Edition		us-east-1f	db.t2.micro	↻ Modifying

Figure 15-22.   RDS instance modifying to apply the new option group

Once the state of the database is Available, you can proceed to set up SQL Server Audit.

Setting Up SQL Server Audit

Some guidelines need to be followed on an RDS instance when setting up SQL Server Audit. These are in addition to any other guidance I've provided on SQL Server Audit in earlier chapters of this book.

- Don't use RDS_ as a prefix in the server audit name.

- For FILEPATH, specify D:\rdsdbdata\SQLAudit. This path is required by AWS and no other path will work.

- For MAXSIZE, specify a size between 2 MB and 50 MB.

- Don't configure MAX_ROLLOVER_FILES or MAX_FILES. This is not allowed and you will receive an error if you try. Leave MAX_ROLLOVER_ FILES set to 2147483647. Don't use MAX_FILES at all. This is why it will be particularly important to not audit everything under the sun. The more audit files you have, the harder it will be to query the audit data.

- Don't configure SQL Server to shut down the DB instance if it fails to write the audit record. I don't normally recommend this anyway, but definitely, don't do this in AWS.

Note   SQL Server Audit in RDS will work on any edition of SQL Server, including Express.

To set up SQL Server Audit, you need to connect to your RDS instance with SSMS. I recommend setting up your audit with the script in Listing 15-1.

Listing 15-1. Create server audit

```
USE [master];
CREATE SERVER AUDIT [AuditSpecification]
TO FILE
(       FILEPATH = N'D:\rdsdbdata\SQLAudit\'
        ,MAXSIZE = 10 MB
        ,MAX_ROLLOVER_FILES = 2147483647
        ,RESERVE_DISK_SPACE = OFF
) WITH (QUEUE_DELAY = 1000, ON_FAILURE = CONTINUE)
WHERE ([database_name]<>'rdsadmin');
```

Next, you will need to set up a server or database audit so it will collect audit data as shown in Listing 15-2.

Listing 15-2. Create server audit specification

```
USE [master];
CREATE SERVER AUDIT SPECIFICATION [ServerAuditSpecification]
FOR SERVER AUDIT [AuditSpecification]
```

```
ADD (DATABASE_OBJECT_ACCESS_GROUP),
ADD (SCHEMA_OBJECT_ACCESS_GROUP),
ADD (DATABASE_ROLE_MEMBER_CHANGE_GROUP),
ADD (SERVER_ROLE_MEMBER_CHANGE_GROUP),
ADD (AUDIT_CHANGE_GROUP),
ADD (DBCC_GROUP),
ADD (DATABASE_PERMISSION_CHANGE_GROUP),
ADD (SCHEMA_OBJECT_PERMISSION_CHANGE_GROUP),
ADD (SERVER_OBJECT_PERMISSION_CHANGE_GROUP),
ADD (SERVER_PERMISSION_CHANGE_GROUP),
ADD (DATABASE_CHANGE_GROUP),
ADD (DATABASE_OBJECT_CHANGE_GROUP),
ADD (DATABASE_PRINCIPAL_CHANGE_GROUP),
ADD (SCHEMA_OBJECT_CHANGE_GROUP),
ADD (SERVER_OBJECT_CHANGE_GROUP),
ADD (SERVER_PRINCIPAL_CHANGE_GROUP),
ADD (SERVER_OPERATION_GROUP),
ADD (APPLICATION_ROLE_CHANGE_PASSWORD_GROUP),
ADD (LOGIN_CHANGE_PASSWORD_GROUP),
ADD (SERVER_STATE_CHANGE_GROUP),
ADD (DATABASE_OWNERSHIP_CHANGE_GROUP),
ADD (SCHEMA_OBJECT_OWNERSHIP_CHANGE_GROUP),
ADD (SERVER_OBJECT_OWNERSHIP_CHANGE_GROUP),
ADD (USER_CHANGE_PASSWORD_GROUP)
WITH (STATE = ON);
```

The server audit in Listing 15-2 will only get the schema and permissions changes. This will keep your audit files smaller and fewer in number.

Querying SQL Server Audit Data

Until each file reaches its max size, it will be stored on the database instance. Those audit files are stored in D:\rdsdbdata\SQLAudit\. Once it reaches its max size, it will be uploaded into S3. At that point, the file is moved into the retention folder, which is named transmitted. Then, your audit files will be stored in D:\rdsdbdata\SQLAudit\ transmitted.

To query the audit data, use the script in Listing 15-3.

Listing 15-3. Query audit data not transmitted to S3

```
SELECT DISTINCT
      event_time,
      aa.name as audit_action,
      statement,
      succeeded,
      database_name,
      server_instance_name,
      schema_name,
      session_server_principal_name,
      server_principal_name,
      object_Name,
      file_name,
      client_ip,
      application_name,
      file_name
FROM  msdb.dbo.rds_fn_get_audit_file ('D:\rdsdbdata\SQLAudit\*.
sqlaudit',default,default) af
INNER JOIN sys.dm_audit_actions aa
ON aa.action_id = af.action_id
WHERE event_time > DATEADD(HOUR, -1, GETDATE())
ORDER BY event_time DESC;
```

Tip   AWS has done a good job with auditing to mimic SQL Server as much as possible. You can use `*.sqlaudit` to query all the audit files at once. It's harder to query audit data in Azure SQL Database Managed Instance. This is because you have to know the exact names of the files. You can't use `*.sqlaudit` to query all the files at once in Azure SQL Database Managed Instance.

Even with the audit set up in Listings 15-1 and 15-2, it's going to capture a lot of actions happening in the background. You will need to filter it. There's going to be a user something like WORKGROUP\EC2AMAZ-QG7G9L3$, depending on your instance.

You will need to filter that user out to avoid having issues with too much audit data. You may also be seeing a lot of sys schema, which you won't need to audit. Also, rdsa may be audited a lot, and that will be more background actions you don't need to audit. The filter you need will depend on what you see coming through cluttering up your audit. Listing 15-4 gives you a way to filter your audit.

Listing 15-4. Filtering your audit

```
USE [master];

ALTER SERVER AUDIT [AuditSpecification] WITH (STATE = OFF);

ALTER SERVER AUDIT [AuditSpecification]
WHERE [database_name]<>'rdsadmin'
AND session_server_principal_name <>'WORKGROUP\EC2AMAZ-QG7G9L3$'
and schema_name <> 'sys'
and server_principal_name <> 'rdsa';

ALTER SERVER AUDIT [AuditSpecification] WITH (STATE = ON);
```

If you need to query audit data that has already been moved to S3, you will need to change your query as shown in Listing 15-5. The only difference from Listing 15-3 is the filename path.

Listing 15-5. Query audit data transmitted to S3

```
SELECT DISTINCT
        event_time,
        aa.name as audit_action,
        statement,
        succeeded,
        database_name,
        server_instance_name,
        schema_name,
        session_server_principal_name,
        server_principal_name,
        object_Name,
        file_name,
        client_ip,
```

```
        application_name,
        file_name
FROM  msdb.dbo.rds_fn_get_audit_file ('D:\rdsdbdata\SQLAudit\transmitted\*.
sqlaudit',default,default) af
INNER JOIN sys.dm_audit_actions aa
ON aa.action_id = af.action_id
WHERE event_time > DATEADD(HOUR, -1, GETDATE())
ORDER BY event_time DESC;
```

My recommendation is to query the audit data while it's still in the database instance and not yet transmitted to S3. If you set up your server audit like Listing 15-2 and added an appropriate filter like in Listing 15-4, you won't be getting a lot of audit data. You could probably collect it every hour and never miss any audit data. The best way to make sure you don't miss audit data is to keep a close eye on how fast it collects. Then you can set the schedule for querying it based on that.

Note   For more information about SQL Server Audit in RDS, visit `https://docs.aws.amazon.com/AmazonRDS/latest/UserGuide/Appendix.SQLServer.Options.Audit.html`

Nicely, AWS RDS allows you to use SQL Server Agent and Linked Servers. You could do a centralization setup like in Chapter 11, "Centralizing Audit Data." This will make it easier to query and report on multiple RDS instances.

AWS RDS Extended Events

It's pretty straightforward to use extended events in AWS RDS. The main thing to note is the filename. You have to put your extended events in the path `D:\rdsdbdata\Log\` as I've done in Listing 15-6

Listing 15-6. Extended event setup in RDS

```
CREATE EVENT SESSION [auditxel] ON SERVER
ADD EVENT sqlserver.rpc_completed(   ACTION(sqlserver.client_app_
name,sqlserver.client_hostname,sqlserver.database_name,sqlserver.sql_
text,sqlserver.username)
```

```
    WHERE ([sqlserver].[username]=N'josephine')),
ADD EVENT sqlserver.sql_batch_completed(   ACTION(sqlserver.client_app_
name,sqlserver.client_hostname,sqlserver.database_name,sqlserver.sql_
text,sqlserver.username)
    WHERE ([sqlserver].[username]=N'josephine'))
ADD TARGET package0.event_file
            (SET filename=N'D:\rdsdbdata\Log\auditxel',
max_file_size=(10),max_rollover_files=(5))
WITH (MAX_MEMORY=4096 KB,EVENT_RETENTION_MODE=ALLOW_SINGLE_EVENT_LOSS,MAX_
DISPATCH_LATENCY=30 SECONDS,MAX_EVENT_SIZE=0 KB,MEMORY_PARTITION_
MODE=NONE,TRACK_CAUSALITY=OFF,STARTUP_STATE=ON);
ALTER EVENT SESSION [auditxel] ON SERVER
STATE=START;
```

Note   Extended events will only work on Enterprise and Standard editions.

To query your extended event, use the script in Listing 15-7.

Listing 15-7. Query extended event data in RDS

```
SELECT n.value('(@timestamp)[1]', 'datetime') as timestamp,
      n.value('(action[@name="sql_text"]/value)[1]', 'nvarchar(max)')
      as [sql],
      n.value('(action[@name="client_hostname"]/value)[1]',
      'nvarchar(50)') as [client_hostname],
      n.value('(action[@name="username"]/value)[1]', 'nvarchar(50)')
      as [user],
      n.value('(action[@name="database_name"]/value)[1]', 'nvarchar(50)')
      as [database_name],
      n.value('(action[@name="client_app_name"]/value)[1]',
      'nvarchar(50)') as [client_app_name]
FROM (SELECT CAST(event_data as XML) as event_data
FROM sys.fn_xe_file_target_read_file('D:\rdsdbdata\log\auditxel*.xel',
NULL, NULL, NULL)) ed
CROSS APPLY ed.event_data.nodes('event') as q(n)
```

```
WHERE n.value('(@timestamp)[1]', 'datetime')
>= DATEADD(HOUR, -4, GETDATE())
ORDER BY timestamp DESC;
```

Tip   AWS has done a good job with XEvents to mimic SQL Server as much as possible. You can use `*.xel` to query all the files at once. It's harder to query XEvent data in Azure SQL Database and Managed Instance. This is because you have to know the exact names of the files. You can't use `*.xel` to query all the files at once in Azure SQL.

The results from Listing 15-7 will look something like the results in Figure 15-23.

	timestamp	sql	client_hostname	user	database_name	client_app_name
1	2022-05-20 22:32:58.783	(@Param1 datetime,@Param2 nvarchar(9))SELECT TOP...	DESKTOP-15	josephine	auditing	Microsoft SQL Se
2	2022-05-20 22:32:58.723	(@_msparam_0 nvarchar(4000),@_msparam_1 nvarchar...	DESKTOP-15	josephine	auditing	Microsoft SQL Se
3	2022-05-20 22:32:58.657	use [auditing]; if (db_id() = 1) begin -- contained auth is 0 ...	DESKTOP-15	josephine	auditing	Microsoft SQL Se
4	2022-05-20 22:32:58.603	DECLARE @edition sysname; SET @edition = cast(SERV...	DESKTOP-15	josephine	auditing	Microsoft SQL Se
5	2022-05-20 22:32:58.540	select col.name, st.name as DT_name, case when (st.n...	DESKTOP-15	josephine	auditing	Microsoft SQL Se
6	2022-05-20 22:32:58.427	(@timestamp datetime,@description nvarchar(9))INSERT ...	DESKTOP-15	josephine	auditing	Microsoft SQL Se
7	2022-05-20 22:32:58.317	(@_msparam_0 nvarchar(4000),@_msparam_1 nvarchar...	DESKTOP-15	josephine	auditing	Microsoft SQL Se
8	2022-05-20 22:32:58.257	use [auditing]; if (db_id() = 1) begin -- contained auth is 0 ...	DESKTOP-15	josephine	auditing	Microsoft SQL Se
9	2022-05-20 22:32:58.203	DECLARE @edition sysname; SET @edition = cast(SERV...	DESKTOP-15	josephine	auditing	Microsoft SQL Se
10	2022-05-20 22:32:58.143	select col.name, st.name as DT_name, case when (st.n...	DESKTOP-15	josephine	auditing	Microsoft SQL Se

Figure 15-23. *Extended events query results example*

Note   For more information about extended events in RDS, visit `https://aws.amazon.com/blogs/database/set-up-extended-events-in-amazon-rds-for-sql-server/`

Auditing Google Cloud SQL Databases

Google Cloud has an offering called Cloud SQL, which allows you to set up a fully managed SQL Server. This does not support SQL Server Audit or extended events.

Note   For more information about Cloud SQL, visit `https://cloud.google.com/sql/docs/features#sqlserver`

There is a way to audit Cloud SQL via the Google Cloud portal. This will not mimic the functionality of SQL Server Audit or extended events. It will give you access to the SQL Server Log only.

For these reasons, I recommend using a VM in Google Cloud, if you want to have any auditing capability.

Please refer to Appendix A to get a comparison and overview of auditing options. It will provide you with use cases, pros, and cons. It will also give links back to the chapters for additional information.

PART V

Appendix

APPENDIX A

Database Auditing Options Comparison

Here's a quick review of the options for auditing. This chapter has use cases and pros and cons for each auditing option along with references back to specific chapters for additional information.

Auditing Options

- **SQL Server Audit** – This built-in SQL Server auditing feature can be used to set up auditing with SQL Server Management Studio or with SQL scripts. This feature makes it easy to see what is changing on your SQL Server. To make SQL Server auditing work, you need two or three things depending on what you want to audit. The server audit specification is generally good for auditing server-level changes and/or all the databases at the same time. The database audit specification is good for auditing one database or a subset of activities in one database.

- **Extended events** – This built-in SQL Server auditing feature that can be used to set up auditing with SQL Server Management Studio or with SQL scripts. It doesn't have auditing capabilities as nuanced as SQL Server Audit; so if you are looking to audit a subset of activities for a user or database, then it's best to use SQL Server Audit for that instead. To make extended events work, you need to set up a session. That's the only piece that's required, instead of the two or three pieces for SQL Server Audit.

293

© Josephine Bush 2022
J. Bush, *Practical Database Auditing for Microsoft SQL Server and Azure SQL*,
https://doi.org/10.1007/978-1-4842-8634-0_16

- **Change data capture** – This feature uses the SQL Server Agent to track DML changes made to a table. This allows you to see the changes made to data, the details of which are in a format that is easily consumed. This can be particularly useful to extract, transform, and load (ETL) applications or processes.

- **Change tracking** – This feature is a lightweight method to track DML changes. This is typically used by applications to query database changes.

- **C2 and Common Criteria compliance** – This feature is internationally recognized to follow specific security guidelines when auditing. These types of auditing are a comprehensive type of logging of all activities on your database server. If you don't have an auditor requiring you to turn this on, leave it off. It can be very impactful to server performance.

- **Successful and failed login auditing** – Both SQL Server Audit and extended events allow you to audit successful and failed logins. You will need an audit to store the audit data and a server audit specification to collect the login information.

- **Triggers**

  - **Server triggers** can be set up to prevent people from changing databases or preventing them from logging in at certain times.

  - **DDL triggers** can be set up to prevent certain actions from occurring, such as CREATE, ALTER, DROP, GRANT, DENY, or REVOKE. They can have another action occur in response to these actions, or they can record these actions.

  - **DML triggers** can be set up to prevent or have another action occur in response to INSERT, UPDATE, or DELETE statements.

- **Cloud auditing**

  - **Azure SQL Database** – With SQL Server Audit functionality via the Azure portal or with extended events

  - **Azure Managed Instance** – With diagnostic settings via the Azure portal, SQL Server Audit, or extended events

- **AWS RDS** – With SQL Server Audit and extended events

- **Google cloud** – Only on a VM

Caution   Any auditing technique can overload your server depending on how much you audit with it. Best case, you can't weed through all the data, and worst case, you overload your production servers. Always remember to do the least amount of auditing needed for your situation.

Pros and Cons of Auditing Choices

	Pros	Cons
SQL Server Audit	Easy to capture very specific audit events Don't need to parse XML	More complicated to set up than XEvents No templates to guide you
Extended events (XEvents)	Easy to get started with templates Feels familiar if you used SQL Trace or Profiler	Need to parse XML to query results
Change data capture (CDC)	Useful for ETL processes Allows you to see before and after data changes	Performance and storage may be an issue on large, busy tables
Change tracking	Useful for applications to track changes on a database table	Performance may be an issue on large, busy tables Database needs snapshot isolation level for consistency Table needs a primary key Can't see how many times or the values of each change
C2 and Common Criteria compliance	Internationally recognized to follow specific security guidelines when auditing	It can be VERY impactful to server performance

(continued)

	Pros	Cons
Azure SQL Database audit	Easy to set up in the Azure portal Easy to centralize into Log Analytics	Default auditing policy audits everything, but you can modify it with PowerShell Need to query audit data in Kusto
Azure SQL Database extended events	Works a lot like SQL Server extended events	Need to use a storage account Hard to query multiple .xel files
Azure SQL Managed Instance diagnostic settings	Easy to set up in the Azure portal Easy to centralize into Log Analytics	Need to query audit data in Kusto
Azure SQL Managed Instance extended events	Works just like SQL Server extended events	Same cons as SQL Server XEvents Hard to query multiple .xel files
Azure SQL Managed Instance SQL Server Audit	Works just like SQL Server Audit	Hard to query multiple .sqlaudit files
Google Cloud		Can only audit on a VM with SQL Server installed

SQL Server Audit vs. Extended Events

The following table gives a comparison of SQL Server Audit vs. extended events to help you decide which is best for your use case.

Feature	Extended events	SQL Server Audit
Setup via GUI or scripts	Yes	Yes
Query via GUI or scripts	Yes	Yes
Delete in GUI or script and it deletes history	No, xel files are left on disk if disk location is configured	No, audit files are left on disk if disk location is configured
Can delete and modify it while it's enabled and running	Yes	No
Save to locations	event_file as .xel file on disk ring_buffer event_counter histogram pair_matchingetw_classic_ sync_target	.sqlaudit file on disk Application Log Security Log
Ability to customize number, location, and size of files	Yes	Yes
Query without parsing XML	No	Yes
Gives you host info about changes made	Yes	Only in SQL Server 2017 and later versions
Templates	Yes	No
Ability to filter what is captured	Yes	Yes
Ability to audit what a user does	Yes	Yes
Ability to capture server metrics like waits stats or connection tracking	Yes	No
Setup multiple on a server	Yes	Yes
Number of items required to make it work	One	Two to three

Use Cases

- **Everything happening on a database server**

  - **Extended events** – Capture rpc_completed and sql_batch_ completed without a filter. Be careful with this because it can produce a lot of audit data. For more information, review Chapter 7, "Implementing Extended Events via the GUI," and Chapter 8, "Implementing Extended Events via SQL Scripts."

- **DDL and security changes across the entire server**

  - **SQL Server Audit** – This will require an audit and a server audit specification. For more information, review Chapter 4, "Implementing SQL Server Audit via the GUI," and Chapter 5, "Implementing SQL Server Audit via SQL Scripts."

- **DDL and security changes on one database**

  - **SQL Server Audit** – This will require an audit and a database audit specification. For more information, review Chapter 4, "Implementing SQL Server Audit via the GUI," and Chapter 5, "Implementing SQL Server Audit via SQL Scripts."

- **DDL changes on one table**

  - **SQL Server Audit** – This will require an audit and a database audit specification that specifies this one table with the associated actions you want to capture. For more information, review Chapter 4, "Implementing SQL Server Audit via the GUI," and Chapter 5, "Implementing SQL Server Audit via SQL Scripts."

- **DDL and security changes at the server level and only one database**

  - **SQL Server Audit** – This will require an audit, a server audit specification, and a database audit specification. For more information, review Chapter 4, "Implementing SQL Server Audit via the GUI," and Chapter 5, "Implementing SQL Server Audit via SQL Scripts."

- **Everything a user does**

  - **SQL Server Audit** – This will require an audit with a filter to capture only that user's activities and a server audit specification. For more information, review Chapter 4, "Implementing SQL Server Audit via the GUI," and Chapter 5, "Implementing SQL Server Audit via SQL Scripts."

  - **Extended events** – Capture rpc_completed and sql_batch_completed. Put a filter on server_principal_name for each of your selected events. For more information, review Chapter 7, "Implementing Extended Events via the GUI," and Chapter 8, "Implementing Extended Events via SQL Scripts."

- **Everything happening in a database**

  - **SQL Server Audit** – This will require an audit with a filter to capture only that database's activities and a server audit specification. For more information, review Chapter 4, "Implementing SQL Server Audit via the GUI," and Chapter 5, "Implementing SQL Server Audit via SQL Scripts."

  - **Extended events** – Capture rpc_completed and sql_batch_completed. Plus, put a filter on server_principal_name for each of your selected events. For more information, review Chapter 7, "Implementing Extended Events via the GUI," and Chapter 8, "Implementing Extended Events via SQL Scripts."

- **Everyone executing a stored procedure**

  - **SQL Server Audit** – This will require an audit and a database audit specification that captures execute on your stored procedure. For more information, review Chapter 4, "Implementing SQL Server Audit via the GUI," and Chapter 5, "Implementing SQL Server Audit via SQL Scripts."

  - **Extended events** – Capture rpc_completed with a filter on object_name. For more information, review Chapter 7, "Implementing Extended Events via the GUI," and Chapter 8, "Implementing Extended Events via SQL Scripts."

- **Configuration changes**

  - **SQL Server Audit** – This will require an audit and a database
    audit specification that captures execute on sp_configure. For
    more information, review Chapter 9, "Tracking SQL Server
    Configuration Changes."

- **DML changes**

  - **SQL Server Audit** – If you don't need to track the actual data
    changes themselves, but the DML statement itself. This will
    require an audit and a database audit specification that captures
    INSERT, UPDATE, and/or DELETE on each table you want to
    audit. For more information, review Chapter 4, "Implementing
    SQL Server Audit via the GUI," and Chapter 5, "Implementing
    SQL Server Audit via SQL Scripts."

  - **Change tracking** – If an application needs to track whether
    data changed, but not the exact value of the data. For more
    information, review Chapter 10, "Additional SQL Server Auditing
    and Tracking Methods."

  - **Change data capture** – If you need to track the exact values
    before and after the data change. For more information, review
    Chapter 10, "Additional SQL Server Auditing and Tracking
    Methods."

- **Successful and failed logins**

  - **SQL Server Audit** – You will need an audit to store the audit data
    and a server audit specification to collect the login information.
    For more information, review Chapter 10, "Additional SQL Server
    Auditing and Tracking Methods."

  - **Extended events** – You will need to create a session that uses the
    login event and the error_reported event. For more information,
    review Chapter 10, "Additional SQL Server Auditing and Tracking
    Methods."

- **Audit Azure SQL Database**

  - **Azure SQL Database audit via Azure portal** – This is similar to SQL Server Audit. It makes it easy to centralize audit data in a Log Analytics workspace. For more information, review Chapter 13, "Auditing Azure SQL Databases."

  - **Extended events** – This is similar to extended events in SQL Server. The only issue is it's hard to loop through multiple .xel files to query all the XEvent data at once. For more information, review Chapter 13, "Auditing Azure SQL Databases."

- **Audit Azure SQL Managed Instance**

  - **Diagnostic settings** – Configured via the Azure portal. Makes it easy to centralize audit data in a Log Analytics workspace. For more information, review Chapter 14, "Auditing Azure SQL Managed Instance."

  - **SQL Server Audit** – Similar to SQL Server Audit, but audit files need to be stored in an Azure storage account. The only issue is it's hard to loop through multiple audit files to query all the data at once. For more information, review Chapter 14, "Auditing Azure SQL Managed Instance."

  - **Extended events** – Similar to SQL Server extended events, but .xel files need to be stored in an Azure storage account. The only issue is it's hard to loop through multiple .xel files to query all the XEvent data at once. For more information, review Chapter 14, "Auditing Azure SQL Managed Instance."

- **Audit AWS RDS**

  - **SQL Server Audit** – Similar to SQL Server Audit, but audit files need to be stored in a folder specified by AWS. For more information, review Chapter 15, "Other Cloud Provider Auditing Options."

- **Extended events** – Similar to SQL Server extended events, but
  .xel files need to be stored in a folder specified by AWS. For more
  information, review Chapter 15, "Other Cloud Provider Auditing
  Options."

- **Google Cloud**

  - Only on a VM with SQL Server Audit or extended events

Index

A, B

Advanced settings, 99–101, 133, 143

Amazon Web Services (AWS), 20, 268, 269
    See also AWS RDS SQL Server Audit

Application log, 40, 41, 53, 54, 67, 69

Audit
    categories, 26
    configuring, 39, 40
    creation, 38
    database specification, 46–51
    destination, 39, 40
    enabling, 43
    HTML (*see* HTML reports)
    specification, 24, 44–46

Audit action groups
    database audit action groups, 28–30
    server audit action groups, 27, 28

Audit actions, 228

Audit distribution, 221

Audit files, 40, 44, 70, 81, 184, 185, 251,
    254, 259, 261, 269, 271, 276, 301

Auditing, 18, *See also* Database auditing
    Azure SQL databases, 18, 19
    Azure SQL Managed Instance, 19
    choices, 295, 296
    database problems, 6, 7
    enabling and configuring, 214–218
    Google Cloud, 20
    management, 4
    modifying, 224–226
    official examination, 3
    options, 293–295
    policy, 226–229
    SQL server, 296–298
    types, 4, 5
    value, 3
    viewing, 219–225

Auditing Azure SQL databases
    centralizing, 241–245
    credentials, 236, 237
    extended event, 237, 238
    modifying, 224–226
    portal, 213–224
    querying extended event, 238–240
    and reporting, 241–245
    storage account and
        container, 230–236

Auditing Azure SQL
        Managed Instance
    centralizing, 265–268
    with diagnostic settings, 246–252
    reporting, 265–268
    with SQL Server Audit, 251–261
    XEvents, 261–265

Auditing event actions, 140

Auditing events, 139

Auditing option, 275–279

Auditing user, 183, 188, 189

Audit-level actions, 27

Audit log failure, 68

Audit logs, 259

Audit name, 39, 67

Printed in the United States
by Baker & Taylor Publisher Services